Famous
The
World Forgot
Volume II

Also by Jason Lucky Morrow

The DC Dead Girls Club:
A Vintage True Crime Story of Four Unsolved Murders in Washington D.C.

Famous Crimes the World Forgot: Volume I
Ten Vintage True Crime Stories Rescued from Obscurity

Deadly Hero:
The High Society Murder that Created Hysteria in the Heartland

FAMOUS CRIMES
THE
WORLD FORGOT

VOLUME II

More Vintage True Crime Stories
Rescued from Obscurity

JASON LUCKY MORROW

Copyright © 2017 Jason Lucky Morrow

All Rights Reserved
No part of this book may be reproduced, distributed, or transmitted in any form or by any means, including photocopying, recording, or other electronic or mechanical methods, without the prior written permission of the author, except in the case of brief quotations embodied in academic works, critical reviews, and certain other noncommercial uses permitted by copyright law.

Published by: Historical Crime Detective Books, Tulsa, OK
Primary Editor: Cherri Randall
Secondary Editor: Tiffany McNab
Cover Design: Jason Morrow

ISBN-13: 978-1544677026
ISBN-10: 1544677022
ASIN:
First Edition, 2017
10 9 8 7 6 5 4 3 2 1

.

for Alison

Your mother was seven-months pregnant when your dad started this book, and you were nineteen-months old when it was published.

I will always love you more than anything else in this world.

Halloween 2016. You were dressed as a strawberry.

Contents

Preface — 1

Chapter One — 5
The Last Supper, 1897

Chapter Two — 51
The Crystal Cool Killer, 1922

Chapter Three — 83
The Love Song of Archie Moock, 1928

Chapter Four — 99
The Highway Hunter, 1930

Chapter Five — 145
The Destiny of Luther Jones, 1936

Chapter Six — 175
The Tomato Killer, 1944-45

Chapter Seven — 209
A Soft Touch, 1955

Chapter Eight — 287
The Stiletto Slayer of Milwaukee, 1966

Images Available Online	327
Acknowledgments	329
Sources	331
About the Author	373
One Last Thing…	374

Preface

Purpose

IN 2013, I BEGAN MY journey into the world of historical true crime with the creation of my blog, HistoricalCrimeDetective.com, "where you will discover forgotten crimes and forgotten criminals lost to history. You will not find high profile cases that have been rehashed and retold *ad infinitum* to *ad nauseam*."

My purpose for creating the blog, and writing this book, my fourth, was to salvage obscure true crime stories and repackage them in an entertaining fashion to appeal to a wide audience that shares my appreciation for their educational and historical value. My personal mission is to research, write, and present stories from our past that I believe are being lost and ignored. I believe they still have value, and that the lives of those who lived them are still important. I truly care about discovering these forgotten crime stories, researching each case as thoroughly as I can, digging up all the pieces, and then carefully crafting those pieces into what I hope is a well-written story that informs and engages the reader.

Although a long line of researchers and authors better than I have also taken on this same mission, I wanted to embark on my own explorations and make a humble contribution to the historical true crime genre.

The selection process for the eight stories in this book had to meet a simple criterion—that they were once very famous crimes, nationally publicized, that have not been written about or adequately explored in decades. If they have been covered recently by other authors, then I wanted to dig deeper, go further, and present readers with an accurate retelling of the full story. If you have heard of one of these stories before, I hope that my research and retelling of it provided you with more information than you knew before.

Additionally, I wanted this book to feature a cross-section of cases that covered different locations, decades, and types of killers.

From there, the decisions of which stories to include were completely arbitrary. I relied on my "reporter's instinct" to tell me if a certain case was worthy of further examination. Because of that, I make no assertion that the stories presented here are the *most* famous and forgotten, or that these eight are *better* than any others.

As enjoyable as it was to dig into these cases and write about them, I look forward to exploring more 'famous crimes the world forgot' and presenting them in future volumes, as well as on my blog. Thank you for purchasing this book and I sincerely hope you enjoy it.

A Special Note on Historical Accuracy

As a former journalist, my approach to writing is to make the story entertaining, but to also stick to the facts. I go where the research leads me and in the end, the story is the story. All of the dialogue, quotes, and events in this book are how they appeared in the original source material—with one exception I describe below. To help make the characters come to life, I relied on clues and statements within the research material to guide me with how I portrayed their body language, facial expressions, mannerisms, gestures, and voice inflections. These character traits are used to enhance the scene and set the mood without altering the facts.

The stories in this book were assembled together over the last twenty-one months like a jigsaw puzzle from approximately 700 newspapers, magazines, books, maps, census reports, interviews, prison documents, and other resources. In any work of nonfiction, it is inevitable that some facts will be incorrect. In the rush to meet deadlines, newspaper reporters often got primary and secondary facts wrong. Readers who explore these cases on their own may find newspaper accounts with conflicting information. This is not uncommon, especially when it comes to dates, the spelling of names, and other minor details. When confronted with those issues, I did my best to verify the information I have included for accuracy. I apologize in advance for any mistake I may have misrepresented or overlooked.

Exception

There is one exception to the historical accuracy statement above. In **Chapter Five, The Destiny of Luther Jones, 1936**, there is an interrogation scene that is indented and set-apart in italics. That scene is the author's recreation based on bits and pieces he gathered during his research. I thought it was important to write this mostly-fictional scene to show how Luther's actions had backed him into a corner from which there was no escape. However, since it is indented and placed in italics and not direct quotes, I used that formatting style to remind the reader that this is not a direct capture, and the scene is fictional. That is the only place in this book where I have taken that liberty, and I am pointing this out to the reader here, and again in chapter five in a footnote.

Comparison of Volume I and Volume II

Readers of the first book in this series, *Famous Crimes the World Forgot: Ten Vintage True Crime Stories Rescued from Obscurity*, may notice significant differences between that book and this one. In volume one, there were ten stories that averaged 6,953 words each. In this one, the average story is nearly 12,000 words long.

I never plan the length of the story I am working on for my books and prefer to let each one sort-of play itself out from beginning to end. However, the reason for the increased story length in this volume is simple: all of the crimes presented in this book are fully resolved.

In volume one, only six of the ten stories featured a complete conclusion of the case by trial and punishment. The other four included: two cases, which were never solved and no suspect was identified; a third case that ends abruptly after the killers fled the country; and a fourth case, in which the suspect was mortally wounded and died several days later.

In this volume, all eight cases were solved and went to trial. Each crime story has a beginning, middle, and end. Because there are no 'loose ends,' each account commanded more narrative.

Footnotes

Like most other history books, this one relies heavily on footnotes to clarify, explain, expand, and further illuminate a particular item for the benefit of the reader's understanding without disrupting tight organization, pace, and flow of the story. Different eBook devices may present these footnotes in different ways. Regardless of how they are formatted, **I want to encourage the reader to explore the footnotes while reading the text, and then return to the main body of the story.** These footnotes were carefully selected and included to augment your enjoyment and understanding of the narrative, without disrupting the main storylines.

Chapter One: The Last Supper, 1897

DURING THE LAST TWENTY-FOUR HOURS of her life, Susie Belew suffered the excruciating abdominal pains of a tormented body trapped in a violent, hopeless struggle to survive by expelling massive amounts of vital fluids that rapidly led to a collapse of her circulatory system, heart failure, and a death that was inhumane, undignified, and came two days before her wedding.

Susie's last day alive began like any other when she awoke Monday morning, November 8, 1897, in her brother Louis's small home in Dixon, California, where she lived and kept house. It was an arrangement that would end that Thursday when she and Charlie Ehmann were to be married. Before they left for their honeymoon in Nevada, the newlyweds would attend Louis's wedding to Clara Ferguson the following week. The back-to-back weddings were joyous occasions that were eagerly welcomed by them and their three brothers following the death of their father the previous year, and their mother in 1894.

That morning, Susie fed the wood stove, boiled water in the teakettle, and prepared a breakfast of cornmeal mush, eggs, potatoes, and coffee. Although it was her brother Louis's house, he was spending his nights inside the livery stable[1] he owned. This was done on Susie's behalf to allow her and Charlie some privacy before their nuptials. As the sun was rising, Louis walked the three blocks to his house and ate

---

[1] The Arcade Livery Stable was the largest in Dixon. Louis had purchased the business four years earlier with Susie as one of his investors.

breakfast with his sister. Upon returning to the stables, he sent hired hand and boarder, Bruno Klein, for his meal.

Entering through the back door, Klein walked across the kitchen and peered into the parlor. He was surprised to see Susie lying down on the sofa, clutching her stomach, moaning about how sick she felt. He knew her as a serious woman, not one who gave voice to petty complaints. He served himself and ate quickly to return and inform Louis of his sister's condition. As Klein gobbled his food and drank his coffee, he noted to himself that the mush tasted as if it had been seasoned with peppers. Susie rarely cooked with peppers.

When he reached the livery stable, he found Louis in a similar condition; vomiting and purging himself. Minutes later, Klein began to feel those same symptoms. He was the one now clutching his stomach and moaning.

A local doctor was summoned. He first suspected they had eaten something poisonous, but when he discovered sauerkraut in their vomit, a meal all three had eaten the night before, the physician changed his mind and declared they were suffering from acute indigestion. After the Bromo-Seltzers he offered failed to relieve their symptoms, and his patients continued to complain of intense abdominal cramps, he injected them with an unspecified pain reliever. Whatever the medicine was, it immediately eased their discomfort, but only for an hour or two.

And then the pain came back.

Louis knew better. As soon as Klein told him about Susie, Louis calculated they had been poisoned and thought he knew the cowardly provocateurs behind it. By his reckoning, it was either the work of Walter de Carlo, or it was Harry Allen, Susie's ex-boyfriend.

De Carlo, a known thief and liar, was convicted of perjury after Louis testified against him as the state's primary witness. He was now over at Folsom serving an eight-year prison term, and could easily have enlisted one of his pals to do his dirty work.

In this image from a San Francisco newspaper, the spelling of Louis's name is incorrect.

Or maybe it was Harry Allen, Susie's ex-boyfriend. Louis and his brothers, Frank, Arthur, and Thomas had convinced their sister to break-up with Allen, and warned him to stay-away. Allen was a hardworking ranch hand who didn't own property and hadn't built up his own stake. He was still untamed, a bit of a hothead, and invested too much of his time in Dixon's saloons.

But Allen wasn't easily intimidated, and when Susie broke-off their relations, he swore to get even—with Louis.

At the house, Susie's caretakers were unnerved by her thrashing, and wailing, and vomiting, and diarrhea, which continued hour after hour after hour. Everything she eliminated contained blood—including her sputum expelled by hyper-salivation. They sent for more bedding and rags, and cleaned what they could as this once proud and strong thirty-year-old languished and cried for mercy from an invisible fury that could not be subdued.

She was being looked after by Charlie's mother, Clara's mother (the mother of Louis's fiancé), neighbors who came and went, and a nurse the town doctor sent over. Following 'Dr. Sauerkraut's' advice, they boiled water in the teakettle and prevailed upon her to consume a warm beverage. But with each drink the liquid seemed to reactivate the demonic force within, and a roaring fire would surge across her bowels.

By the early evening hours, Susie was refusing to ingest anything they made. They switched to beef broth, and hoped the thicker consistency would nourish her body that was rapidly wasting away from dehydration. Again, Susie rejected their offer. Charlie's mother tried to show her it was safe, and in her enticement for Susie to consume the broth, drank some herself. She soon felt sick and retreated outside where she vomited.

News that Susie and Louis were suffering with a mysterious illness from something they ate was passed on to brother Frank at his humble ranch a few miles west of Dixon. He reached Susie early that night, took a seat beside her bed and wrapped his thick fingers around her hand. She was dying, he was told. Probably poisoned, he was told. He sat there, quietly, offering no advice and only a few words of comfort to his dying sister. He seemed fearful and overwhelmed by her suffering. Just the evening before, Frank had made a rare visit to the house and ate dinner with Susie, Louis, Klein, and Thomas and his fiancé. Frank and Bruno had lightly teased Susie about her upcoming wedding, and it was fun.

Sometime after eleven o'clock, word came that Louis was unconscious and his blood pressure was dropping. Frank made it there in time to watch as his brother died in a place that smelled of horse manure and human waste. It visibly disturbed him, and "he looked almost dead himself."

"Oh, why should he die when he seemed so happy?" Frank cried out.

When he returned to the house, it was clear that Susie was in her last hours. Someone told her she had been poisoned and, at first, she refused to believe it. Possibly delirious, Frank listened as Susie spoke of how happy she and Louis were going to be since they were each about to get married. He smiled and agreed.

No one told her Louis was dead.

Frank Belew

But in her final moments, after her kidneys had failed, as her lungs and heart struggled to circulate oxygen and blood, she told Charles where he could find the ring he had given her. He spoke with her, briefly, until she was unconscious. Twenty minutes later, at five o'clock Tuesday morning, under the ghoulish glow of an oil lamp, Susie Belew died.

All eyes turned to Bruno Klein as he fought his way through the first twenty-four hours. Over the next two days, newspaper reports predicted Klein would die, but he surprised everyone and survived.

News of the Belew deaths circulated throughout central California within hours and carried the conclusion that it was murder. Outrage grew exponentially as the story spread, its velocity propelled by the anxiety that an unknown assassin lurked within their realm—capable of poisoning the wells from which they nourished their own families.

Veteran reporters from the San Francisco dailies, the *Chronicle*, *Examiner*, and *Call*, caught the first train to Dixon, a small town located thirty miles west of Sacramento. Although the *Chronicle*, *Examiner* and even the Sacramento papers gave the story routine coverage, the *San Francisco Call* resolved that first day to make the Belew double homicide case their special project. *Call* reporters went further than the others by digging deeper, devoting more copy space, inserting themselves into the story, and then boasting of their achievements. By the end of the week, the *Call* had the answer to who they thought did it, how they did it, and why they did it.

It wasn't enough, however, because what they didn't have was evidence of guilt, an arrest, or a confession.

Solano County District Attorney Frank Devlin and Sheriff Benjamin Rush began their investigation with the assumption that the Belew siblings were intentionally murdered by a cowardly devil that snuck into their yard and simply dumped poison down their well. It was the easiest, most covert way to go about it. Wait until the coal-black hours, the hours when good men slept and bad men roamed, and let hunger and thirst do the rest.

"One thing is certain, the poison did not get into the well of its own accord," District Attorney Devlin told a newspaperman the day after Susie died. "Someone put it there and what the officers have to find out is who it is that put it there."

To confirm that assumption, Sheriff Rush took water samples from the well and sent them to San Francisco chemistry professor William T. Wenzell, along with the pump valve, food from the kitchen, and Susie's stomach and liver, which had been removed during the autopsy. When local doctors turned their attention to Louis's body, they were disappointed to discover he had already been embalmed by an enthusiastic undertaker eager to experiment with a new brand of solvents.

Rush then drafted local high school chemistry teacher J. R. Grinstead to apply the Marsh test to water from the teakettle and the beef broth-that had apparently made the other women sick.

Until the Marsh test was invented by British chemist James Marsh in 1836, arsenic was the preferred method for wives to eliminate abusive husbands, and for nephews and grandchildren to collect the wealth of their elders who inflicted upon them the inconvenience of living too long. Arsenic trioxide is an odorless, white powder that is easily mixed into food and beverages. When consumed, the poison takes a direct path to the gastrointestinal tract where it wreaks havoc, causing symptoms that could easily be mistaken for more naturally occurring illnesses. Without a test for it, arsenic was undetectable and its use could not be proven at trial. As the primary ingredient in rat poison during Susie's time, it was cheap and easily available.

Before the Marsh test, arsenic was used in one-third of all criminal poisoning cases, researcher Sandra Hempel reports in her 2013 book, *"The Inheritor's Powder."* That was the name given to the poison by the French during the early 19th Century: *poudre de succession.* By the time Wenzell and Grinstead were analyzing items from the Belew home, the Marsh test had been around for sixty-one years. A state law mandating the record keeping of all who purchased rat poison was passed in 1891. Although it was often used by those committing suicide, its popularity as a means for covert murder had sharply declined.

Not long after the *Call* reporter arrived in Dixon, the town's grapevine revealed an intriguing back-story to the Belew family. When their father, Thomas Belew, died the year before, he chose to bequeath his $7,000 life insurance policy to just three of his five children. Susie received $3,000, and Louis and Arthur each collected $2,000. Thomas Fletcher, his youngest son, had received the family farm some years before.

Frank, the brother who rushed to his sister's bedside, got nothing.

But local gossip had a pretty good explanation for that as well: Frank was the black sheep of the family. He was the rotten apple, the troubled son with a disturbing ledger of misdeeds for which he had never been held to account. When he discovered his father had cut him out, Frank fixed his resentment toward his siblings, but never directly. It was done on the sly. That was the way Frank liked to do things, on the sly.

In all his jealousy and indignation, Frank had forgotten something. Shortly after his marriage to Tennessee Dixie Martin in 1888, his parents gave him $1,100. He used that money to buy a small ranch and the young couple had two boys over the next three years. It wasn't much of a place, however, and didn't have the resources that his father's ranch had—the one his younger brother Thomas now owned.

In the years leading up to the death of his father and siblings, it was said that Frank grew bitter, disappointed over "his portion of life's feast." His desires exceeded his capabilities. He believed he deserved more and to get what he wanted he did bad things, and brushed-off the consequences. But men and women of his nature are driven by an enduring discontent that fuels frustration which turns to anger; anger that morphs into violence; violence that is often directed at those closest to the source: his own family, and wife in particular.

She didn't tolerate his abuse for long. Earlier that year, she took her children and moved to Davisville[2] to live with her sister and her husband. She told folks she was afraid to live with Frank and declared, "There would never be a reconciliation."

By Wednesday, November 10, the day of Louis and Susie's funeral, the *San Francisco Call's* second story on the case pointed the finger at Frank Belew. It was a bold proclamation—one that completely ignored any other theory of who may have committed the murder. It wasn't a stranger. It wasn't some deranged bughouser. It wasn't Charlie Ehmann (who was the last one to leave the house). It wasn't one of Walter de Carlo's pals, and it probably wasn't Harry Allen. Maybe it was Allen, the paper hedged, but that's only because the Belew clan was pointing their finger at him.

"The most startling facts that have yet to come to light concern Frank Belew, whose reputation has not been good for some time," the *Call* confided to its readers. "It is known that he was in such financial straits that he resorted to methods that caused his dead brother a great deal of pain and worry."

The *Call* also revealed the thirty-nine-year-old's "domestic troubles," and that "he bitterly opposed the marriage of his sister, which was to have taken place tomorrow."

But the *Call* may have known more than they let on in their November 11 article when they applied Sherlock Holmes' style logic.

"…Frank Belew was a guest at his sister's table at the last supper she ever ate. The breakfast following the supper at which Frank was a guest and Louis the host, contained the fatal poison—or *it was in the water of which the tea was made.*"

They were on to something, for the next day, the results of the Marsh tests performed by Professor Winzell and high

---

[2] The name was later shortened to Davis.

school teacher Grinstead were revealed: negative on the well-water and table salt, positive on the water in the teakettle. There was so much arsenic in fact, that Grinstead could visibly observe the sugar looking substance on the underside of the lid. When the water was boiled, the steam lifted it up where it clung to the cast iron.

Several witnesses from the Sunday night dinner noted to Sheriff Rush that the water in the teakettle had been drawn from the well the *night before*. It was then used the next morning to make breakfast, as well as the hot beverages, soup, and beef broth by Susie's caretakers throughout that Monday. When those items were tested, Wenzell and Grinstead found arsenic in them as well.

Grinstead's discovery narrowed the focus of the investigation to just two possibilities: that someone snuck into the house during the night and put the poison in the teakettle, or, it was an inside job—someone close to the family.

That someone was probably Frank, the *Call* advocated over the next two weeks. During that time, the newspaper slowly and methodically laid-out the case against him. Their reporters conducted a parallel investigation to the authorities, dug into his past, checked his alibis, and pushed his neck into the noose of public opinion.

On the Sunday during which the family held their last supper, Frank Belew arrived in Dixon around 4:30 in the afternoon. About an hour later, he sat down for dinner with Susie, Louis, Thomas and his fiancé, Louisa Bremley. At one point during the meal, Louis left for the livery stable and sent Klein to the house to eat dinner. The family gathering ended at 6:30 and Klein, Thomas, and Miss Bremley went outside where they chatted briefly as Thomas prepared the buggy for departure.

After arsenic was discovered in the teakettle, Frank revealed to a *Call* reporter that he also got sick from the poison. "He claims that he was attacked by a sick headache after supper, and that after the three other persons had left the house, his sister gave him a headache powder [with a] a glass of water," the *Call* reported on November 15.

Glass of water? Did it come from the teakettle? If so, he had just received a double-dose. If he poisoned the water, why take a drink from it? But of course, no one left alive saw him take that drink of water.

The following day, Frank's claim included a new detail. "I admit I was in the kitchen at one time Sunday night and *I lost my supper*," he declared.

When he left shortly after the others, Susie was arranging her hair in preparation for Charlie who would be there in a few hours. Frank finished by stating he left town around 7:30 and was home in bed by 8:30.

Charlie Ehmann's account of that night reinforced the circumstantial evidence that was building against Frank. Charlie said he arrived around 9:30 p.m. Sunday and found the back door unlocked. When he entered the house, he locked it. At one point during the evening, he briefly went outside to get a drink of water from the well and noticed the teakettle was on the wood stove. After he said goodnight to Susie at 11:30, he made sure to lock the back door by engaging a double-latch system, which provided additional security against intruders.

In case their readers did not understand the significance of who did what and when, the *Call* explained it in detail.

"These facts become interesting when it is remembered that every circumstance seems to point to the fact that the poison was placed in the teakettle on Sunday night sometime between 6:30 and 9:30. Ehmann says he locked the door at 9:30. ...there is no evidence that any one entered the room violently, the locks and windows being undisturbed."

Although the backdoor was unlocked for three hours that evening, Sheriff Rush and the *Call* correspondents were confident that no one entered the house after Frank left. Their claim was supported by "a savage little watch dog that barked whenever he heard strange footsteps," and "no one could have entered the Belew home without making a noise, the floor being squeaky."

Harry Allen, in contrast, had a strong alibi for that Sunday night. He was in one of Dixon's saloons between seven o'clock and 11:30. Witnesses confirmed it.

County authorities and the *Call* detective-slash-writers noted the inconsistencies in Frank's claims. No one saw him vomit or profess he had a headache. There were no headache powders in the house and Susie had never purchased any, according to her account at Kirby's Drug Store. The teakettle couldn't have been poisoned before 6:30, because no one else got sick after dinner. And he didn't leave Dixon at 7:30 p.m., he left around nine o'clock, the town's night watchman reported. He had spoken to Frank, and was sure of the time, although Frank swore he left at 7:30.

"It has therefore been shown beyond question," the *Call* declared in their newfound Arthur Conan Doyle style of writing, "that Frank Belew could have done the deed, for he admits that he was in the kitchen at an hour when the fatal dose might have been placed in the kettle."

They also pointed out that before that night, Frank was on bad terms with both Susie and Louis. It was the first time he had been to their house in a month, and for good reason, the San Francisco newspaper uncovered. Earlier that year, Frank had signed his brother's name to some checks.

"Louis Belew had told me that Frank had forged his name to two notes, one for $75,[3]" Constable Frank Newby told a *Call* reporter on the day of the Belew funeral. "He told me he had paid both notes, but warned Frank that if any more forgeries occurred, the law would take its course."

The president of Dixon Bank, Steve Little, confirmed the forgery story and added one of his own. During the course of routine business a few weeks before, Frank and Little took a

---

[3] The 2016 equivalent of $1,829. In 1897 one dollar is the same as $24.24 in 2016.

carriage ride out to the country to visit some Belew family property. As the two men rode together, Frank engaged in his favorite topic of conversation: his anger over his disinheritance and his feelings toward his sister.

"He did not like the idea of Susie and Louis prosperous while he was forever at the door of want," Little said. "His manner was that of one deeply hurt, and he seemed to brood over the matter and frequently referred to it."

Frank also blamed his sister for prejudicing his wife against him, "Susie has interfered with my affairs, and she shall never enter my house again," Frank told Little.

It was laughable that Frank should blame Susie for his wife leaving him. If Frank's wife was set against him, the $400[4] he once stole from her father likely contributed to why she was sour on her estranged husband.

"It was raining one day about five years ago," Frank's father-in-law, William Martin, later explained to a *Call* man, "and as I had a wad of greenbacks, something like $400, I asked Frank to take care of it for me at the house while I was out in the storm on business. He took it and wrapped it in a piece of newspaper. A day or two later, I asked for the money, and he went to the drawer to get it. The paper was empty, and he at once declared he had been robbed."

Frank then blamed a ranch-hand he had conveniently discharged earlier that day. "[Frank] had him arrested on his way from the ranch to Woodland.[5] The hired-hand did not have a cent and was cleared at once, as there was no evidence against him," the father-in-law continued.

There was anecdotal evidence against Frank, however, who was hard up for money when the $400 disappeared. "About a week later, he came back from Chico with a fine gold watch, which he gave his wife. He also had about $150 in his

---

[4] The 2016 equivalent of approximately $10,000.
[5] A city thirty miles north of Dixon. It is the seat of Yolo County.

possession. When she asked him where he got it, he said he had won it gambling."

Frank's skullduggery didn't end there; the father-in-law had another story to tell. It was about the time a neighbor's prized hog made the fatal mistake of trespassing on Frank's property.

"One day, [Tennessee] came home and saw the remains of a white hog about the place. The head had been burned, and the skin buried. The girl knew the hog was not theirs, so she said 'Frank, this is not right.' He replied that he was hard-up and needed the meat, and that the hog 'had no business on his place.'"

Just as he had blamed his sister for his wife leaving him, Frank blamed the hog. Like all the other times, Frank was never rectified. He had a knack for getting away with misdeeds, even when he tried to murder ranch hand Charley Hough[6] twice in one day. After it happened, Hough reported the incident, but it was a he-said, he-said situation, and the poorer man lost because "Hough was generally believed to be crazy."

Charley Hough crazier than Frank Belew? It hardly seemed possible. But Hough's suggested motive didn't make much sense to anyone at the time: that Frank wanted to get out of paying $47 he owed him. Although the *Call* mentioned the incident in their funeral article, Hough's account wouldn't emerge until much later.

By taking stock of Frank Belew's transgressions, the *Call* was able to show that he was a bit of a snake. A dangerous, venomous snake. But they weren't the only ones to think so. Susie thought he was one, too. She shared her parent's aversion to Frank, and like them, sought to cut him out of her will. Two weeks before her funeral, on October 27, Susie approached an official with the Dixon Bank and stated she

---

[6] Hough spelled his first name with an "ey." Ehmann spelled it with an "ie."

wished to change her will to exclude her brothers Frank and Arthur.[7]

During her meeting with the bank's notary public, Susie purportedly said that Frank "had always been a financial burden to the family," a newspaper reported. She died before her new will could be completed.

As bad as things were starting to look for Frank, the investigation was in danger of fizzling-out like a Bromo-Seltzer. Sheriff Rush was left scratching his head. The Belew brothers were pointing their fingers at Harry Allen, and everyone else was pointing the finger at Frank. Both were strong in their denials. With two suspects, there was only one thing Sheriff Rush could do: put them in a hotel room together and see what happens.

On Sunday, November 14, Rush, a deputy, and a *Call* reporter watched as the two men were thrown together in what was, more or less, a human cockfight to see which rooster made the most noise. It was arranged without their prior knowledge and organized with the idea "to involve them in a wrangle, with the hope one or the other might involuntarily make some damaging admissions."

By the *Call's* judgement, Frank clucked and Allen crowed.

"Harry Allen's language was coarse, brutally direct, and cruelly vindictive," it was reported. "Allen seemed to revel in his epithets, and to enjoy the meeting. Belew regretted it, and tried to evade his accuser."

Although Frank attacked first, Allen quickly retaliated and finished strong.

"What motive had I for committing such a crime?" Allen asked when he was accused.

"Revenge," Frank answered, "the revenge of a rejected lover. Susie was to marry you and you threatened to get even on Louis. My brother told me that you had declared that you

---

[7] Arthur had lost entire inheritance in the saloon business and began drinking too much.

would get even on all the Belews. I tell you frankly, Allen, that I believe you are the man. The murderer of my brother and sister stole into the kitchen by the back door and poured the arsenic into the kettle. He did it while she was with her lover in the parlor, in my opinion."

From there, it was all downhill for Frank who was forced to admit that Susie had never said one bad word about Allen, who didn't consider himself the "rejected lover" because it was the Belew brothers who warned him to stay away.

"I didn't call [on Susie] anymore because I heard that you and some of your brothers had threatened me with personal violence. I had heard that you had taken a shot at one of your hired men when his back was turned and I didn't want to give you the opportunity to shoot me," Allen roared as he pointed his finger. He then accused Frank of threatening to "blow his head off if he didn't leave town." That was a direct quote he had heard from Frank's own son.

"You charge me with murder," Allen continued, "then assign a motive. You are the real murderer and let me tell you what your motive was. It was both revenge and greed. You haven't got a dollar. Your life has been a failure. Your wife has left you and for good reasons. You squandered all your father ever gave you.

"Because you were cut-off in his will, and the bulk of the property–left to your brother and sister–you have been angry ever since. You have been kicking about your treatment ever since your father died. You wanted revenge, and you wanted $3,000, which you claimed was your part of the estate."

Allen paused to catch his breath as Frank stared mule face, unsure of how to respond. The climax came when he professed his innocence.

"One or the other of us has got to hang for this murder, and I hope to God the guilty man will be hung," Allen shouted.

"So do I!" Frank replied.

"No, you don't," Allen snapped. "You are the guilty man and you don't want to hang. If I had anything to do with that murder I hope God may strike me dead and that my soul will burn in hell for all eternity!"

If Frank was still a rooster after that exchange, the foxes were closing in. The press was after him. The investigators were after him. Harry Allen was after him. The whole county seemed to be against him, and soon, the greatest private detective in San Francisco would be after him.

"Belew has the hunted look," the *Call* observed the following day. "He is nervous, and his brothers fear he will end his life if he is harassed further. His friends say his actions are caused by deep sorrow over the death of his brother and sister, and by the fact that he is being hounded and denounced. His enemies say he exhibits all the signs of guilt and remorse."

His brothers, Thomas and Arthur, were his only real defenders. By their calculation, Frank couldn't have been the one to poison Susie and Louis, and then stood vigil with them as they thrashed and moaned through a slow, painful death.

"No matter what they say about Frank, and no matter how black the storm may gather around my brother," a teary-eyed Thomas said with Frank sitting next to him, "just one picture makes me know he is innocent. I can see him now at the deathbed of Susie, holding her hand when she died. I can see him again watching over Louis until the last, like a slave, to save them both. And he stayed until the tide of life had ebbed away. No man can make me believe that my brother had the heart to poison those he loved this way. It is inhuman and unnatural. He has not that kind of a heart."

For a man who had "the hunted look," his brother's eloquent defense overwhelmed the suspected murderer.

"Frank Belew suppressed the sob that strove to break the silence," the *Call* described, "swallowed the great lump in his throat, [wiped] the tears from his deep blue eyes, drummed nervously with his right foot, and said: 'I never poisoned them. It was someone else.'"

Frank, Allen, someone else—the first legal procedure necessary to unmask the killer was to hold a coroner's inquest. Jury members would hear witnesses and submit their judgement on the manner and cause of death. Occasionally, a coroner's jury could give an informal ruling on *who* caused the death. An inquest is typically held soon after the death is discovered, but in the case of Susie and Louis Belew, District Attorney Frank Devlin took time to gather more evidence. This delay only added to the excitement that was building as those in Solano and adjacent counties eagerly anticipated the hearing, which, they hoped, would answer the question: *did Frank do it?*

To help provide an answer, Sheriff Benjamin Rush invited Captain John Curtin, a highly-regarded private detective from San Francisco, to assist with the investigation. Curtin began his career with the Pinkerton Detective Agency where he rose to the rank of captain. In recent years, he had started his own private firm. His name and accomplishments were frequently cited in San Francisco newspapers during the 1890s.

On November 16, just one week after Susie died, Captain Curtin began his investigation with a systematic interrogation of all the witnesses, which included a three-hour grilling of Frank.

"He was greatly disturbed when he left the inquisition chamber," an observer wrote. "His story was replete with vital contradictions, and he was crowded to the wall."

Curtin next searched the Belew home for clues, read Susie's private letters, and traveled to Davisville to interview Frank's wife. She was reticent to discuss anything concerning her estranged husband, good or bad. As much as she disliked Frank, she was a mother who was trying to protect her sons. If their father was a double-murderer, they would become outcasts. Like Frank's blue eyes and dark hair, his murderous instinct would be passed down to his sons—or so people would assume. Curtin then turned his attention to finding the smoking gun—Frank's name on record as having purchased arsenic. "Of course, this piece of evidence is vital," Curtin told the *Woodland Daily Democrat*. "If we ever get it, there are many circumstances of value already in our possession which will be made more valuable by that discovery."

They never found it. Not in San Francisco, not in Sacramento and not anywhere in between. They didn't find Allen's name either.

That elusive clue may have been why District Attorney Devlin delayed the coroner's inquest until November 23, exactly two weeks after Susie died. Without inculpatory evidence, Devlin decided to change tactics, and refrain from pushing the coroner's jury to name Susie and Louis's killer. He only wanted to show they were murdered, and use the proceeding to question witnesses whose statements could later be used to build a criminal case.

"It was his policy at the outset to reserve the strongest evidence until a more serious inquiry...the coroner's jury will not accuse anybody of foul play," a *Call* reporter foretold.

The inquest was held in a public meeting hall packed with several hundred people, mostly women, who had come from all over central California. Despite the public fervor, the hearing was anti-climactic, with only a handful of new revelations.

One of the first to testify was the father of Louis's fiancé, Eugene Ferguson. He shocked those in attendance when he reported that during the funeral, Frank told him: "Tommy wants to be administrator [of the estate], but I want a stranger. They got the best of me before, but they cannot get the best of me this time!"

The women in the audience gasped when they heard this—that Frank's bitterness and greed should emerge in those callous words on the day of his dead brother and sister's funeral. It was still unclear if Frank broke the Sixth

Commandment, but his heart seemed settled firmly against the Tenth: *Thou shalt not covet the neighbor's house…*

Eugene's wife, who cared for Susie, Louis and Klein, stated that after she made a whiskey toddy from the water in the teakettle, she was ill an hour later. Faring even worse was the nurse who said that after she dipped a slice of bread in the beef broth, she got sick, and was temporarily blinded. This brought the poison count to six: two dead and four sick.

When Frank was called, he was "the coolest, most-intelligent, and best witness of the day," the *Call* declared. His confidence may have been bolstered by the presence of his new attorney, Reese Clark. During his questioning, Frank revealed that he, or maybe it was his wife, had purchased *Rough on Rats* a few years earlier. However, he was sure the box was empty, that he hadn't seen in it in over a year, and that he had buried it to prevent his children from finding it.

It was a smart move on his part. Instead of trying to conceal his purchase of rat poison, he admitted it, but downplayed its importance and diverted its relevance.

His admission helped Devlin's case, but it wasn't a noose knot. Every farm and ranch throughout Solano County probably had rat poison on hand. It was as common as the family bible.

Frank was then asked to repeat his earlier statement that he left Dixon at 7:30 that Sunday night, and was home in bed by 8:30. Before he sat in the witness chair, Dixon's night watchman, Joe Staton, testified that he spoke with Frank around nine o'clock that night. It was an important discrepancy. Why would Frank lie about when he left town? Did he sneak back into his brother's house to poison the teakettle?

Harry Allen, by contrast, emerged from the inquest practically cleared of any wrongdoing. He welcomed the chance to tell his story, was sincere in his denials, and able to account for all his time that Sunday night.

"In fact," the *Woodland Daily Democrat reported*, "the story he told on the stand made a very favorable impression on nearly everybody who heard it and there does not appear to be the remotest possibility that he will ever be a defendant in any criminal proceedings."

The jury deliberated one-hour before returning the verdict Devlin wanted: "…that Louis Belew and Susie Belew came to their deaths from arsenic poison administered by a person or persons unknown to this jury."

After the inquest, the Belew case took an unexpected turn—it disappeared from the newspapers. Devlin, Rush, and Curtin swore to continue their investigation into Frank Belew, but without physical evidence or a surprise witness, there wasn't much to go on. And if there wasn't much to go on, there was nothing to report on.

Although it was possible someone else snuck into the house and poisoned the teakettle, folks didn't think it was likely. Susie would have easily discovered the intruder and told Charlie about it. They knew it had to be Frank. He had the motive, he had opportunity, and he had the dark history of Abel's brother, Cain.

To resolve this case, they needed to catch a break. They needed a miracle. They needed divine intervention. They needed *Ecclesiastes 10:20:* "Do not revile the king even in your thoughts, or curse the rich in your bedroom, because a bird in the sky may carry your words, and a bird on the wing may report what you say."

And that's exactly what they got—a little birdy that told them who did it.

JOHN W. BIRD WAS A LITTLE MAN with a big problem. His brother-in-law wanted to kill him. He never said it directly, but Bird knew. He knew Frank Belew was going to kill him—on the sly.

His predicament started on Saturday, November 6, when Frank stopped by Bird's photography studio to talk about his favorite subject: the money from his father's estate that should have been his.

"I've just been down to see Susie," Frank began, according to a statement Bird later gave to authorities. "She showed me her wedding clothes and said she and Charlie Ehmann were going to Nevada on tour."

Her marriage to Charlie, and Louis's to Clara, was the spark that lit his dynamite. His anger exploded inside the gallery, launching him into a verbal vilification of them both for having the impertinence, the pompous arrogance, the gall to introduce "new people in the family to divide the hard-earned wealth of his parents."

Susie was showing off that wedding dress, that's what she was doing. Puttin' on airs and acting like one of them Gibson Girls[8]. Not only that, Louis spent $40[9] on a new suit. Forty-dollars!

And then he said it. He said what he was going to do and it was so horrible, Bird could scarcely believe it.

"They have not treated me right in regard to the estate, but I'll have some of it yet. They'll not live to enjoy it," Frank blasted through gritted teeth. After a long pause, and a change of subject, Frank circled back to an idea he had. He was going to do something about their mistreatment of him.

"Bird, I'm going to commit a terrible crime tomorrow," Frank said as he looked him in the eyes. "I'm going to commit a tragedy that will shock the whole community!"

"Do not do anything foolish, old man. Think of the consequences of such a crime," Bird warned.

---

[8] According to Wikipedia, "The Gibson Girl was the personification of the feminine ideal of physical attractiveness as portrayed by the satirical pen-and-ink illustrations of artist Charles Dana Gibson during a 20-year period that spanned the late 19th and early 20th century in the United States"

[9] Close to $1,000 in 2016, when adjusted for inflation.

His wife, Ellen, was the sister of Frank's wife, Tennessee. If Frank did something wicked, it would bring shame to Ellen. But he kept this to himself, and said nothing more to Frank.

John W. Bird

The next time Bird saw him was the day of the funeral. Frank, wearing a black suit underneath a long black coat, moved through the mourners shaking hands and nodding his head solemnly when they gave their condolences.

Later, when they were alone, Bird approached him. "Well, you did what you said you would," he commented.

"Did what?" Frank replied.

"Murdered Louis and Susie."

"Did I tell you that?" Frank asked.

"Yes."

"Yes, I do remember that I made that threat. *BUT,* I didn't tell you that I did it," Frank countered.

"Well," Bird snapped, "but I know you did it."

NOW THAT BIRD KNEW HE did it, Frank carefully cultivated his relationship with his brother-in-law. He had to. The man could send him to the gallows. Even so, of all the people who could preserve Frank's secret, it was John W. Bird. When the *San Francisco Call* described him as the "strange brother-in-law," they were being polite. In verbal exchanges with one of their reporters, Bird displayed a riged personality with a curious propensity to act difficult for the sake of being difficult.

His motive for keeping Frank's secret for several months seemed even more bizarre. During those two weeks in November, when the pressure against Frank was building to a crescendo, and the social outrage and clamor for justice was heard all over California, Bird kept his secret "to save his wife from the disgrace of being known to all the world as the sister [in-law] of an infamous moral monster."

It didn't seem reasonable. He lived in Sacramento and commuted by train to his photography studio in Dixon. His wife wasn't even related by blood to the "moral monster." She was a Martin, not a Belew, and the Martins had a good reputation in those parts. There was also a combined $1,350 reward[10] for information that led to the person who poisoned the teakettle. Yet, Bird kept his mouth shut.

When Frank threatened to kill Susie and Louis that Saturday before the family's last supper, it wasn't the first time. His obsessive anger had been building up to that moment just days after his father died on September 21 the year before.

"He first began to threaten murder shortly after the death of his parents," Bird later said. "In many conversations, he told me he would get revenge."

---

[10] The 2016 equivalent of $32,728.

After the coroner's inquest, when the pressure on Frank was relaxed, he met often with Bird with whom he shared his dark pride for setting things right, and boasted of how he had outsmarted the authorities.

"He never expressed remorse for the murders, but has often laughed at the way he eluded the officers and perpetrated what he threatened," Bird described later. "He said he did a good job and thought he was pretty smooth in getting away [from] the sleuths."

Frank had gotten away with it, just like he had gotten away with everything else, including the attempted murder of Charley Hough. Now that it was just him, Arthur, and Thomas, he could patiently bide his time until the estate was settled and get his share of what Susie and Louis had. He was about to receive the blessings he had always deserved.

But Frank couldn't leave well-enough alone. He had hornswoggled everybody but he couldn't leave the bull in the barn. That December, he came up with a plan to take Bird on a hunting trip to the tules—the marshlands of California's Great Central Valley. A hunting trip with his pal Bird was the perfect way to reward the man for his loyal friendship. It was such a grand idea, Belew didn't ask Bird, he insisted on it. He damn near demanded it.

"Frank [had] been trying to get me to go out hunting in the tules for a long time," Bird later reported. "He has been persistent in this request, and has planned in every way to get me to some lonely spot. When I refused, he seemed more determined than ever, and I read, unmistakably, that he wanted to murder me because he wanted to get me out of the way."

Bird was no simpleton. Frank had gone bughouse if he thought Bird couldn't see what he was up to. He knew about Charlie Hough—and that was over $47. Frank had tried to claim the gun "accidentally discharged" when the shotgun pellets tore through the brim of Hough's hat. After he realized he'd missed, Frank apologized and said it was an accident.

Hough believed him. But that was just one incident. There were two other times he attempted to kill Hough that most people didn't know about. Frank managed to convince everyone that Hough was crazy and had tried to commit suicide. Folks believed him, until they heard the real story.

Soon, everybody would know that Louis, Bruno, Susie, as well as her caretakers, were not his poison first victims.

After Frank realized his brother-in-law was not one for hunting geese, he came up with a new idea: he began talking about how they could get rich by hunting for gold in the Klondike. When Frank got his share of the estate, the two men would have a real nice stake when they reached Alaska. Real nice.

But Frank wasn't foolin' him. Bird knew "that the object was to murder him rather than hunt for gold." The only hunting Frank was interested in was Bird hunting.

"Then, dark days of fear and suspicion came to Bird," the *Call* dramatized. "His secret grew heavy. It became a burden that bore him down, drove sleep from his eyelids, and made him suspicious that every morsel he ate contained poison. It was for these reasons that the secret of the dreadful murder came to the ears of authorities."

Now that a little birdy confirmed what they had suspected all along, Sheriff Rush, prosecutor Devlin, and Captain Curtin concocted a simple but brilliant trap for Frank Belew. According to Bird, Frank would visit him at his Dixon studio on Sunday, January 30 (1898). While the two men were chewing the fat, Deputy Frank Newby would be squirreled away in an adjacent room listening to everything he said through a peephole.

At ten minutes to noon that Sunday, Frank entered the studio. A table and two chairs had been carefully arranged to give him no choice but to take a seat with his back to the wall—just two feet away from Newby's secret perch. Bird, sitting across from him, carefully introduced Frank's favorite topic: the money and the estate, which was working its way through probate. He then steered his brother-in-law toward discussing the grand jury proceedings and District Attorney Devlin. It was the perfect topic for Frank because it gave him the opportunity to crow.

"I'm as good as pie," Frank said with pleasure, leaning back in his chair. "There is another election coming up and Devlin wants votes, and thinks he wants my help, and won't bother me anymore; but I won't be here at election. I will be in Alaska. If everything goes well, I want to go as soon as I get settled up, which I think can't be done before the middle of April."

"Well, Frank, you fooled them all in grand shape in this poisoning case, not to get caught," Bird said.

"Yes."

"Frank, that was a terrible thing; but you would not have poisoned Louis and Susie if they had treated you right with the estate before, would you?"

"No."

"They were after you pretty hot for a while. You must have been pretty slick in getting the poison so they could not find out where you got it, for they hunted every drug store in Sacramento and all around."

"Yes, and they went to you, didn't they?" Frank asked.

"Yes."

"Who?"

"The reporters," Bird replied. "All of them—*The Call*, *Examiner*, and *Chronicle*—they were all after me and also wanted your picture. I would not tell them anything or give them the photo. I have been a friend to you, Frank."

"Yes," Frank said as he nodded his head, "and if I can ever do anything for you, Bird, I will do it."

"Yes, Frank, after you told me beforehand that you were going to poison Louis and Susie, and then it happened as you said, it worried me so I couldn't hardly eat or sleep until after I had a talk with you about it. Then I felt better and haven't thought so much about it since."

"Bird, you have been a friend to me and when I go to the Klondike I want to take you with me. Ellen (Bird's wife) don't know anything about it, does she?"

"No, she don't know you did the poisoning."

"Don't tell her," Frank said as he looked Bird directly in the eyes. "I don't want anyone to know I did it, but you and I."

"No, if I should tell her, she might tell some friend, and then some other friend, and it would get out, so it's best for only us to know it," Bird answered in a reassuring tone.

"I don't think she would tell; she is a good friend to me, but it would worry her if she knew it and it's best to keep it from her."

"It's enough for you and I to know you poisoned them."

"Yes, and I am grateful to you for the friendship you have shown me, and I would do anything for you," Frank said as he shifted in his seat. "I won't go to Alaska alone and I hope you will go with me."

At that moment, two young women entered the studio to pick-up some photographs. When they left, Frank brought up the name of the man who was listening to everything he said.

"Newby thought he was raising hell for a while, but he has let up now," Frank said. "Guess he was out for the money[11] there was in it."

"Does he talk to you about the case anymore?" Bird inquired.

"No, but he patronizes the stable and sends business there. Guess he is all right now," Frank said in a confident tone.

By then, local church services were over and more customers began coming into the studio. At 1:50, Frank left, saying he had to get home.

---

[11] The reward money.

FOUR DAYS LATER, FRANK BELEW was arrested at his ranch. The law arrived after ten o'clock on February 3, when they knew he would be in bed. Sheriff Rush, and two "stalwart" deputies banged on the door, identified themselves, and when Frank opened the door, guns were pointed at this head.

It was all over.

Frank Belew, a tall man with a powerful frame, the man who boasted about his crime, who took pride in outsmarting everyone—wept as he was arrested. A *Call* reporter, who stayed behind in Dixon after the November 23 inquest, was there to relish the moment for his patient readers.

> The climax was a terrible surprise to him. He is a strong man physically, but his hands shook within their [shackles]. His eyes filled with tears as he stood helpless in the presence of the officers of the law. His voice faltered, but faltering it still denied the charges.
>
> "Gentlemen," he had said when the click of the manacles first made him realize the clutch of justice, "you have the wrong man."
>
> This he repeated many times.
>
> "I never did it," he added, but there was no confidence in the tones, and they did not impress as being sincere. He licked his lips with feverish persistency. He looked about him, as if in each shadow there might be something to fear.
>
> The scene was a striking one.... The officers do not try to question him. They have no care what his answer might be.

In the Solano County Jail, described as "the darkest, most dismal jail in California," Frank Belew melted into a pathetic, loathsome creature. With the evidence they had, county officials took no real interest in him. Unsurprisingly, San Francisco reporters roamed the jail corridor. Over the next thirty-six hours, they observed and noted Frank's every move. The portrait they painted with words was more animal than human.

"Abject despair." —— "Belew is much depressed. He feels that his friends are falling away from him." —— "His strong frame trembling, his blue eyes filled with tears and his throat is pulsating with the visible sign of emotion. He gulps as he speaks, his tongue moistens his feverish lips." —— "At times, he checked an impulse to speak and bit his twitching lips. His strong hands clasped and unclasped (the flat-iron slats of his cell door) convulsively."

FRANK BELEW IN HIS CELL.

During those thirty-six hours, *Call* reporters took Frank's mind to the psychological woodshed where they whipped him mercilessly with guilt. They appealed to whatever sense of right and wrong was left in him, and reminded him that a confession might bring mercy. Occasionally, they directed his attention to Newby's sworn statement, and Bird's affirmation of its accuracy. The evidence was strong, they assured him.

"But what of the admission you made to Bird which Newby overheard?" Leigh Irvine from the *Call* asked.

"Bird and Newby both lied," Frank snapped back. "They are after blood money. They want the reward. They lied. I would not have murdered my brother and sister for all the wealth in California."

BETWEEN THE EARLY MORNING HOURS of Friday, February 4, when he was thrown in his vault-like cell with only a barred window in the iron door, to Saturday evening, Frank held out hope that his friends, his brothers, and his attorney would come to his aid.

They didn't. Arthur reacted as predicted, by getting drunk. "I will not believe Frank is guilty until I hear him say so," was his only statement from a saloon forty miles away. When pressed by reporters, he could only muster a repetition of those words.

Tom, the emotional, sensitive sibling, broke down and wept "twenty-times today" when he visited Frank. Tom didn't want to believe it either, but he couldn't ignore the evidence. He wasn't any help to his brother and could only pass on a message from attorney Reese Clark: don't talk, and not to see any of the newspaper men.

But Clark underestimated the tenacity of Leigh Irvine, star reporter for the *Call*. Frank was no match for Irvine who realized that the doomed man was holding on to belief that his friends and brothers would bolster him. In the early evening hours of Saturday, February 5, Irvine removed that last trace of hope by stating the obvious: nobody was coming to his rescue.

> At first, he made no sound except one impossible to describe. It was the suction as he gulped, vainly striving to control his convulsive lips and the throat which would vibrate. Then he asked if his friends, his brothers, his lawyers had been heard from. It was hard to tell him that in his extremity he was friendless; that his brothers, convinced of his blood guiltiness, had cast him off; that his lawyers had sent no word. The man

writhed on his pile of blankets, his right hand fumbling the leaves of a magazine he had been vainly trying to read.

"Frank, think of how your mind would be relieved if you told the truth," Irvine said softly.

But Frank was thinking of his betrayal by Bird, and it gnawed at him. He had done so much for Bird.

"I want you–to tell the world," Frank pouted, "that–for four years–I supported Bird; that he used my horse–without charge, and lived off me–when I could not afford to keep him."

And then it slipped out, through a narrow crack in his ridged willpower to maintain his innocence, Frank spilled the beans.

"Why did you tell Bird what you had done?" Irvine tried.

"He pumped me."

In an instant, Frank realized what he had just said, and although he tried to recover, he didn't seem to regret it, Irvine reported.

An hour or so later, Frank's will was broken, overwhelmed by guilt. The words, held inside him for so long, blew out of his mouth like dynamite exploding in a Nevada silver mine.

"I DID IT! OH, I DID IT!" he cried out to a *Call* reporter. "I killed my brother and sister. I did it!"

Irvine, and his associate, Henry James, could scarcely believe what they had heard. It was the dramatic moment they needed, and they were afraid it would slip away—that Frank's see-saw mind would tilt back toward denial. They pushed him to sign an informal confession and pressed him for details of everything that transpired that Sunday. He gave a partial account that was printed the next day under the full-page headline:

FRANK BELEW HAS CONFESSED

News of his confession made it onto the pages of most newspapers west of the Rocky Mountains, and even spread as far east as Indiana, Ohio, and New York. In California, the story was on the front page of nearly every daily newspaper that weekend.

The day after he came clean to Leigh Irvine, Sunday, February 6, Frank was escorted to District Attorney Devlin's courthouse office, where he gave a full, written confession.

The poison he used was the number one brand name in rat poison, suicides, and arsenic murders, *Rough on Rats*. He had purchased it in 1892. Before he left for Dixon that Sunday, Frank poured several grams in a rolled-up piece of paper.

Like Curtin, Rush, and Devlin expected, Frank dropped the white powder in the teakettle at the first opportunity.

"Tommy and his sweetheart, Miss Brimley, had left the supper table," Frank said as he trembled with fear. "There was some delay at the carriage while they were all saying good-bye. I then went through the kitchen and dropped the poison through the top, after lifting the lid. After I was sure that the poison was in the water, I walked into the room where Susie was preparing to meet Charlie Ehmann. She was fixing her hair at the time, and we chatted as if nothing had happened."

Beginning with his confession to *Call* reporters Saturday night until approximately twenty-four hours later, Frank Belew repeatedly claimed that he couldn't understand why he killed his sister and brother. Irvine pushed him for an explanation.

"I had no reason," Frank blubbered. "I cannot understand it myself. I don't know. I would tell you if I could."

"Were you jealous of their prosperity?"

"No, I had nothing against them," Frank whispered.

"Were you dissatisfied about the division of the estate?" Irvine asked.

"I was not. I had no reason. I just did it, that's all."

He continued to make his 'I don't know — I can't understand' claims until six o'clock Sunday night when he concocted a new version, one that might cast him in a better light.

He did it because Susie and Louis slandered his wife Tennessee—whom he still loved and was the mother of two boys.

"When I heard Susie and Louis speak evil words of my wife," he said in a firm tone blended with the proper amount of self-righteousness, "I conceived the idea that there ought to be some way to make them suffer. I do not think I had the idea of poisoning them in my mind for over three hours, but out on the ranch–I suffered at the thought–that my wife was not with me–and that she was separated–partly because of financial worries. I said to myself–that it was not right for them to talk as they had done.

"When any human being steps between a man and the woman he loves as I loved my wife–and as I love her now–let him beware of the consequences. I did not kill them–for the paltry money in question."

Frank repeated that last sentence "again and again," and ridiculed the idea that he killed for money. It wasn't about the money, it was about his wife's honor, he assured his listener.

Even though he was defending his wife, the one who was physically afraid of him, on the day he signed Devlin's written confession, he was eager to plead guilty.

"I do not want a trial," Frank said to Deputy Newby. "I want to plead guilty and have it all over with."

Later that night, when he was alone with a *Call* reporter, Frank was described as genuinely remorseful and resigned to his fate, which he knew was death.

"You know what they do with men who do what I have done?" he asked rhetorically. "I suppose there is no way of escape. I do not want to escape, as there is nothing in life for a man who has done what I have done."

But those were just words to Frank. They didn't mean a thing. By the following day, he was given hope—hope that washed away his sins and fed his desire to save his own neck from the noose. Of all the people to influence Frank to change his mind it was Arthur, who sobered up long enough to visit him late Sunday evening, February 6.

"Frank," Arthur began, "was that confession all right?"

"Yes. I poisoned them."

"Why did you do it?" Arthur cried, as he broke down into tears. "Oh, why did you do it? You must have been out of your head."

When he composed himself, Arthur considered his brother with a confused look on his face and said, "I do not see how I could have been with you all these weeks and had no suspicion. Many a night you have gone to bed, first, and I have heard you sleeping soundly with this on your soul."

That did not paint a pretty picture. Knowing the *Call* reporter was standing within earshot, Frank had to fix that.

"But I was not always sleeping as well as you thought," he replied to his brother. "For this thing has been weighing on me like a thousand tons of pressure."

Arthur wanted to believe him. The newsmen did not.

Away from his brother's cell, Arthur gave a clue of what was to come. "It seems to me impossible that he committed that crime while he was in his right mind. I think some strange emotion controlled him, and he could not resist the idea to do what he did."

The bughouse defense. Frank was crazy when he did it. The next day, Frank declared he was coerced into confessing because Irvine tricked him into believing his friends and family had abandoned him. He would, he announced, plead not guilty, and rely on a technical defense—code words for an insanity plea. Afterward, he was more cheerful, buoyed by the hope that a noose may never touch his neck.

"I do not feel as I did when arrested, and have no desire to die," Frank told a group of out-of-town correspondents. "I think that imprisonment would suit me better."

His change of heart was fertilized by the knowledge that Arthur was talking to lawyers and telling newspapers that,

"Frank must have been insane...I do not think he should suffer the extreme penalty."

Frank himself may have had "no desire to die," but he didn't feel the same about Charley Hough's life. He was finally located in Stockton by *Call* reporters who found him to be an intelligent, reasonable man—nothing like the suicidal lunatic Frank had described.

During the spring of 1894, Hough worked on Frank's ranch for two months. "I never worked for a man more agreeable to my face. When we got through, he owed me $47, but as I had some money, I told him not to inconvenience himself as I was not broke."

Hough moved on to another farm nearby where he found more work. There, he had an accident and hurt his ribs. He went to Dixon to rest and heal, and while there, met Frank Belew on the street one day.

"He said he was alone at the ranch and suggested that I come out and eat supper with him," Hough recalled. "I went, and after the meal I had to go and lie down for some time. It seemed that every bone and muscle in me was paralyzed. I got better, however, and returned to town that evening. The idea that Belew tried to poison me never crossed my mind, as I supposed I was merely sick from some [unknown] cause."

By September of that year, Hough was broke and had no place to live. "I got hard up and I went out to Belew and asked him if he would not help me out by letting me board out that debt. I thought it [would be] all right, as Mrs. Belew had told me several times to come out and feel at home."

Everything was fine, as long as Mrs. Belew was there, but when she went away for a few days, Frank changed—from affable employer to cold-blooded killer. Hough told the *Call* reporter the strange story of how Frank tried to shoot him in October.

> Frank asked me if I wanted to drive across to his other place with him. He harnessed up and I went with him. He took his

shotgun with him, but I thought nothing of that, as he frequently carried the gun around with him. We arrived at the place and after looking around, I started to get back to the wagon, supposing that Belew was going home.

Since it has turned out as it has, I can see that his actions were wrong, but I thought nothing of them at that time. He hesitated and finally suggested that we walk over to the road fence and see how things looked in that part of the country. We went, and he kept hesitating and gaining time by small talk.

We were near the haystack at the time and he said he was going over on the other side of the fence. I told him I guessed I would lie down on the straw and wait until he returned.

I lay down with my head resting on my hand and my elbow on the straw, and was dozing when I heard the report of a gun, which was followed by a charge of shot tearing off my hat brim. My first thought was that it was an accidental shot from long-range, but when I got up and went around the stack, I saw Belew walking away from me over on the other side of the fence.

I thought this was funny, so I jumped up and overtook him. He looked rather white, and when I told him he had almost struck me by a wild shot he grew very nervous and seemed to be making no preparations to go home. I never suspected anything up to this time, but now I feel a little uncertain.

On the way home, he told me not to say anything about the close-call, as it might worry his wife.

But Hough's problems didn't end there. Frank tried to kill him again later that same day. Since it was the early part of October, a fine time to enjoy the evening hours, he sat outside while Frank made supper. When dinner was ready, Frank called him inside to eat.

We had hardly sat down when he jumped up and said the gun accident had made him so nervous that he could not eat. I reached over, and, breaking a biscuit, buttered it. The first mouthful was so bitter that I spat it out on the plate. I noticed some white powder. Then I was scared, and jumping up I went over and got my coat. Belew was out in the yard, and so I went back to the table, got a piece of the bread, and put it in my pocket. Without waiting further, I cut across the fields and did not stop until I got into Dixon.

The next day a druggist examined the biscuit and said it was full of poison. I complained to the constable up there and he told me I was a stranger and Belew well thought of, and it would do me no good to press the case. I even told Frank's brother, whom he poisoned, and he made no comment. I talked, some, [about] the attacks on me and to contradict me, a report was started that I was crazy and had tried to commit suicide.

More than anything, Hough's story was a sad one. The constable was Deputy Newby. If Newby had inquired with the pharmacist and taken Hough more seriously, Frank Belew could have been exposed as a poisoner and Susie and Louis would still be alive.

IN HIS DISMAL CELL, THEIR killer was in high spirits and slept peacefully during the cold nights of February and March. The insanity defense would save his life and he began saying things about the murder like, "I cannot understand…" and that the "terrible crime…was beyond my control." He would never say the word "murder."

On February 23, a smiling Frank pled not guilty to the lone charge of murdering his sister. If he slithered out of a guilty verdict, Devlin would charge him for the murder of his brother. But Frank wasn't worried about his brother's trial. He was convinced he would be sentenced to life in prison. His disposition at his arraignment reflected that sentiment, and his demeanor was noted in the press as "cheerful" and "perfectly at ease."

Besides his new defense strategy, Frank's mood was lifted by the fact that he would soon receive his share of the estate. Even though he had murdered his brother and sister, confessed to it, and was due to stand trial, California had no law in place that would block him from inheriting his share of their estate. When his wife requested that he cede his rights of familial inheritance for the benefit of his children during a jailhouse visit on March 8, he politely refused. As long as he had hope that he could escape the hangman's noose, Frank Belew wanted that money for himself.

"It was obvious that the question of standing trial, with a possible sentence of life imprisonment, was of more importance to him than the maintenance of his children," a special correspondent wrote. For all his declarations that the motive wasn't about money, Frank was too stupid to realize his selfishness had just invalidated those claims.

On the human being scale, Frank had sunk pretty low, but it was not the bottom.

On March 30, Belew surprised everyone by changing his plea. He had thought better of his insanity defense. His trial would have been held in Solano County, and in Solano County, he was despised. Susie and Louis were two of the most beloved young citizens of Dixon. Residents there also knew Frank: like him or hate him, they knew he wasn't loco. Degenerate poisoner, yes. Bughouse, no.

He didn't stand a chance.

His only hope was to plead guilty and throw himself on the mercy of the court.

"I warn you," Judge Abraham Buckles began, "that in pleading guilty you need expect no greater leniency than though you were tried by a jury. The jury's duty is to determine your guilt, whether you be hanged or sent to prison, and the court has the same duty. This crime is one of the worst kinds of murder, if it is as rumored, and as you have confessed. What is your plea?"

"Guilty, and I ask the mercy of the court," Frank replied. This was it. If it failed, if there was no mercy, Frank just stuck his neck in the noose.

Which is exactly what happened. After two days of witness testimony to evaluate if mitigating factors would warrant a jury trial to fix his punishment, Judge Buckles ruled against him. "My decision is that there are no mitigating circumstances, or facts, or anything whatever which can relieve the defendant from the extreme penalty of the law for such cases," he said on April 9. Four days later, the judge read the death warrant to him in court. "…hanged by the neck until you be dead. And God have mercy on your soul."

God's mercy wasn't the mercy he was hoping for. He had just sixty-five days to live.

But Frank Belew wasn't one to go to hell without dragging someone else down with him. On May 3, the *Woodland Daily Democrat* reported that his nemesis, John Bird, filed a claim to receive Governor James Budd's reward offer of $600[12]. At the time, Frank's wife and children were living with Bird and his wife. It is unclear what his intentions were for that money, but he was "severely criticized" for seeking the payment.

There was one person who especially didn't like it—Frank Belew. He was determined to put Bird's neck in the noose like that Judas had done to him. On May 13, Sheriff Rush met with Frank at Folsom Prison to listen to the death row prisoner who declared, "I am now ready to open my heart." He wanted to tell the *real* story. The big secret he had been carrying with him all this time is that his brother-in-law, John Bird, was his co-conspirator to wipe out his entire family.

"The murders were planned by J.W. Bird and me some time before I killed Susie and Louis. Our original intention was to murder Arthur and Tommy but I did not get a good chance to do the job."

"What was Bird to get out of this?" Sheriff Rush asked.

"Well, you see I was to kill them all and the property would then go to me and my children," Frank answered. "He was to be administrator, and he would have made a haul that way (profited). If I got into trouble, Bird was to stand by me and

---

[12] The 2016 equivalent of $14,545.

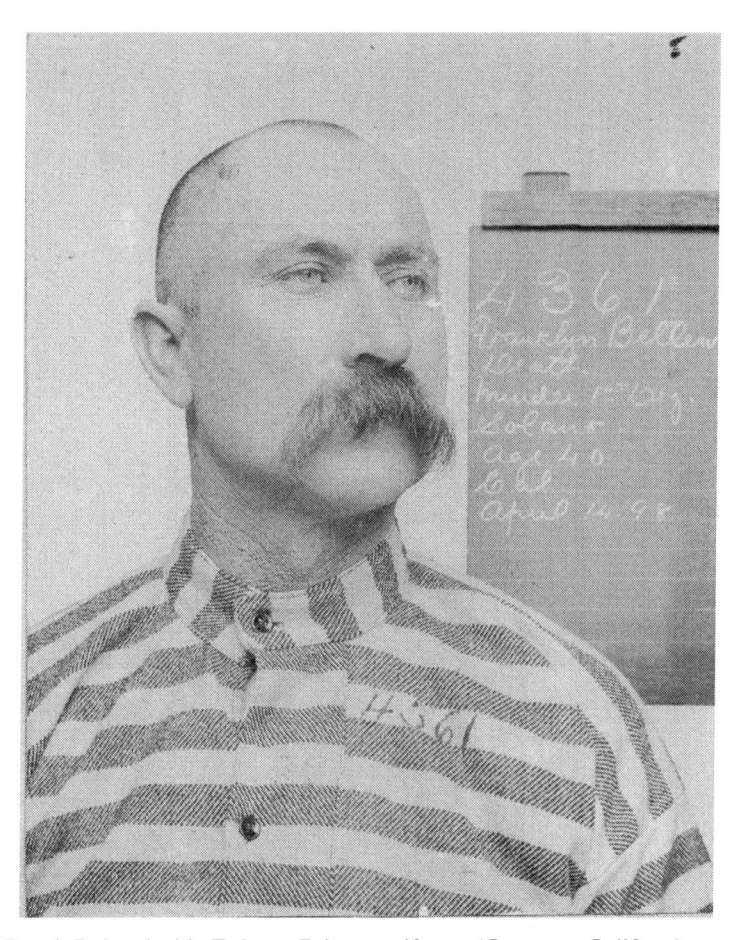

Frank Belew in his Folsom Prison uniform. (Courtesy California State Archives.)

do all in his power to save my life; but he went back on me, and that is why I want to tell the whole truth. Bird knew all the time I was going to murder them."

This wasn't the first time a death row inmate tried "to tell the whole truth," and Frank's story was widely regarded as fertilizer. Bird, however, never did collect the $600 reward.

June 16, 1898

DURING THE LAST TWENTY-FOUR HOURS of his life, Frank Belew found God, "professed his religion" to a minister, slept peacefully in his Folsom Prison death cell, then arose early to eat a hearty breakfast and was allowed to spend one hour visiting with friends who came to say good-bye[13]. With his pals present, he was in a jovial mood and possessed a stoic indifference to his 10 a.m. meeting with the hangman. And in that final hour, instead of expressing remorse, instead of repenting, he dedicated the last moments of his life to the spiteful destruction of the man who betrayed him.

"An hour before he was led to the gallows, he was visited by his friends and companions, and when one of them asked if he thought he could go through with the ordeal without breaking down, he laughed in the most apparent good humor," observed a *San Francisco Chronicle* reporter.

"Why should I break down?" he queried. He knew the *Chronicle* reporter was jotting down everything he said, and was eager to wreck Bird's life. "I killed Susie and Louis and I'm perfectly ready to pay the forfeit. I have nothing to say except I am guilty. I have signed a full confession in which I have named my brother-in-law, J.W. Bird, as an accessory and that is true."

Frank then launched into a denunciation of Bird, but was interrupted by the minister who reminded him of a promise made the night before during his better-safe-than-sorry religious conversion. Frank nodded, and then grew silent for a moment. With ten minutes left, he turned to a *Sacramento Bee* reporter and inquired about his wife and two sons. The night before, Frank finally got around to making his will. According to a report in the *Woodland Daily Democrat*, he bequeathed his property, valued at $1,300, in trust for his two sons. Each would receive $15 a month until they reached the age of

---

[13] They were allowed to meet him at his death cell—the cell he occupied prior to his execution.

twenty-one, and then the remainder would be divided between them. His last charitable act was coupled with a genuine concern for Merritt and Thomas Raymond, both under the age of ten.

At ten o'clock that Thursday morning, Frank, with his head shaved and arms strapped to his sides, was led from his cell to a large room where one hundred men stood silently. Without any hesitation or guidance, Frank walked directly to the scaffold and ascended the steps.

"He walked firmly, with head erect and paid no attention to anybody, not even Sheriff Rush, who greeted him with a 'Hello Frank,' as Belew brushed past him," the *Chronicle* reported. "On the gallows, Belew glanced over the upturned faces, but if he recognized any of them, he gave no sign but just before the cap was adjusted, he recognized Sheriff Rush and nodded to him."

Seconds later, the trap door gave way and Frank's body fell ten feet. There was no report of his neck breaking. As he swung there, suspended above the floor, Charlie Ehmann, who was in the audience, grasped a prison guard and exclaimed so all could hear: "This is too good to be true!"

Eleven and one-half minutes later, Frank Belew was declared dead. His brothers buried him in Sacramento—twenty-three miles west of the family plot in Dixon.

Epilogue:

AFTER FRANK'S EXECUTION, HIS BROTHER Arthur filed an objection with the Solano County Superior Court arguing that since Frank had caused the death of Susie and Louis, the estate of Frank Belew, represented by his children, was not entitled to receive any part of Louis and Susie's property. A demurrer was filed on behalf of Frank's estate, and Judge Buckles ruled in favor of Frank's children arguing that unless the Code of Civil Procedure were changed, the estates of Louis and Susie Belew must be distributed in equal parts to both surviving brothers and the murderer's estate.

Judge Buckle's surprising decision made news across the country and in death, Frank Belew's name became more infamous then when he was alive. Legal journals covered the story and *The American Lawyer* speculated "Had Frank Belew been alive when the petition was filed, we [anticipate] a different ruling would have been made."

John W. Bird's application for the governor's $600 reward was rejected by both the governor and attorney general who declared, "The reward was offered for the arrest and conviction of the poisoner, and not for information leading to such arrest and conviction. They held that only the arresting officer could lay valid claim to the reward," the *Sacramento Daily-Record* reported. One short news item reported that Sheriff Rush and Deputy Newby flat-out refused to file for the reward. It probably would have made them extremely unpopular had they done so.

After Frank was executed, public opinion in Solano County and central California turned against Bird, not because he knew about the murders and kept it a secret, but because he betrayed his friend and then tried to claim the reward. He closed his Dixon photography studio sometime before 1902.

Frank's brother, Thomas, married his sweetheart, Louisa, and they had two children together, a daughter they named Susie, and a son they named Frank. Thomas never spoke to his brother again after he heard him confess in February 1898. Frank's son, Merritt, went on to become a horse showman and trainer for circuses. He spent most of his adult years living in Texas but moved to Phoenix, Arizona, in 1953 and died there in 1967. According to findagrave.com, Thomas Raymond may have changed his last name to Kavanaugh— possibly to escape the notoriety of being the son of Frank Belew. Their mother, Tennessee, remarried. Findagrave.com contains short biographies with more information about their lives after Frank's 1898 execution.

Chapter Two: The Crystal Cool Killer, 1922

IN HIS DREAMS, FRANK PETERSON could hear a woman cry for help. It was soft at first—faraway. He couldn't see her, but he could hear her. *Help! Help me!*

"SOMEBODY HELP ME!"

That time, it was loud enough that he bolted from his bunk, and looked around in the dark at his railroad chums inside the caboose they were sleeping in during the early morning hours of August 14, 1922. Louis Chasen and William Ayers were up too. The men looked at each other, unsure of what they'd heard.

"Help! Help me!" a woman screamed.

It wasn't a dream. It was coming from a two-story building just beyond the tracks, diagonally opposite of the train station in Lakehurst, New Jersey.

Then as now, the sand-colored brick structure sits at the corner of Union and Railroad Avenues. The first floor was designed to accommodate two businesses while the second-floor comprised a large, seven-room apartment.

When Frank and his pals reached the front of the building, they could hear the woman calling out from behind the second of three doors—the one that led to the upstairs apartment. Peering through the upper-glass of the door, they could make out the crumpled figure of a heavy-set woman.

It was locked, they told her.

Break it down, she cried.

The Giberson building at it appears today, 3 Union Avenue, Lakehurst New Jersey. (Photo Credit: Google Maps.)

Inside, the railroad employees found forty-one-year-old Ivy Giberson at the base of the stairs with her ankles trussed and her wrists tied behind her with package twine. A cloth napkin hung from her neck, apparently used to gag her. As Frank broke the twine with his fingers, the woman "babbled an incoherent story of a robbery," shouting that "two robbers had killed her husband," he later told police.

Upstairs, in a back bedroom adjacent to the kitchen, Frank turned on a lamp and found William Giberson dead from a gunshot wound to the base of the skull. The body was cold to the touch and from the looks of it, the thirty-four-year-old died instantly.

Frank found a telephone and called the sheriff's office.

By breakfast time that Monday morning, Ocean County deputies and New Jersey State Troopers were searching the Giberson property, talking to neighbors and checking on all the strangers in town. Although the sheriff would normally lead the investigation, his skills were not up to the standards of District Attorney Wilfred H. Jayne Jr.

Murder victim William Giberson

"Mr. Jayne...told the sheriff...that he was not satisfied with the way he conducted criminal investigations, and would develop his own cases hereafter," explained a New York City newspaper.

Thirty minutes into the case, Jayne understood he was still going to need a lead detective. That morning, after listening to the woman's story, he knew she wasn't telling the truth. He couldn't put a finger on it, but Ivy Giberson's account of what happened "didn't ring true for a minute," he later said. To help him sort it all out, the ambitious thirty-three-year-old prosecutor called in one of America's most famous investigators, Ellis Parker, chief of detectives in neighboring Burlington County. By August of 1922, Parker was near the peak of his profession with ninety murder arrests resulting in eighty-nine convictions over twenty-nine years. He would later wreck his career and reputation over the Lindberg kidnapping, but his investigation into William Giberson's murder would be recounted in psychology classes for more than a decade.

Like Jayne, when he heard Ivy Giberson's story, he knew she was lying and correctly identified the flaws in her account. He kept that from her, however. He knew the prosecutor was playing a ruse on the peculiar woman by leading her to think they had believed every word she said. Loud enough so she could hear, Jayne ordered his men to look for the two perpetrators. Privately, two of his officers had drifted into the background, nonchalantly observing everything she said and did.

The plan worked. By early afternoon, her actions led them to nearly all the evidence they needed to convict her—if she were a man. In what became one of New Jersey's most sensational murder cases of the 1920s[1], everyone in the state knew that sending a woman to prison for killing her husband was statistically improbable.

---

[1] As sensational as it was at the time, the William Giberson murder was overshadowed by one of the most famous crimes of the early Twentieth-Century, the Hall-Mills murder. On September 16, 1922, the bodies of Eleanor Mills and Edwin Hall, an Episcopal priest, were found on a rural pig farm in Somerset County. The two had been having an affair. Eleanor's throat had been cut, her tongue cut out, and she was shot three times. Hall was shot once in the head. Hall's wife and two of her brothers were tried four years later but were found not guilty due to insufficient evidence.

IVA M. RICHMOND WAS BORN on January 7, 1882, in Sidney, New York, a small town fifteen miles north of the Pennsylvania border. She was the second of four children born to Almira and Leroy Richmond. As a carpenter, her father's profession forced the family to move often as he followed different construction projects throughout New York and New Jersey.

Ivy Giberson

After graduating high school, Iva married John C. Meehan in Oneonta, New York, on September 13, 1899. Their marriage was a mistake from the start and the 1900 US Census reported she was back living with her parents in Manchester, New Jersey, just five miles southwest of Lakehurst. During a brief reconciliation, Iva became pregnant and in 1902, she gave birth to a son, Joseph. Four months later, she left Meehan, left Manchester, and gave Joseph to her parents who adopted him as their own son, changing his last name to Richmond.

By 1909 she was living and working in Trenton, New Jersey, as a waitress in a small restaurant owned by William Giberson, the man whom she would later marry. With an eye toward William, six-years younger than her, the twenty-seven-year-old got around to divorcing her first husband, charging him with desertion, although *she* had left *him*. Later that year, Iva made the front pages of Trenton newspapers as the victim of a robbery under circumstances that would seem familiar thirteen years later.

According to the *Trenton True American* newspaper, at approximately 8:30 on the night of November 23, Iva Richmond was alone in the restaurant passing the time with sewing work when she heard the backdoor rattle. Thinking it was a neighbor boy named John Wooley, who had left just a few minutes before, she went through the kitchen and opened the door to let him in. When she did, she was confronted by a "burly Negro" who shoved her back into the kitchen, and wrapped his big hands around her throat and began choking her.

"She struggled desperately with the man," the newspaper reported, "upsetting chairs, pans, and glasses, but she was unable to make an outcry as the other robber (his accomplice) clasped his hands over her mouth and finally, consciousness left her."

Around nine o'clock, William returned from a theater performance, and was surprised to find the front door of his restaurant unlocked. Inside, the place was pitch-black. He relit the gas lamps and called out for Iva. She had agreed to stay behind while he attended the play alone. He found her unconscious on the kitchen floor, her clothing soaked in water from a pot that had turned over.

"The small room bore evidence of a violent struggle," the newspaper continued. "His first act was to attend to Miss Richmond. By bathing her head with water, he restored her to consciousness and was told the story of the attack made upon her by the Negroes."

When William checked the cash register, $22 was gone, and only $2 in change was left in a cup nearby. It took Iva some time to recover from her ordeal and when she did, she was "unable to give any description of her robbers."

That may have been what the *Trenton True American* reported, but another local newspaper, the *Daily State Gazette*, took a different slant to the story. In their report, they quoted a "Detective Pilger" who concluded that no robbery had occurred and Iva Richmond had not been assaulted. Giberson's restaurant was located directly across the street from Trenton City Hall, an impressive building completed just two years earlier. This made it an unlikely choice for either experienced or inexperienced robbers. No witnesses saw the black men enter or leave the premises. The Wooley family, who lived just behind the kitchen, never heard a thing that night.

When Iva read the *Gazette's* version—that she had faked the whole thing—she reportedly became livid and telephoned the Trenton police chief to "express great indignation." After suffering through her verbal reprimand, the chief replied that he did not doubt her story, that he believed everything she said, and vowed to catch the men who attacked her.

Sensing an opportunity to discredit a rival, the *True American* defended Iva, attacked the *Gazette* in a front-page article, and interviewed witnesses who reported seeing the lights out in the restaurant during the time she was unconscious in the kitchen. Other witnesses in the kitchen that night reported seeing marks on Iva's neck and judging by her disoriented state after she regained consciousness, believed her story.

The "burly Negro" and his accomplice were never captured.

Three years later, William and Iva married after he sold his restaurant. Her husband used that money to purchase a sawmill. In 1917, he transitioned to the taxicab business when the war in Europe brought thousands of soldiers and sailors to the area. He saw financial opportunity shuttling servicemen between Camp Kendrick, near Lakehurst, and Camp Dix in nearby Burlington County. The taxi business thrived and three years later the couple moved to Lakehurst[2] where they bought the two-story building on Union Avenue. By then, Iva was Ivy and she wasn't content to just sit at home. She wanted her own money and to get it, she bought her own automobile and became a taxi driver. She quickly developed a reputation and was regarded as, "…an expert driver, reputed to be fearless and aggressive…driving cars herself at all hours of the day and night," the *New York Evening World* reported after her husband was killed. "On her night trips, she went armed with a pistol."

However, after eight years of marriage, the relationship had apparently soured. Ivy would later claim that she never loved either husband, and that she and William were more like "pals." The younger man enjoyed drinking and gambling, while Ivy attended church regularly and supported prohibition. Whatever he saw in her when they were married in 1912 was gone by 1920. She had transformed herself from a tall, attractive twenty-seven-year-old to a frumpy, matronly woman who wore Pince-nez spectacles that were popular in the 1890s. Her face was framed in an old-fashioned hairstyle and her thin lips seemed permanently fixed in a dour expression.

At some point during her formative years, Ivy developed what mental health professionals today might term as a reduced affect. Her ability to manifest normal emotions with

---

[2] In 1937, Lakehurst would be known around the world as the site of the *Hindenburg* crash.

her face and voice was limited to just two expressions: apathy and anger. When she wasn't yelling at her husband, her face was known to be "cold and expressionless."

There was no poetry in her. Music did not flow between her red and white blood cells. She could not feel the mournful cello or hear the merry flute. Art was just pictures, culture was for cheese, and her intellectual ambitions went undetected.

She did have feelings, but they leaned toward the egocentric. For all those hours she spent at the Methodist Episcopal Church, aversion to the deadly sins eluded her. She could feel wrath. She could feel greed. She could feel lust, she could feel pride, and over the next two years, they would all come out.

Ivy's devotion to the Methodist Episcopal Church and the temperance movement helped her forge a reputation that was "above reproach" and "immune to gossip." However, the image she projected to others didn't match what she was doing at home. During their marriage, Ivy took it upon herself to take charge of the family finances and in 1920, she began a clever campaign to embezzle money from her husband. Money that was to be deposited in his private bank account was never actually deposited. Although she recorded the deposits in his personal bankbook, she was spending his money on herself and her family. When the local bank mailed monthly account statements to William, she would intercept those letters, erase the true figures, and substitute false amounts with her own personal typewriter.

By July 31, 1922, William believed he had $2,369.69[3] in the bank when the actual amount was only $2.89. Ivy had plundered all of it.

William's parents, who also lived in Ocean County, never liked their daughter-in-law. They knew what kind of person she really was, despite the reputation she had built for herself.

---

[3] The 2016 equivalent of $33,853 when adjusted for inflation.

"She had a violent temper, was extravagant, and although she had money of her own, she always wanted his," his mother, Martha, later told a newspaper reporter. "Ivy quarreled often with [William] and was never home when they visited him," she added.

Some of that money may have also been spent for the benefit of an emotional affair she was having with a handsome new arrival to Lakehurst. In January 1921, a mutual acquaintance introduced Ivy to Harold Ga Nun, a thirty-one-year-old mechanical engineer from New York City. Ga Nun was a supervisor for a construction company tasked with building an airship hangar at the local Naval Air Station. It was a temporary job for the married father, who resided in Lakehurst during the week, and went home to his wife and daughter on the weekend.

Most of them, anyway.

It was a peculiar relationship, with the motherly-looking Ivy doing everything she could to get closer to the tall, athletic, and much younger Ga Nun. Whatever magic she had over men, Ivy applied it to Ga Nun—a man his own wife later said was "susceptible to flattery."

Ga Nun's work on the hangar project ended in June 1921 and he returned to his wife and daughter in Brooklyn. His absence provoked Ivy to grow more obsessive. In him, she saw an escape from William, and a chance to trade up on the husband ladder. She wrote to him several times a week and bought him an expensive silk shirt, which she mailed to his office on West 55th Street. Her letters were flirtatious, spoke of her desire to run away together, and attempted to manipulate him with talk of suicide.

Suicide?

That was enough for Ga Nun, who wanted nothing more to do with the unstable woman. To get the job done, he asked his wife, Helen, to write a note demanding that she stop pursuing her husband.

Harold Ga Nun

August 1, 1921.

At Mr. Ga Nun's request, I'm writing to ask that you stop trying to communicate with him. He has confessed the whole miserable thing to me, though it was unnecessary, for I have known for several weeks how things were done down there.

Perhaps my strongest feeling was faith in his wholesomeness and morality. Harold is susceptible to flattery, but he is not morally weak. He says he felt sorry for you in your trouble...that if he ever dreamed of turning away from me, you would not be his type.

I don't feel from what Harold says that you are a bad woman, and in a way, I am sorry for you, but you are dishonorable, and that is shame enough. That you should stoop so low as to try and infatuate a man who is married and has a little daughter, that you had no scruples—well, you put your own valuation on yourself.

Helen's appeal did not stop Ivy; she grew more desperate to connect with Ga Nun through intermediaries, telephone calls, and letters addressed to his sister. Several times in August 1921, she traveled to New York City and would send her taxi driver up to his apartment to attempt to lure him outside.

Ivy's persistence forced Helen to write a second and final letter, dated September 2. She was able to convince Ivy to leave her man alone after threatening, among other things, to turn over her letters to the judge at Ivy's "divorce trial," a fictitious claim that was part of her ruse to entice Ga Nun away from his wife.

"I have consulted my lawyer and he assures me that I have a case against you for attempted alienation of affection, and I warn you I shall push it to the limit unless you cease your disgusting performance," Helen fired back before ending with a powerful insult. "You are a disgrace to womanhood. Very truly yours, Helen M. Ga Nun."

The false divorce claim fit perfectly with Ivy's pattern of creating a fabricated narrative to get what she wanted through emotional manipulation. She was getting a divorce, she told Ga Nun. She was going to commit suicide, she told Ga Nun. She was going to have "an operation," she later told Ga Nun. She had created these stories before, and she would create them again.

The next one came in April 1922, when Ivy happily informed her husband that she had secured for him a position with the United States Secret Service that paid the incredible amount of $3 an hour, the equivalent of $42 in 2016. She had gotten him the job after talking with a chief inspector assigned to the Lakehurst Naval Air Station. His mission, Ivy told her husband, would be to patrol the railroad station in Mount Holly in search of "a German spy with a poison gas formula."

Since the mission was top secret, she would handle all the communications with the chief inspector. Ivy was so excited, however, that she informed William's sister, Nellie Bowers, all about it when she came to visit the month he started "sleuthing" around the rail yards.

Mount Holly was more than thirty miles away and almost every evening, agent William Giberson, spy hunter, made the fifty-minute drive[4] both ways each night. Sometimes, he got out and would roam the area for ten hours each night; at other times, he would sit in his car and watch the comings and goings of others.

When the taxi drivers in Mount Holly asked the taxi driver from Lakehurst what he was doing in their area, he lied, and told them he had special contract driving government employees for $30 a day.

Toward the end of July 1922, after just three months on the job, William told his wife he was growing tired of snooping around the Mount Holly rail station. It was boring. He wanted to quit. Fortunately, she was able to convince him to continue with his patriotic duty after receiving secret messages from the chief inspector encouraging him to stay.

Shortly after he started grumbling about his boring job, Ivy drove to a department store in another county and purchased two expensive mourning outfits that included two dresses, two veils, a black hat, black stockings, and black shoes. A few days later, she wrote a letter to Ga Nun, asking him to meet with her. The two met on August 4 at a Jersey City hotel dining room, where Ivy told Ga Nun that she would soon undergo an operation.

A day or two after meeting with Ga Nun, Ivy sent a telegram to her ex-husband that read: "Iva dead. Come at once."

He ignored the telegram.

---

[4] An approximation based on the average speed of automobiles in the early 1920s.

Two days before he was killed by robbers, William quit his secret service job on Saturday, August 12, and told his wife to prepare an invoice for his services to submit the chief inspector. The bill came to $5,385.[5]

On Sunday, August 13, Ivy woke-up early and despite feeling sick and nauseous, prepared her husband's breakfast. He then left their second-floor apartment to answer a taxi call in Asbury Park. He returned around 6:00 p.m. with one of his drivers, Edward Howard. The three ate dinner. Howard and her husband then discussed business matters until 9:30 when the two left. She stayed up until he returned home a few hours later. When he did, Ivy said he stood in front of the rear window—a window that was open—and counted out $700 in cash, which included three one-hundred dollar bills. He then went to bed around one o'clock on the morning.

According to the story she told District Attorney Wilfred Jayne, Ivy was awakened around three o'clock in the morning when she heard noises in the kitchen. Curious, but not alarmed, she got up to discover the source and found two men in their apartment. One of them was tall and strong, and the other was short and heavy. She had never seen either one of them before.

The tall one grabbed her arm and told her to keep her mouth shut. He then pushed her back into the front room where he sat her down in a chair and tied her feet and hands with twine. He then found a napkin in the kitchen, wrapped it around her mouth, pulled it around her head and tied it in the back. While he was finishing up, the other intruder, the short one, entered the bedroom.

"Just then, I heard a shot from the rear room," Ivy declared to Jayne. "The man who had tied and gagged me called out: 'What the hell did you do that for?'

"'Had to. He started to move,'" his partner replied.

---

[5] The 2016 equivalent of $77,500 for just four months of work.

In the dark, the men were able to find her husband's $700. They then left the apartment the same way they had entered; out the back door by the kitchen which exited to a second-floor balcony, and then down the back stairs. That door, she explained, was often kept unlocked.

After they had left, Ivy got off the chair and was able wiggle the gag out of her mouth, which slid down to her neck. She then slithered and squirmed to the front door, unlocked it, and from there, she rolled and crawled down the rubber padded stairs to the front stairwell where she screamed for help, attracting the attention of the railroad crew asleep in a caboose approximately one hundred yards away. After breaking the lock on the door, she told them that her husband had been killed by burglars who took his $700.

When District Attorney Jayne listened to the story later that morning, he knew it was hogwash. Although he didn't believe a word she said, he knew famed detective Ellis Parker would figure it out when he arrived later that morning.

As he began his investigation and search of the property, Jayne "...lulled the suspicions of the widow by making her think they had an entirely different theory from the real one—that she was the slayer," the *New York Evening World* reported later that night. With her mind at ease, two detectives nonchalantly observed Ivy Giberson as she milled around her apartment while officers began searching the property and all of Lakehurst for her husband's killer.

Before Parker interviewed Ivy, he was informed of Jayne's secret plan. With a soft voice and sympathetic disposition, Parker listened carefully as she told her story again. With his sharp mind and twenty-nine years of experience as a detective, he found the flaws immediately.

When most housewives hear a strange noise in the middle of the night, they invariably wake their husband, he would later explain. They do not investigate it themselves.

Second, when the short man went into the bedroom and shot her husband, how did the tall man know it was his partner who fired the shot? In any scenario like the one Ivy described, the burglar tying her to the chair would have assumed it was his companion who had been shot. In a dangerous situation like the two men were engaged in, they would be hyper-vigilant to anything that could go wrong.

Third, when Ivy rolled off the chair, opened the unlocked door, and rolled down the stairs, she told the railroad men that her husband had been killed in a robbery. How did she know her husband had been killed? How did she know the men had found his $700? They never said anything else after the short man said, "Had to. He moved." They just left according to Ivy. From the chair she was tied to until she was discovered at the foot of the stairs, she never went into the bedroom.

Frank Petersen said that when he freed Ivy, he easily broke the twine with his fingers. The knot was a simple slipknot—the kind one would use if wanting to make it look like someone else had done it. More alarming, Petersen said Ivy had no reaction to his report that her husband was dead.

"Several witnesses to the scene just after Mrs. Giberson gave the alarm said that the woman displayed not the slightest emotion in the presence of her dead husband's body," the *New York Times* reported. "She shed not a tear, they declared, and she did not seem to be nervous."

Even more telling than her lies was the physical evidence. The apartment showed no signs of a struggle. It was in perfect order—not what you would expect from burglars used to ransacking a place, looking for something of value. In the bedroom, the forensic evidence clearly showed that William was shot in the back of the head while he slept.

"No one heard the single shot that killed Giberson," the *Times* continued. "It was fired into the base of the skull as he lay in bed, face pressed into the pillows, so close that both his neck and the pillow case were burned by gun powder. The bullet ranged upward through the brain, coming out under the eye and dropping on the bedclothes (on the floor next to the bed). Death was instantaneous. It was apparent that the man was shot as he slept, without the faintest warning of danger. The sounds of the struggle between a robber and herself, which Mrs. Giberson said preceded the shooting, also went unnoticed."

One neighbor who lived above his tailor shop twenty-five yards away said he never heard the gun shot that killed William Giberson. He did, however, hear Ivy's screams for help from the stairwell.

When they looked closer at the bullet hole in William's head, they made a shocking discovery. Ivy had trimmed the hair around the wound with scissors. When she shot her husband, the barrel was so close the flash singed his hair. Ivy did this, a newspaper later reported, "to prevent ascertaining whether the shot was fired at close range or from a distance."

The bullet found on the bed clothes was badly damaged, but looked to be a .38 caliber. Ivy told detectives her husband had two guns in the house, which they found. One was a .45, the other a .32 caliber. Neither one of them appeared to have been fired recently.

The detectives assigned to monitor Ivy Giberson noticed that she had two points of interest as she flittered around her property. The first was a spare bedroom and the second was an outhouse in the backyard.

"When she went to the spare room the first time, she was seen to push a dressing table," the *New York Evening World* reported the next day. "Whenever she got near it, she gave it a shove as if to get it out of the way. Finally, she moved the table against the wall. Suspected as she was, her action aroused keen interest in the detective, who noted at once that the table had been so moved that the side from which its drawers opened now faced the wall and the drawer might easily be overlooked."

The detective reported the peculiar movements to Jayne, who then ordered the detective to coax Ivy to another part of the house to explain some trivial matter. When she was a safe distance away, Jayne moved the table, opened the drawers and found the letters from Ga Nun, as well as some from her ex-husband, John Meehan. Also inside one of the drawers was William's wallet with his driver's license and business cards but no money. It was the wallet he carried every day and it was found hidden inside a dressing table drawer in a spare room, not the master bedroom where he normally slept.

During his course of observation, the other detective noticed that Ivy made five trips to an outhouse. The fifth time she went there, he saw a strange flash of light through a ventilator. When she left, he searched the building but found nothing. He then followed Ivy back to the house where he overheard her make a self-pitying remark. "It's bad enough to have your husband killed without being held," she told two of her friends from church.

Later, Ivy returned to the outhouse a sixth time. After she left, a different lawman conducted a more thorough search and discovered a .38 caliber revolver in a crevice. To get the weapon out, he had to use a long wire with a hook fashioned at one end. When Parker examined it, he concluded that it had been fired sometime in the last twelve hours.

By then, detectives had uncovered more circumstantial evidence inside the apartment. A holster, which fit the gun, was found buried in a dirty clothes hamper. Two .38 caliber bullets were discovered wrapped in cloth, and tucked down inside a coffee can. A ball of twine and a pair scissors were found underneath a piece of furniture. The string matched perfectly with the twine removed from Ivy's wrists and ankles. And finally, the brand-new mourning outfits were discovered tucked away in a box in the attic. The price tags were still attached to some of the items.

At approximately three o'clock in the afternoon, twelve hours after she claimed robbers killed her husband, Ivy Giberson was arrested and taken to the Ocean County Jail in Toms River. There, she was interrogated for five hours by

Parker before being led to her cell. If he thought his interrogation was going to go his way, he was mistaken. In this case, "the famous sleuth" was outmatched by the headstrong, emotionless Ivy. She never budged from her story. She declared she had never seen the .38 caliber revolver before and that they would not find her fingerprints on it, which they didn't. Eventually, she refused to answer any more questions.

Reporters marveled at her demeanor. In an era when women were expected to swoon and catch the vapors, her detached indifference puzzled them. She did not possess the usual "female hysteria" that a woman in her situation was presumed to have.

"Mrs. Giberson's cool demeanor in jail earned her the title today of 'the woman of iron nerve.' She mourns not, and neither does she worry," one senior news reporter observed. The *New York Times* also had a viewpoint on her peculiar attitude. "She is described as the calmest woman who ever has occupied a cell in the jail. Nothing nonpluses her, not even the discovery in her home of affectionate letters from two men to her."

The so-called "affectionate letters," combined with shooting her husband while he slept in his bed, and the made-up bit about robbers, was the kind of story news editors dream about. For the next forty-eight hours, the Harold Ga Nun angle was blown out of proportion and then quickly faded until the trial. At first, Parker and Jayne believed that Ivy, being a woman and all, couldn't have been the one who shot her husband while he slept. Women can't shoot people, only men could do that. It had to have been that Ga Nun fella, or one of her other boyfriends.

To prove their short-lived point, they arrested Ga Nun in Brooklyn the following day. Prosecutor Jayne, an Ocean County detective, and two state troopers took the train to New York City, and questioned him for several hours at a local police station. He provided them with an ironclad alibi for the night of the murder and explained his involvement with Ivy the previous year. The last time he saw her was eleven days ago, after she requested to meet him. They had dinner in a restaurant and she informed him that she was to have some unspecified operation. He then volunteered to travel with them back to Toms River where they arrived at 10:30 Tuesday night.

In the mind of one reporter, Ga Nun's cooperation with police was supposed to provoke an emotional breakdown in Ivy. When he informed the woman that her beau was in Jayne's office, she had no reaction except to lie. "I have not seen Ga Nun or heard from him for a year. I had no idea where he was."

Over at the courthouse, Jayne, a detective, and Ga Nun cooked up a ridiculous scheme that revealed they had no clue as to the kind of woman they were dealing with. At 2:20 in the morning, the three men, accompanied by two state troopers, walked over to the county jail and informed the jailor they wished to speak with Mrs. Giberson. She was awakened, allowed to dress, and then carefully composed herself as she sat on the edge of her bed. When the five men took their positions in front of her cell, they just stood there, staring at her. A minute went by. Ivy, puzzled, looked at them with curiosity—as if something was wrong *with them.*

"What do you want?" she finally asked.

"We want nothing from you," Jayne retorted.

The silent staring continued for another awkward minute or two, and then Ga Nun said: "Mrs. Giberson, I've told Mr. Parker everything, and he thought you should know."

Ivy stared back at him—as if she couldn't understand why that was supposed to mean something.

"Very well, Mr. Ga Nun," she replied after a long pause. "But you don't know anything. Therefore, anything you have said is of no concern to me."

Defeated, the men left. Thirty minutes later, Ivy was sound asleep.

NEWS ABOUT IVY'S ARREST FOR THE murder of her husband dominated east coast newspapers, and spread to the west coast where it made the news in California, Washington, and Oregon. In New Jersey, the story was met with shock and disbelief and "stirred Lakehurst to a high pitch of excitement," the *New York Times* reported.

This excitement was on display just hours after Ivy's arrest. "During the five-hour grilling of Mrs. Giberson, the courtyard of the Toms River courthouse presented a lively scene," the *Philadelphia Public Ledger* reported. "Hundreds of residents crowded about the jail entrance, and rumors [spread] fast among the assemblage. Motorcars and wagons crowded the nearby thoroughfares, the hum of automobile motors adding to the din of motorcycles of the state police who dashed up and departed at brief intervals."

Among those in the mob were Ivy's father, one of her brothers, and Ivy's twenty-year-old son, Joseph. They stood vigil outside the county jail, keeping a watchful eye on the light that lit Ivy's cell. If it was on, she was there, and Joseph stared long and hard at it in the hopes that his mother would look out and see him. She never did.

The Richmond family ignored the evidence against her, and defended her to the press.

"My daughter is innocent and she will certainly be cleared of this charge," her father Leroy told the *Public-Ledger*. "I am positive my son-in-law was murdered by robbers and I will not see my daughter persecuted in this manner. I will stand by her to the end."

The Giberson family had a different opinion. William's parents told the press all about their daughter-in-law's anger issues, her obsession with their son's money, her extravagant spending, and the phony Secret Service job. When William's sister, Nellie, telephoned Ivy at the jail to enquire what kind of flowers she thought were best for her husband's funeral, she coldly replied: "Use your own judgement."[6]

Despite the strong circumstantial evidence against her, Jayne and his investigators were having trouble coming up with a motive. After the Harold Ga Nun/love triangle theory collapsed, they began to gravitate toward a money angle. William was prosperous, known to have a lot of money tucked away. They hadn't yet uncovered Ivy's embezzling, or the $5,385 owed to William for his phony spy work, but they told the press that motive didn't matter. She did it, and that was enough for the jury to know.

"There isn't a thing to this case," Parker told New York City reporters three days after Ivy's arrest. "Of course, outside of the money Giberson is known to have, we haven't a motive as of yet, but in New Jersey, we don't need a motive in homicides. But what more do you want? Here's a dead, open-and-shut proposition. There were no accomplices and we are convinced that Mrs. Giberson bound herself up."

Parker was bluffing. He was living in a peculiar era—an era where women were seldom convicted of murder. According to a 2010 *Chicago Magazine* interview with Jeffrey S. Adler, author and professor of history and criminology, there was only a slim chance that a white woman was going to be convicted of murdering her husband.

"It was exceedingly rare for a white woman to be convicted of homicide," Adler said. He went on to explain that all male juries had trouble believing that white women could commit premeditated murder.

Black women? Definitely. But white women? Not likely.

Douglas Perry, author of *The Girls of Murder City,* agreed with Adler in that same *Chicago Magazine* interview.

"If a woman were to commit a terrible crime, there had to be reasons for it," he explained. "She was drunk, and of course, her boyfriend made her drunk. Or, it was a crime of

---

[6] In an ironic twist, Ivy did order a floral embroidered pillow that would support her husband's head for eternity—the same head she fired a bullet through.

passion. Women were fragile beings; they needed their men, and they were possessive of their men. The man was cheating on them, and it made them snap, and it was forgivable for that reason."

Ivy's lawyer was William Jeffrey, a former county judge who had gone into private practice. Jeffrey was a natural when it came to defending his client with the style of an early twentieth-century spin-doctor. He knew how to snort and scoff and guffaw and mock the prosecution's "manufactured evidence" against his client—all before the jury was selected. He soon hired his own detectives and ordered them to "get the two men who killed and robbed Giberson and bound and gagged his wife."

This was another one of his public counter attacks against Jayne and Parker. Parker's reputation was held in such high regard throughout the entire region that if he said you did it, you did it—even if you were a white woman. Jeffrey was able to cast doubt on this presumption through his own private detectives.

"Jeffrey said the progress of his investigators had already been so satisfactory he saw an excellent chance of being able to prove Mrs. Giberson's story that the murder was committed by two robbers," the *Evening-World* reported on August 18.

But in case there were any lingering doubts among the potential jurors in Ocean County, Jeffrey was ready with a strategy still in use today: attack the victim's character.

"It was intimated that the defense hopes to show that Giberson was slain as a result of differences with a gambling and bootlegging ring," the *World* continued in the next sentence. "In fact, it was stated that the defense has two certain men (who were lingering around Lakehurst at the time) under suspicion. They might have committed the crime, according to the theory of Mrs. Giberson's friends, either for the money they knew Giberson had or for revenge, or both."

Mrs. Giberson's friends said that? The defense lawyer was smart. He wanted someone else to be attributed for that unsubstantiated bit of housewife gossip.

But the attack on William's character was more effective when it came out of his widow's mouth. Ivy confirmed her husband was a gambler and bootlegger before adding that he beat her, he wouldn't give her "enough money to buy bread," and he was cheating on her with a younger, prettier girl—a girl nobody could seem to find.

Jeffrey certainly knew what he was doing when it came to pre-trial strategy. In addition to ridiculing the prosecution's evidence; insinuating misconduct; directing blame elsewhere; and attacking the victim's character, the final step in his plan was to have Mrs. Ivy Giberson the widow, Mrs. Ivy Giberson *the victim*, dramatically proclaim her innocence during a carefully managed press conference on August 19.

"This may seem to you to be a silly question," a *New York Times* reporter carefully began, "but will you tell us if you killed your husband?"

Appropriately dressed in mourning clothes, Ivy rose quickly, looked up to the ceiling—as if she was looking into the eyes of God in heaven who was looking down just at her—and dramatically proclaimed: "I stand in the presence of my God, innocent and unafraid, and that is the whole secret of my calmness since I have been here, about which the newspapers have been wondering. And that's all I have to say."

As profound as that was, it didn't explain her lack of emotion when she was in the presence of her dead husband—and his blown-out eyeball.

But Jayne's fivefold strategy seemed to have worked. When told that women everywhere believed she was innocent, Ivy smiled and replied: "I am glad someone likes me."

County Attorney Jayne employed some pre-trial stratagems of his own. He misled reporters into believing they were either searching for an alternative suspect or an accomplice. It was a ploy to mislead Jeffrey. In those days, the prosecutor didn't have to turn over his evidence to the defense—who had no idea what kind of case they would present. Jayne and his investigators were tipped off to William's finances, or lack thereof. Nellie Bowers told them about the Secret Service job, which turned out to be a complete sham. They found out that forty-eight hours before he was murdered, William had quit that job and asked his wife to submit a bill for $5,385. Ivy didn't have $5,385 to pay her husband. Inside that two-day window, Ivy was desperate to borrow $500 from another man—a man who came forward and told police.

Where Jeffrey liked to run his mouth, Jayne preferred to keep his shut until it was time for the real battle—inside the courtroom.

But Jayne and his men did explode one little bombshell to the press. It was one they knew would never be admitted at trial—that the August 14 incident was the *third* time Ivy had been incapacitated and robbed by two men. They told reporters about the Trenton robbery, and a second robbery in Lakehurst a few years back when the couple lived on Pine Street. In that case, two men entered the home when Ivy was alone, tied her up, and made off with $200.

Ivy Giberson was the unluckiest woman in the world when it came to being robbed by two men.

WHEN THE STATE OF NEW JERSEY versus Iva M. Giberson began on October 11, 1922, the *New York Evening World* predicted she would be found not guilty. "It is commonly believed here that the state's case is weak and that an acquittal is likely, unless the prosecution submits evidence which is not now a matter of general knowledge."

Ivy was also feeling confident about her chances. Her lawyer had already won her case in the court of public opinion, and she knew she would be acquitted.

"I slept like a log," she told newspapers the morning of that first day. "I know I am innocent and I am confident that the jury will so decide."

By the end of that first day, her defense attorney would lose all his confidence. Jeffrey thought he knew everything there was to know about the case—until he heard the prosecution's opening arguments. He didn't know that his client had embezzled more than $2,300 from the victim. He didn't know that his client had convinced her husband that John Kangetten,[7] a chief inspector with the Naval Air Station, had hired William to be a counter-spy for three dollars per hour. He didn't know that his client held all their property in her name, and that she had failed to pay the property taxes because she was $12,000 in debt.

Money was the motive and Ivy shot her husband to cover-up her crimes, the prosecution asserted.

It certainly looked that way.

For the next two and one-half days, Jayne carefully revealed his circumstantial, but strong case to the jury. Frank Petersen recalled finding the defendant bound with twine that he broke apart with just his fingers, and that the knot was a simple slip knot. The young prosecutor then called as witnesses two bank employees who stated that the deposits and dates listed in William's bankbook were false, and that he only had $2.38 in his account. Both employees were also able to verify that the monthly bank statements mailed to William Giberson had been altered by an eraser and a different typewriter.

Jayne wrapped-up his financial malfeasance line of inquiry by calling John Kangetten, who denied knowing anything about the Secret Service position Ivy claimed she had obtained for her husband. Leon Craypool, a Mount Holly police officer,

---

[7] The correct spelling of his last name is unclear. Eight newspapers spelled it eight different ways. A search of Ancestry.com did not clear up the confusion.

"told of seeing Giberson around the [train] station night after night throughout the summer."

As preposterous as it seemed to everyone in the courtroom, William Giberson sincerely believed he was working for the Secret Service.

To show that Ivy was the one who pulled the trigger, Jayne had to connect her with the .38 caliber revolver found in the outhouse. He did this by calling a former Navy ammunition inspector who stated that the bullet that killed William Giberson was a .38 caliber.

The serial number on the outhouse revolver identified it as one that was issued by the United States Army to Camp Kendrick, Lakehurst, between 1917 and 1922. One of William's drivers, Earle Fowler, testified that he received the pistol in-lieu-of-payment for a taxi-fare. He then sold the gun to William. The holster found in the clothing hamper was consistent with what the military issued for that revolver.

Jayne then laid out the rest of his circumstantial evidence which included: the mourning dresses found in the attic; the bullets found in the coffee can; the twine; the scissors used to cut the twine; the fact that singed hair was cut around the wound to conceal the close proximity of the gun barrel when it was fired; that the .38 caliber revolver had recently been fired; and finally—the love letters, which an embarrassed Harold Ga Nun was called forward to explain.

During most of the trial, Ivy seemed unaffected by the impressive case that was being built brick-by-brick. She didn't show emotion until the letters from Harold's wife were read aloud. The "You are a disgrace to womanhood," insult from Helen was met with approval by nearly everyone in attendance. "The words drifted over the courtroom," the *New York Tribune* reported. "As their sting was felt (by Ivy), there came an involuntary burst of applause."

Her face was flush, but just for a moment. Then she regained her composure.

"Whatever her emotions all through the somber and sometimes ridiculous proceedings of the day, Mrs. Giberson was a poised and defiant figure," the *Tribune* continued. "She scarcely invites the pity of the crowd that gathers to watch a woman fight for her life. She is not the veiled sodden figure that women defendants charged with murder usually are. Her demeanor is like crystal, cool and hard, seemingly immune from shock or impression. Sitting with her back to the morbid gallery, all her attention focused on the witnesses, she has an admirable grip on herself and her ease. Entering and leaving the court, she walks with a quick, self-conscious stride, her head thrown back at a defiant angle, her eyes coolly leveled at spectators."

When the prosecution concluded their case Friday evening October 14, it was clear to everyone the tide had shifted against Ivy Giberson—including William Jeffrey who tried to downplay the state's witnesses. News reporters were impressed with Jayne's evidence, some of it kept secret until the trial.

"The evidence presented by the state in no way surprised the defense," Jeffrey claimed to the *New York Times*. "We know that Mrs. Giberson will be able to explain satisfactorily to the court and jury the alleged falsified bank statements, the Ga Nun letters, and all the other matters the state so strongly relies upon."

For all his pre-trial blustering and bluffing, the crux of Jeffrey's case boiled down to a now discredited defendant explaining herself. Although she was confident she could convince the jury of her innocence, during a brief interview granted the day before she testified, Ivy revealed her true concerns.

"What a fine reputation they are giving me," she said bitterly on October 15. "People think it awful that I didn't cry and faint and carry on. I've never cried in my life. I'm not the crying sort."

As Jeffrey guided her, Ivy began by relating everything that happened that Sunday night in August. Later, when her husband came home, she gave special emphasis to the fact that he always counted-out his money in front of an open window and that night was no different.

When she got to the part about waking up in the middle of a burglary, Ivy gave the court a lively performance in which she acted out the entire crime.

"She did not rely upon words alone to present to Judge and jury her story of having been bound and gagged by robbers who shot her husband," a wire service reported. "Springing from the witness chair, she twisted her body, shuffled her feet and proceeded from the stand to the jury box as she dramatized her account of the way she managed to free herself from gag and bonds after the murderers, as she contends, fled from the house."

In her excitement, the first she had ever displayed to anyone, Ivy spoke too fast, and was warned by the court reporter to slow down a dozen times.

"Her answers came like bullets from a machine gun," the *Times* reported.

Her answers may have been like bullets, but they had only one caliber—deny everything.

She denied killing her husband. She denied pursuing an affair with Harold Ga Nun. She was never in love with him, and she almost divorced her husband because *he* was having an affair, not her. She never sent her ex-husband a telegram that read: "Iva dead. Come at once." She never saw the gun before and didn't know it was in the outhouse. She denied altering the bank records. She wasn't stealing money from her husband. She didn't know anything about the Secret Service job but said her husband was a bootlegger. In fact, he would bring liquor back from Mount Holly and hide it in their apartment, she claimed.

"In her capacity as a wife and church worker," the *New York Morning-Telegraph* began, "she cautioned him several times to stop this practice, but quoted him as saying: 'Don't worry, I won't get caught.'"

On rebuttal, prosecutor Jayne brought in John Riley, a Mount Holly policeman, who testified that William Giberson was not a bootlegger because he had the taxi driver under surveillance. Riley had followed him back to Lakehurst and said William never unloaded whiskey from his car.

During closing arguments Jayne's assistant, Maja L. Berry, hammered the defense with rhetorical questions that illustrated how illogical Ivy's claims really were.

"How did she know a robbery had been committed (when found by the railroad men)?

"How could a robber take such deadly aim and shoot Giberson through the head in the dark?

"How did the tall man tying her up know that the short man shot Giberson?

"If they were robbers, why didn't they take the jewelry that was in plain sight?

"Did you ever hear of a man who tried to fool himself by changing his bank statements?"

In Jayne's closing argument, he began by calling her entire story of the robbery and murder of her husband a "Mutt and Jeff fairy tale."

He then surprised everyone by showing jurors the pillowcase William was sleeping on when he was murdered. It was blood-stained on one side, and on the other, "was an outline, in grease and grime, of a gun."

When Jayne laid the .38 caliber revolver on the pillowcase, it fit the outline perfectly. "This is a tell-tale exhibit which, I believe, was left behind as an act of God to capture the murderer." To Jayne, it clearly showed that if the gun's resting place was under William's pillow, then his wife had to have known about it. He then launched into an adjective-laden denunciation of the emotionless defendant.

"This is the most cold-blooded, villainous, dastardly, cowardly murder in this state, and the murderer deserves no sympathy. Even the foulest and most criminal thief has some sense of honor and, generally speaking, is not a coward. This unfortunate man, Will Giberson, was murdered in his own home while he slept."

Ivy's face remained frozen as he spoke. She never grimaced, shook her head, or teared up. Berry's words bounced off her.

"Of all those in the courtroom," a reporter observed, "she alone seemed unaffected."

The closing argument for the defense was uninspired and lackluster. They belittled the state's arguments and testimony, and declared that "no case had been made out."

In his instructions to the jury on Wednesday, October 18, the judge reminded them that no special consideration should be given to the defendant because she was a woman. After four hours of deliberation, they returned a guilty verdict. Four of the twelve men wanted to sentence Ivy to death, but a compromise was reached and a life sentence was recommended instead.

"Mrs. Giberson," the judge began, "I cannot add anything more to impress upon you the seriousness of the position you now occupy than has been said by the jury. In accordance with the law, I sentence you to spend the remainder of your natural life in the Trenton prison at hard labor."

As she had throughout the trial, Ivy's face revealed no emotions. Her blank face told reporters nothing about what she was thinking. Back in her Ocean County jail cell, she vowed to fight on with an appeal.

"I am innocent," she told to reporters from behind bars, "and if I have to remain in prison for the rest of my life, I will not be the first innocent person punished. I will fight this case to the bitter end."

One month later, Ivy's petition for an appeal was rejected. However, she was fortunate to live in a time when a sentence to life in prison did not mean life in prison. Not even close. She was paroled after serving ten years.

Epilogue

ACCORDING TO HER OBITUARY FROM *New York Daily-News* Service, Ivy Giberson returned to Lakehurst where she redeemed her reputation by devoting herself to church and social work. The 1940 US Census reveals that she lived on Pine Street with her eighty-year-old mother, and her thirty-nine-year-old son, Joseph, who was unmarried. She worked forty-hours a week at a nearby factory.

On January 30, 1956, Joseph, "died suddenly" at his home on Pine Street. No cause of death was mentioned in the available newspapers. He was fifty-four-years-old. Iva Giberson died on September 24, 1957, at the age of seventy-five.

Chapter Three: The Love Song of Archie Moock, 1928

DURING THE SPRING OF 1928, Catherine Clark was lonely and looking for love. Things hadn't worked out with her first husband, Ralph, whom she divorced in 1925. Nearly every day for the next three years, Catherine would wake up early, go to work at her small business repairing oriental rugs, then return home to an empty apartment. There were no children to happily greet her at the door; no sober man to hold her in his big arms; and no in-laws with whom she could plan holidays. Just sore fingers, a meal for one, a depressing light bulb or two, and solitary life in big city Boston—far from her childhood home in Connecticut where she grew up with ten brothers and sisters.

A woman can only take so much loneliness. If men weren't coming to her, the plump, thirty-five-year-old would have to put herself in a position where they could see her better. Three years was enough and in January 1928, Catherine placed her information with one of the many nationwide matrimonial agencies popular during her time. To get a man interested in her, Catherine would not only have to advertise her measurements—*five-feet five-inches, 165, blue eyes, light-brown hair*—in a catalog for men to peruse, but also her net worth—a dowry to be paid to the man who promised to take care of her. He, in turn, was required to list his employment, income, and net worth including property.

It wasn't romantic, but it was practical. True love, Catherine hoped, would come eventually.

Catherine spent very little on herself, and after three years of saving, she had accumulated $2,000.[1] It was a big sum to her, but seemed insignificant to other women in the catalogue who were worth $10,000 or more, and some of them even as much as $100,000.[2]

To her delight, she quickly received a photograph and warm letter from a James Murphy who lived in Spokane, Washington. Like her ex-husband, Murphy was originally from Canada, and moved to Washington in 1925. Jim, as he liked to be called, was college-educated, considerate, and kind-hearted. He had a lucrative job selling mining stocks and bonds, and Catherine quickly found something special in him. She wanted love, but she also wanted stability, and stocks and bonds were the big thing in those days.

Thirty-two-year-old Jim also had a large sum of money. Well, he would have it soon, according to his father's will–God bless his soul. His father had recently died and willed his son $100,000 on two conditions: one, that he would accumulate his own fortune of $10,000—just to show that he could prosper by himself; and two, that he would get married to a nice woman before September 24, 1928. Catherine's $2,000, he assured her, would only help prove to his father's lawyers that he was financially capable of accumulating ten grand on his own, thank you very much.

Their correspondence continued and later that summer, they decided that Catherine would travel to Spokane by train so they could get married and begin their life together in Alberta, Canada. His father had some land there and it would soon be Jim's—after he married. If Catherine's mail order beau had $110,000 and land, her lonely days of repairing rugs would be over. And, with that kind of stake, maybe they could

---

[1] The equivalent of $28,240 in 2016, when adjusted for inflation.

[2] $10,000 and $100,000 in 1928 is the 2016 equivalent of $141,200 and $1.41 million in 2016, when adjusted for inflation.

have children, or at least adopt children. With her hopes and dreams for a loved-filled home, Catherine Clark laughed and smiled more among her friends in Boston. She was more beautiful than ever, for nothing is more beautiful than a woman's tender heart that yearns for love and happiness.

Catherine Clark

In his last letter to her, Jim explained to Catherine that his good friend, Archie Moock, would meet her at the train station and take her to his home where she would stay one night with Archie, his wife Augustina, and their five children. The next day, Archie would drive Catherine to Jim's sister's home in Coeur d'Alene, Idaho, where they would finally meet for the first time. It was an unusual arrangement, but one that could easily be overlooked by a woman who just wanted to love and be loved.

She also ignored other peculiar aspects about Jim Murphy; in particular the great secrecy he imposed upon her in his letters.

"*Tell no one*," Jim wrote

"*Bring only a few personal effects along*," Jim wrote.

"*Say, Catherine dear, will you bring the letters I have written you along,*" Jim wrote, "*We will read them over again together.*"

"*Bring cash, not checks*," Jim wrote.

"*Make no announcement to anyone there* (about the marriage or coming to Spokane)," Jim wrote.[3]

She didn't understand it all, except that it had something to do with the lawyers holding the inheritance from his father. Their love, for legal reasons, had to seem as one that books were written about—to fool the estate attorneys. After all, $100,000 was a lot of money. It was a lot of money for what she hoped would be a happy family.

But for a handsome, younger man who was about to inherit $100,000, and made a good living selling stocks and bonds, Jim was quite interested in Catherine's humble $2,000. It was a frequent subject in their correspondence. If it was necessary for them to inherit the small fortune that would be used to start their new life, then she could understand why it was so important to her future husband. He was a smart man, he explained to her, and she trusted him. She wanted to believe him with lines like "baby, you will have a new home. I like those new style bungalows and you can choose your own car when we return from Europe."

Concerned that she was too much on the heavy side, gentle Jim reassured her: "You are just the right size so do not consider reducing your medicine."[4]

---

[3] In truth, she told her family and friends about traveling across the country to marry her wealthy new beau, James Murphy. They discouraged her from going.

[4] It's unclear if he meant calorie intake, or if she was taking medicine she believed was making her gain weight. Her letters were never published.

Catherine arrived in Spokane on Friday, September 21, and Archie Moock was there to pick her up. A big man, Archie was tall and his pants were pulled-up high over his protruding stomach. This unattractive frame was topped off by his wire frame glasses on a chubby face that was pointy, and rodent-like.

Archie had changed his last name from Much to Moock when he moved from Canada to the United States in 1924. He knew James from the time the two worked at the same lumber mill, he told Catherine. Archie still worked there, but Jim went on to bigger and better things selling them stocks and bonds for mining companies. He was a smart guy, that Jim.

A shy and nervous Catherine met Archie's wife, Augustina, and five children. She was seen by neighbors in the backyard during the evening hours, then went to sleep in Moock's own bed.

The next morning, Archie borrowed a Dodge sedan from his neighbor and friend, Grover Tyree. He needed the car to take Catherine to her beau over in Coeur d'Alene. If all went well, he would be back in a couple of hours.

But things didn't go well and Moock didn't return the car until Sunday morning, September 23. He made some excuses and quickly walked back to his house. Tyree was suspicious. Coeur d'Alene was about forty miles to the east, but the odometer showed the car had traveled a total of only fifty-three miles.

Tyree instinctively knew something was wrong and decided to investigate. He enlisted the help of a friend, and the two drove twenty-six and one-half miles east—exactly half the distance Moock had supposedly driven Catherine the day before. When they reached the half-way point, Grover recognized where he was; it was the abandoned prune orchard where he, Moock, and others had come just a week before to pick fruit and have a picnic. It was located near Foothills Road east of town, close to the Idaho border.

At the start of a path that led to the orchard, the two men found bloodstains and a trail, where something heavy had been dragged. They followed the path until they came to a shallow ravine where they spotted the badly mutilated body of the woman Archie said he was taking to Coeur d'Alene. Her skull was split open. Her light-brown hair was covered in blood. Her face was cut and her eyes, cheeks, and lips looked to be contorted in pain and agony. Her body, her disfigurement, made them uneasy. They didn't know her story. They didn't really know who she was. They didn't know that she was just a hard-working single woman looking for love and security, and now she was dead on some abandoned farm nearly 3,000 miles from home.

It was the saddest thing in the world.

A few feet from the body, Grover found the murder weapon; a bloodstained shingler's hatchet that he himself had left in the backseat of his Dodge sedan—the same car he loaned to Archie. He easily recognized it as one he had purchased second-hand. It had specific defects only he was familiar with.

Tyree reported the body to county authorities who immediately began an investigation that quickly unraveled the whole scheme. On Monday, September 24, thirty-one-year-old Archie Francis Moock was arrested. The next day, while snooping around in his backyard, deputies dug up $1,490 of Catherine's money wrapped in newspapers and buried by the back door. In another part of the yard, they found Archie's love letters inside a hatbox buried near the garden. The letters were mailed to "Jim Murphy," but had Moock's address – 2217 East Hartson Avenue. They also found Catherine's purse and a picture frame where Catherine hid the money beneath her own photograph. The frame was broken, the picture tossed aside, and the money stolen by Moock—perfect symbolism for his heartless, cold-blooded plot.

The story of the "mail order bride," who was fooled, robbed, and killed by Archie "the hatchet-murderer" Moock was great copy for newspapers across the country. The story spread from the west to the east coast across the front pages of several hundred newspapers. In the days to come, more details were released explaining how he duped a lonely woman to travel more than 3,000 miles so he could murder her for $1,500.[5]

Moock's callous greed effectively stained the marriage bureau business and became a cautionary tale for women seeking love and security through such an untraditional and disdainful arrangement.

Quite disdainful.

If Archie was stunned that he was caught so swiftly, he never showed it. He had spent months carefully directing what he thought was the perfect crime. He had piled on lie after lie after lie—to Catherine, his wife, and his friends—only to watch as it all came crashing down in less than twenty-four hours. And now, to get himself out of trouble, he would have to pile more lies on top of his old lies. While he may have thought he planned carefully, Archie Moock's mail-order murder for money scheme had actually boxed him into a very tight corner in which there were no rational explanations.

But that didn't stop him from trying. His account of "the truth," however, only sounded ridiculously stupid. Preposterous. Laughable.

On September 27, three days after he was arrested, Moock gave his version of events, which blamed everything on "James Murphy," and portrayed himself as a naive nice guy, who tried to do his friend a favor and got mixed up in a west-coast matrimonial murder-for-profit ring.

It could happen to anyone.

---

[5] Although she reported having $2,000 in savings, it is unclear what happened to the remaining $500. Some of it may have been spent on traveling expenses.

In an interview with the *Spokane Daily Chronicle*, Moock strongly asserted that he never wrote or mailed those letters—James Murphy did. And for a man no one else knew or could seem to find, Archie Moock knew an awful lot about James Murphy. In fact, his story sounded like a play-by-play confession of how he conned Catherine Clark—but it wasn't him, of course, it was Jim Murphy.

Moock was a modest man, a family man who didn't care about money and was devoutly religious. In fact, after his wife and kids went to bed at night, "God sent him messages," Moock explained. During the reporter's interview, with questions tendered as if they came from a milquetoast prosecutor, Moock had an explanation for more than just his messages from God.

He didn't know how the money got in his backyard, unless Murphy put it there.

He never borrowed Grover Tyree's shingler's hatchet and never saw it before in his life.

He never said he was driving to Coeur d'Alene; Murphy's sister lived in a sixteen-room house just across the state line. In Oregon. Where, coincidentally, they didn't have the death penalty.

He never found the house, but met up with Murphy on the road somewhere. Another man named Jake was with him. They all drank beer, but the beer Archie drank was "doped-up" and he passed-out. When he came-to the next morning, they were all gone. Then, Murphy must have driven Mrs. Clark over to the abandoned prune orchard and killed her there.

"I have told the officers the truth, but they don't seem to believe me," Moock said as he wrapped up his story. "The truth is all I can tell them.

"I am surprised at Murphy—he seemed like a nice fellow to me. Maybe he is living under an assumed name or maybe it was an assumed name that I knew him by.

"The entire thing is a surprise to me. Maybe Murphy has killed a dozen other women for their money. Anyone who knows me can tell you that I never cared for money. My wife and I had enough to live on and we were getting by comfortably. I would not have brought this disgrace on my family for any amount of money."

But he did need money. The *Spokesman Review* reported he was struggling to make his house payments. He was also behind on payments for a new electric washing machine he had bought his wife earlier that year. The day Catherine arrived at their home, Augustina was eagerly trying to get a job as a laundrywoman for a big company in town.

He had five children and a fourth-grade education—they definitely needed the money.

BY THE TIME HIS TRIAL BEGAN in December, Moock had to modify his story of "the truth." During the nine-week period he sat in jail waiting for his day in court, new evidence against him had been developed.

So, okay, yes, it was his handwriting on the letters to Catherine, but that was only because James Murphy told him what to write, Moock was forced to admit on the stand. He had to admit that because the prosecution brought in a handwriting expert who would tell the jury Archie wrote the love letters.

Later, the prosecutor was allowed to read "Jim Murphy's" letters to Catherine. They revealed Moock's clumsy, sappy, but effective prose, which wooed a lonely Catherine Clark to her death. A reporter for the *Daily Chronicle* gave an unvarnished account to his readers.

> As the prosecutor read the matrimonial bureau love letters, the expressions on the faces of the jury members made an interesting study. A few scowled with disgust, others smiled with delight, amused at such endearing terms as "you big darling" and "my baby."

"Jim Murphy" continually assured the Boston woman of his sincerity. Some of his friends, he wrote, even called him "old faithful."

"Honey, my adorable one, I do not expect you to hand no money over to me. No, but I will hand a nice slice over to you to use as your own."

In another letter he wrote: "I think you would be my ideal mate to hold and to love. I should surely make you happy sweetheart."

In one letter he described himself as being thirty-two years of age, dark complexion and grey eyes. He gives his height as six-feet two-inches. According to the letter the man was "not a bad looker" and was "worth $100,000."

Mrs. Clark is addressed as "My dearie," "Sweetheart," and "Baby."

After hearing from Mrs. Clark that she was plump, "Murphy" wrote, "My dearie girl, I like stout people, especially girls. I am no lightweight myself." Again he wrote, "I am experienced in reading handwriting and I feel sure I can love you. I am a one-woman man."

In one letter, "Murphy" becomes philosophical, writing: "Life holds nothing for us if we haven't happiness, does it?" He wrote in another letter, "I wish I could send you a kiss, or a dozen of them. I believe I will still call you sweetheart even when you are old and gray."

Archie Francis Moock was a smooth operator. He knew exactly what a vulnerable woman wanted to read and he could pour the maple syrup on the pancakes. He may have fooled her, but he was having a hard time fooling the jury. The prosecution's closing argument erased any doubt in their minds. His barrage of rhetorical questions resembled Ivy Giberson's prosecutor—but with twice the question marks.

"Who is the only one in this cast who knows anything about Murphy? Moock," the prosecutor bellowed with a pointed finger. "Who was last seen alive with Mrs. Clark? Moock. Who brought back Mrs. Catherine Clark's hatbox after she was last seen alive? Moock.

"Who wrote the letters which lured this poor woman to her death? Moock. On whose premises were these letters and the money found? Moock's. Who knew Mrs. Clark had money? Moock. Who knew she kept her money in the picture frame? Moock. Near whose house was the picture frame found broken in Mrs. Clark's purse? Moock's. Who had the car in which the murder hatchet was last seen before it was found beside the body? Moock.

"Mrs. Clark was killed as you or I would not kill a dog, but not once has an expression of sorrow or regret passed the lips of that cold stoic there."

After deliberating for two and one-half hours on the night of December 13, 1928, the jury voted to convict Archie Moock[6], and recommended the death penalty. One month later, the trial judge sentenced him to hang. Moock's father, who scraped together every dollar he could to finance his son's legal defense, was heart-broken; his life-savings, gone. His son's impending death was announced in newspapers across the country under headlines naming him "hatchet slayer," "mail-order killer," and, at best, "mail-order lover."

Moock's lawyer gave an effective appeal—arguing that police did not have a search warrant when they dug up the money and letters—but he also publicly bemoaned the fact no one was paying him his $1,500 in unpaid legal fees. As the state supreme court considered his argument, the defense attorney announced he would no longer represent the portly defendant.

His departure did not matter. In June 1930, the high court rejected Moock's appeal. His execution was scheduled for Friday, September 12, 1930.

---

[6] His name appears in era newspapers by both the German and American versions of his name, Much and Moock.

But that didn't stop Moock from trying one last time to pin the crime on someone else—someone else besides James Murphy that is. In July, Robert Lee Wilkins arrived on death row for the December 9, 1928, murder of attorney John Brooks in Walla Walla. He was placed in a cell next to Moock. Talking between themselves, Moock came up with an idea he hoped would set him free. It was a simple but clever plan that resembled the scheme that got him into trouble in the first place: when Wilkins went to the gallows one month before Moock, he would give authorities a handwritten confession that exonerated Archie of Catherine Clark's murder.

While he was being led to the gallows on August 15, 1930, Wilkins slipped a folded piece of paper to the prison chaplain and said something to the effect that Moock was innocent. The "confession note" was dated July 25, and gave specific information about Catherine Clark's murder. In order to explain his own involvement in crime, Wilkins had to account for how it occurred, how Moock was completely fooled, and how the letters and money came to be buried in Moock's yard.

It was an incredible tale that weaved in and out and around and around all of the known facts of the case in order to portray Moock as an innocent fool.

There was no mistaking who wrote the confession: it was as preposterous as his first account to the press, and as oversentimental as his letters to Catherine. Towards the end, Wilkins adopts an air of false piety, and begs Moock for forgiveness before finishing with something about Satan, the Lord, and the Kingdom of God.

> Confession time has come lest strength should fail me later as I see an innocent man is on the way here, framed and convicted of a dastardly crime that I helped do in September, 1928. 'Twas on a Saturday aught, September 22, and it was so dark it's doubtful if Mr. Moock will know me here.
>
> I was drawn into this for what was supposed to be in it by a George McDonald, alias James Murphy. We picked up a short,

dark fellow Murphy called Tex, and over near Post Falls, Idaho, went [sic] to meet Mr. Moock and a lady who thought she was going to marry Murphy.

Upon meeting, we changed a tire. Also drugged both Moock and the lady. A hatchet I took from Moock's car. Murphy took some letters from the lady's hand bag. We left Moock beside the road. We took the woman back towards Spokane and then into the hills. We drove in to a yard at the end of a trail. We turned around and came out and took another trail that forked by a pile of cordwood, which I stayed by and kept a lookout while Murphy and Tex went on.

Chloroformed and disposed of the lady, they said she would not talk any more, saying they left the hatchet. Going back to Spokane, Murphy fixed two packages, one of letters and one of some money that I buried about 10 feet apart in some berry bushes or shrubbery in Moock's gardens while Murphy watched the street. We left Tex in Spokane and coming home I was scared to death; Murphy drove so fast but I was glad to get home before daylight and I was so busy too. Murphy headed for Boise. I only heard from him once after that as he had wrote me from St. Paul telling me something about a George White he had met from Spokane.

On the way from Spokane, Murphy told me he got quite a bit of money from a woman that he married that spring in [San Francisco] who drowned in a bathtub. A woman from Los Angeles paid to frame this on Moock. I never knew her name.

I entered Murphy's plot rather blindly NOW I see. However, there wasn't to be a killing but Murphy's plans went wrong somehow. I saw a letter urging Murphy to hurry and be careful. Mr. Moock was being framed when he wrote the letters for Murphy. Moock was kept absolutely in the dark as to what was going to happen and did happen.

There is nothing left for me to do but tell you the honest truth, that I may go in peace when my time comes next month.

The lord has forgiven me for all my unseeming and foolish acts and I know this must be confessed to be forgiven. Also, it will save the strife taking the life of an innocent man that has been framed in a most ridiculous way. I know 'twill be hard to face Mr. Moock after what I have done. And I hope he doesn't know before I cross the divide if such is my lot. If I am granted clemency I will confess it anyway that his life may be spared. Forgive often as God has me and I will meet you in the morning where all acts are that of law and benevolence.

August 14

Well, Mr. Moock, too bad, but you were just framed like many another poor fellow. Untruth was framed against me, too, but never mind, Satan's day is coming.

Brother Moock, forgive me. Am glad to know you better in the spirit of the lord. I feel you will, and that you have attended a school that has revealed to you the real Satanic kingdom. Which am sure will have fitted you for the real service in proclaiming the coming kingdom of God. So the Lord be with you."

The "confession" irritated the authorities, who "branded it a falsehood." In order to satisfy the public and the court that they weren't about to hang an innocent man, they had to alibi an executed prisoner.

"Wilkins' whereabouts (on September 22, 1928) would have made it impossible for the Walla Walla attorney killer to commit the Spokane crime," reported the *Spokane Daily Chronicle* after talking with the prosecutor in Moock's case.

"The prosecuting attorney at Walla Walla has informed me that he has checked Wilkins' whereabouts and found that he was at Lowden, Washington, near Walla Walla, at the time of the Clark murder," Moock's prosecutor said. "The letter by Wilkins is just another of Moock's attempts to shift the blame from himself."

The prosecutor then made a shocking revelation that just prior to Moock's trial, he offered him a life sentence if he would "come clean," and confess everything. As horrible as his crime was, the prosecutor felt sympathy for Moock's five children. He did not want them to lose their father.

Archie Moock's prison mugshot. (Courtesy of Washington State Archives.)

"I told Moock before the trial that if he would admit the killing, I would suggest leniency....I felt sure the jury would inflict the death penalty after it heard the mass of evidence that had accumulated against him."

But Moock couldn't do that. His wife was his childhood sweetheart. His children looked up to him. God spoke to him at night after everyone had gone to bed. He would rather die at the end of a noose than live with the shame that everyone knew what he had done to poor Catherine.

During the last week of his life, Archie Moock faced his impending death with a "calm demeanor." The *Spokane Spokesman-Review* reported that he ate regularly, greeted prison officials cheerfully, but never spoke very much. He also met often with his spiritual advisor.

His wife, Augustina, brought him letters from his four oldest children, and visited with him frequently. But on the night before his execution, she left the prison to personally plead with the governor to spare her husband's life.

She was unsuccessful and at four o'clock on the morning of Friday, September 12, 1930, the warden appeared at his cell door to read the death warrant. Moock was then escorted to the gallows where he calmly climbed the thirteen steps to take his place over the trapdoor. Prison officials secured his wrists, arms, knees, and ankles. When he declined to make a last statement, the black hood was placed over his head at 4:07 a.m. Seconds later, the trap door dropped and Moock went with it, the cracking sound of neck breaking heard by everyone in the large room. He hung there for twenty minutes until the prison official checked his vital signs and pronounced him dead.

His body was cut down, placed in a coffin, and taken to a local undertaker where his wife arranged for his burial. He would have been thirty-four-years-old that November.

Catherine Clark would have been thirty-nine or forty-years-old.

Chapter Four: The Highway Hunter, 1930

SISTERS JESSIE AND ZEXIE GRIFFITH were scared and confused. As they drove south on US Highway 77, they could see the advancing headlights of a fast car behind them. Jessie maintained her speed to let him pass but instead of going around, the other driver rammed the back of their Chevy coupe. Their car lurched forward, swerved a bit, but clung to the road.

They had just crossed over the Salt Fork of the Arkansas River Bridge at the southern edge of Tonkawa, Oklahoma, when a small Buick roared to life in their side mirrors. He had been lying-in-wait beside a lifeless filling station, watching over his hunting grounds, waiting for his next prey.

Zexie[1] turned to look behind as the coupe charged after them. His growling *AHH-OOO-GAH, AHH-OOO-GAH* grew menacingly louder as his headlights blinded her. They were in an odd position. Instead of pointing toward the road, the Buick's lights were directed upwards, trapping their car in dual spotlights that wouldn't let them go.

When the hunter rammed them, he could clearly see their look of terror and bewilderment—as if it were all happening in broad daylight. The women were on a dark highway in the middle of an Oklahoma nowhere and there was a maniac after them. Jessie pushed down on the accelerator. The chase was on.

---

[1] Every resource used for this chapter misspelled her name Zexia, with an "a." However, her tombstone on findagrave.com is spelled "Zexie."

In just fifteen minutes, their entire lives had changed. At five o'clock that Sunday morning, December 28, 1930, they were kissing their parents good-bye at their home in Blackwell, eleven miles north of Tonkawa. They had just spent the Christmas holidays with their folks. The two sisters were going to leave Saturday evening but their frail mother, Cora, asked them to stay one more night and leave early the next morning.

Jessie and Zexie were part of a new breed of American women that emerged between the wars. They were beautiful, college-educated, successful, and independent. Thirty-six-year-old Zexie was the oldest of seven Griffith children. Unmarried, she was in charge of the Home Economics Department at Connors State Agricultural College in Warner, Oklahoma, near Muskogee. At just twenty-four, Jessie was the music supervisor for the Norman Public School System. Both women were accomplished singers on the Oklahoma church circuit, and were known to many people throughout the state. Jessie was scheduled to sing a solo at her church in Norman that Sunday morning.

The two sisters were close. One month earlier, they jointly purchased the late-model Chevrolet coupe Jessie was driving that morning. When they left Blackwell, they would have plenty of time to make the 130-mile trip to Norman. After church services, Zexie would drive the car to Warner.

Before leaving, their mother gave Zexie a ten-dollar bill as dad loaded their luggage in the small trunk. Their father, Jefferson Griffith, was the night captain and assistant police chief of Blackwell. He had been an Oklahoma lawman for several decades, serving in many towns throughout the region including Tonkawa. Although his duty was to serve and protect, he had no idea that when he waved good-bye to his two daughters, they were the ones who would need his protection the most.

Just eleven miles away from where Jefferson Griffith had stood, the hunter was doing everything he could to overcome his prey. He intimidated them by blasting his horn, and bumping them from behind. On the straight shots, he would get alongside their coupe and ram into the side of it, sending them off the hard-gravel road and down into a low-grade draw. Each time, a determined but terror-stricken Jessie kept their car from rolling-over, and corralled the Chevy back up to the main road.

Jessie and Zexie Griffith. (Courtesy of Oklahoma Historical Society.)

They had no way of knowing that they were not the hunter's first victims that night. All throughout those cold dark hours he had been terrorizing motorists south of Tonkawa—forcing other cars into the same shallow draw that ran parallel to the highway. Just three hours ago, he had captured a young couple under the false pretense of being a federal officer named Rogers looking for a bootlegger. He let them go, unmolested, but his victims hadn't always been so lucky in the past.

Although she was a novice driver, Jessie, to her credit, lasted far longer than any of his other victims. It was not in her to relent. In the last two months, she had become acutely paranoid. She was convinced someone was out to get her and told her friends about a mysterious man who was "dogging her."[2] Recently, when the coupe she was driving got a flat tire, she continued driving to a service station for several miles, destroying the tire rim in the process.

If she was too afraid to get out of the car then, she certainly wasn't going to stop now that her darkest fears were unfolding.

But she was never going to make it. After Tonkawa, the next town with a police force was Perry, and that was twenty-six miles away. In between lay Ceres, a collection of houses and a cemetery too small to even be considered a village. In the miles just before that hamlet, the hunter's pleasure had evolved to frustration. His prey had refused to surrender. They were defiant. They were just women and he was a man. It was time to punish them for their insolence. Despite being drunk, despite his reckless driving, the hunter pulled out his small automatic pistol with his left hand, stretched his arm out and around the windshield, steadied the weapon, and fired one round.

He got lucky.

The bullet hit just below the rear windshield and disappeared.

Police would later speculate the gunshot frightened the girls and when they saw the houses near Ceres, they pulled over. The hunter left his car, forced his way into theirs, and squeezed his small frame in-between the two women who were practically the same size he was. With his gun pressed into her ribs, he forced Jessie to drive fifteen miles back to Tonkawa. At a point one and one-half miles south of the Salt Fork of the Arkansas River Bridge–near the spot he had first

---

[2] Stalking.

began his chase—the hunter ordered her to turn on to a wide path the locals called "the old river road."

He was taking them to the river.

In those days, at that time of year, that stretch of the riverbank was a desolate landscape with only a few bare trees scattered near the water's edge. Their twisted and crooked branches stretched out like the arms of some forgotten demon praising a barbaric sacrifice. The songbirds were gone. The prairie grass was dead. The crickets were dormant, and even the slow-moving water, concealed by a morning fog, seemed unimaginably indifferent—as if it had seen this sort of thing before.

With the car pointed toward the river, the hunter pushed Zexie out of the passenger door and marched her back up the gravel road that ran parallel to the bank. When they had gone about twenty-five yards, he shot her in the neck. And then he shot her again, in the abdomen.

Behind him, he could hear the car door open and Jessie running down the road. She threw off her scarf and kept running but her dress shoes slowed her down. Fifty yards away from the car, the hunter tackled her.

She was the young one—the one who had defied him by trying to escape. But there was no escape now. He dragged Jessie off the road to some long-dead bushes and ordered her to remove her coat and gloves. He pushed her down, spread her knees apart, and tore at her undergarments. He reeked of liquor, which seeped through his pores and every breath he expelled. Jessie fought back, clawing at his body until her fingernails broke. She dug and scratched at his arms, his body, his legs—wherever she could grasp.

With the gun at her head, he took his revenge by brutally raping her.

As soon as he was done, while her contorted face moaned in pain and tears poured from her eyes, he shot her in the temple. And then, for no practical reason, he shot her in the head again.

During his attack on Jessie, a wounded Zexie heard her younger sister's cries and began crawling toward her, leaving a large pool of blood behind her where she had first fell. Her sister needed her. She crept forward on her hands and knees; inch-by-inch she crawled on the frozen ground. Her stockings tore. Her dress frayed. After she had gone a few yards, she collapsed. She would rest, then try again.

When the hunter turned back toward the car, he spotted Zexie up the road; about fifteen feet from where he had shot her twice. He sauntered toward her. He took his time. She could hear him coming towards her by his shoes pushing down on the dirt and gravel as he walked. She knew what was coming but the ground was too cold for her bare face, so she slid her left hand under her head and waited. There was nothing she could do. This was it. This was how it would end. The crunching grew louder and louder, closer and closer. When he was next to her, she could see his dirty shoes and felt him hover over her as he leaned down to press the barrel against her temple.

And then it was over.

The last thing Zexie had ever done in this world, before crossing to the next, would doom their killer.

The hunter was about to become the hunted.

The Discovery

THE BODIES OF JESSIE AND ZEXIE Griffith were discovered approximately four hours later by a local hunter and his two young sons. By ten o'clock that morning, Tonkawa Police Chief Charles Wagner and Kay County Attorney Bruce Potter were there leading the investigation.

Searching for clues, they found where Zexie had first been shot in the neck; a pool of blood with a single tire track running through the middle of it. They were able to trace the few yards that she crawled. She looked to be asleep, with her head resting on top of her hand. But the streak of blood running down her cheek told them where to look for a bullet, the bullet that had passed through her head, her hand, and stopped in the frozen ground just beneath.

It was in better condition than it should have been. Good enough for a ballistics match, if they ever found the gun—probably a .32 caliber.

Seventy-five yards south of her, near a sign that read **"$50 Fine for Dumping Here,** [3]**"** they found Jessie's body. Her torn undergarments hung below her dress and it was clear to them she had been violently raped. Her pinched face broadcast the agony she had endured—her killer's bullets had frozen the moment like a photograph.

It hurt just to look at her.

But these were not men who cried and they channeled their emotions back into their chests, where it pushed on their lungs and their ribs before it settled in their throats and choked them.

Chief Wagner studied their familiar faces and eventually realized they were the daughters of Jeff Griffith, who had once served as an officer in Tonkawa during the oil boom days. He was over at Blackwell now. A phone call had to be made.

Captain Griffith arrived at the "old river road" later that afternoon, about the same time as Kay County Sheriff Joe Cooper. Griffith confirmed they were his daughters. When they showed him Jessie's gloves, coat, and both of their open and empty pursues, he recognized those items as well. He remembered the $10 his wife had given their oldest daughter. It was gone.

This was going to break Cora's heart.

They continued searching into the afternoon hours and found three .32 caliber shell casings. They were fresh.

---

[3] The 2016 equivalent of $720.

In those first few hours, it was believed the sisters were murdered for their car. The girls were here, but the car was gone. How did they get here?

But later that day they were notified that their Chevrolet was found on a dirt road, just south of Ceres. Looking it over, they saw the bullet hole just below the rear window. Tracks on one of the tires matched those driven through the pool of Zexie's blood. Her blood was splattered under a front fender.

Nearby, they found fresh tire tracks from a different automobile. The killer drove his own car. Their minds started working out scenarios of what could have happened. The killer spotted them; chased them down; shot at their car; ran them off the road; got in their car; and took them back to the old river road where he killed them.

It must have been a nightmare.

The Investigation

DESPITE OKLAHOMA'S RICH OUTLAW HISTORY, nothing like this had ever happened in Kay County before. The double-murder of two beautiful sisters, both of them educated, successful, and known for the musical abilities astounded Oklahomans. Their shock turned to horror when the county medical examiner publicly confirmed that Jessie had been "criminally assaulted," – 1930s newspaper code for raped.

In the minds of Chief Wagner and prosecutor Potter that Sunday evening there was only one kind of man who could have done this: a crazy one. It had to be a mental reject from an insane asylum and in those first twenty-four hours, police between Tonkawa and Oklahoma City rounded-up the known lunatics.

Lyman Constant, a recently released mental patient from the Central State Hospital in Norman, was the first to be arrested near Enid, fifty miles southwest of the murder scene.

The second was William T. Capehart, who wandered into the Oklahoma City Salvation Army headquarters Sunday afternoon with three lady's handkerchiefs in his pocket. He, too, had recently been released from the Norman hospital. Both men were held, questioned, and eventually turned loose.

News of the Griffith sister murders spread to all forty-eight states across thousands of newspapers. From Rochester, New York, to Palm Beach, Florida, and west to Los Angeles and then north to Oregon and Washington, and every state in between, the two women were the most famous sisters in America that last week of 1930.

As the case progressed, the story grew and eventually became one of the top on-going crime stories in America during 1931.

While the papers reported heavily on Constant, Capehart, and a few other unfortunate men during those first forty-eight hours, local residents were coming forward to tell of the bizarre and dangerous actions of a small-time bootlegger and hustler from Kansas City. From midnight Saturday to when he was last seen at 4:40 a.m. Sunday, a drunk, belligerent "Earl Howard" made a lasting impression on everyone who had the misfortune to cross his path that fatal night.

According to Lillie "Fern" Rogers, proprietor of the Carlton Hotel[4] in Tonkawa, she had seen the drunk and foul-minded twenty-six-year-old enter and leave his room several times between Saturday afternoon, and three o'clock Sunday morning. She had known Earl and his pal, "Butch" Colwell, ever since they had moved into her Tonkawa rooming house with their wives about four months prior. They said they were from Kansas City, where they hinted they had underworld connections working for a large bootlegging operation.

That September, they decided to strike out on their own in quiet little Kay County, which shares a border with Kansas,

---

[4] Like many hotel owners during the depression, she ran most of it as a "rooming house" for long-term guests.

and is fifty-miles south of Wichita. Since they were from the big-city, they thought it would be easy for them to swoop right in and take over the area.

Yet, Kay County had its own bootleggers, small-timers, but they were men everybody knew. They didn't know Butch and Earl, who weren't from around them parts. To make inroads with the locals, they would have to be patient and build the trust of their customers.

Like many criminals, Earl's ambitions exceeded his mental capabilities. He was a simple man with a simple mind that was punctuated by a low-frustration tolerance. Chief Wagner later described his failed bootlegging ventures in a crime magazine article published two years later.

> Colwell and [Earl] were both bootleggers and at one time had been pals, but had had a falling out. In the underworld, Colwell had a rather engaging personality. He was able to mix with the golf players and country club set and so found many customers among men who were financially able to pay a good price for their hooch. This rankled [Earl] who was jealous of Colwell's ability to get business denied to him. After many heated arguments, Colwell, tiring of [Earl's] continual fault-finding, had moved to Oklahoma City.

Left on his own, both Earl and his wife Jeanne didn't fare too well. On November 6, Earl and an unknown associate barged their way into a private home in Blackwell where six couples had gathered to play bridge. A newspaper report claimed the two bandits got away with $1,500[5] in money and jewels. This amount was likely an exaggeration since Earl and his wife, Jeanne, were known around Tonkawa as a couple of moochers.

Jeanne was a beautiful, slender blonde, who dressed well and could turn men's heads. She described herself as a "good little bad girl who her knew way around." She could talk men

---

[5] The 2016 equivalent of $21,560, when adjusted for inflation.

into loaning her money, which infuriated Earl, but he seldom did anything about it since he needed the money too. Although his wife had sex appeal, she was really, really, really crazy—especially when Earl was fooling around or not treating her right. Although he was a small man, only five-foot-six-inches tall, Earl was a sharp dresser and handsome in the way young men in their twenties can be handsome, before they lose it in their thirties. He used his looks, nice suits, and silver tongue to his advantage.

"We found that he had been involved in numerous unsavory affairs with women," Chief Wagner later explained in the magazine article.

On Wednesday, December 24, Earl and some friends, including women, were having a private Christmas party when Jeanne got wind of where he was and a particular woman he was with. Like every inconsiderate thing Earl did, it boiled her kettle. Before she could pour hot water on the female-friendly festivities, Jeanne first made a stop at Blubaugh's Hardware Store in Tonkawa.

"Jeanne entered the store laboring under great excitement," the store clerk later recalled. "She bought six cartridges of .32 caliber. I believe that woman bought those cartridges with the intention of killing her husband."

Jeanne was not the passive-aggressive type. There was no subtlety with her. When a situation called for an outburst, a frequent occurrence, the fine points of her argument were best expressed with a human explosion of shrieking, crying, name-calling, and threats with a little bit of slapping, punching, and kicking incorporated when necessary.

On that particular night, the appropriate response was to shoot Earl.

Jeanne loaded those six bullets into a magazine for a .32 caliber automatic pistol. By theft, persuasion or payment, Earl acquired the roscoe from Butch, who apparently stole it from someone else.

The chief learned later, second hand, how Jeanne crashed the party.

"She burst into [the] room, with a gun in her hand. [Earl] was perceptibly frightened as he faced the angry woman," Wagner stated, "but Jim McElreath succeeded in disarming her."

Afterward, Jeanne went back to their room at the Carlton Hotel, packed a small suitcase, and took the next bus out to Wichita. She left the pistol behind.

Jim McElreath was a part-time bootlegger and part-time friend of Earl. After Jeanne left him, Earl went on a three-day bender, McElreath later reported. By Saturday afternoon, December 27, Jeanne sent her husband a telegram saying *all is forgiven, come to Wichita.* Slurring his words, Earl told his landlady, Fern Rogers, he would leave the following morning. He left his trunk behind as collateral for the bill he couldn't pay.

Without a nickel to his name, Earl had to borrow five dollars from McElreath to get back to his wife. Although he would return to his femme fatale, he wanted to get a little action before he left town. The place to meet women that night, the friendly kind, was at a dancehall in nearby Ponca City. But by the time he and McElreath arrived after midnight, Earl was full-blown belligerent and looking for trouble. He wasn't there long before a deputy sheriff working security kicked him out for being drunk. Too drunk.

In his typical alcohol-induced bravado, "Earl said as a personal favor to me, he would bust [the deputy] on the jaw," McElreath later said. After giving McElreath a ride back to Tonkawa, Earl told his drinking pal he was "restless," and was off to go "hijack some bootlegger."

At 2:30 in the morning, Earl was next seen at a Tonkawa gas station owned by William "Dutch" Winchell who nearly got into a brawl with his combative customer. Earl berated him for not moving fast enough. After he put gas in the Buick, Earl "ordered" him to check the oil.

"Before I could [check it], he said to put a quart in," Dutch Winchell later recalled. "[Then] he said, 'now damn you, test that radiator!'"

Dutch said he was walking back to the garage to get the tester when Earl came up behind him yelling, "I told you to test that radiator."

By then, Dutch was tired of his smart mouth and was about to smash the short, little bootlegger with a bottle of oil he was carrying. When Earl saw what was coming, he pulled out a dark, automatic pistol. Dutch put the bottle down. Just then, another customer drove in. His arrival defused the situation and Earl left.

Approximately fifteen minutes later, Virgil Davis and Ruby Herd were driving south out of Tonkawa on US 77 when Earl spotted them pass-by his concealed position alongside a closed filling station. He chased after them.

To get away from the "road hog," Davis was forced "to swerve onto side roads and to take ditches[6]," Miss Herd later told authorities. "We left a bridge party at Blackwell. We drove [through] Tonkawa, and near a filling station, were run into the ditch several times. We finally turned into a farmhouse driveway and the man chasing us came in after us."

Earl then identified himself to them as a federal officer named "Rogers" who was searching the highways for a known bootlegger.

"He pulled a gun out and we got into his car. He drove about a half-mile with us [in his car]. He said he was looking for Charlie Jenkins," Miss Herd later said.

Earl wasn't looking for a Charlie Jenkins, he wanted a piece of Miss Herd, who was reported to be exceptionally beautiful. As much as he wanted the attractive young woman, Earl thought better of it and he let the two go.

---

[6] The "ditches" were wide, shallow dips just off the main road.

"I guess you're not the people I'm looking for, you can go back to your car," the 'federal officer' told them. Then, he opened his door and had the young couple exit from his side, not the passenger's side, which would have been easier. They walked back to their car and drove away. When Virgil Davis told Chief Wagner about the strange incident late Sunday afternoon, he said the man was driving a green Buick.

But his story didn't stop there. After he had taken Ruby back to her home in Three Sands,[7] southwest of Tonkawa, he was driving back north on US 77 when he spotted the same Buick stuck in a ditch. Apparently, agent Rogers' hunt for bootlegger Charlie Jenkins wasn't going so well.

Leaving his Buick, Earl walked partway back to Tonkawa and then caught a ride to Dutch Winchell's garage. Two young men delivering newspapers that morning said they gave him a lift into town.

Although he had pulled a gun on him earlier, Dutch agreed to tow Earl's car out of the ditch. When Virgil Davis drove by, that's what he saw. But what Davis didn't see was that the tow-truck then ran out of gas. To help Dutch out, Earl pushed the tow-truck back to Tonkawa with his Buick and in the process, damaged his headlights.

"You've bent the hell out of your headlights," Dutch said when he saw them. Earl shrugged his shoulders and drove off. Dutch later told Chief Wagner that was around 4:30 in the morning. He never saw him again.

Ten minutes later, Carlton Hotel tenant Cecil McFrederick claimed he saw Earl enter his room, and then leave shortly before five o'clock in the morning. After that sighting, it would be a long-time before anyone from Kay County ever saw Earl again.

Anyone alive, that is.

---

[7] It's now a ghost town. There's a video of what's left of it posted on YouTube.

BY THE TIME FIFTEEN HUNDRED people massed inside and around the First Baptist Church in Blackwell for one of the largest funerals that small city had ever seen on Tuesday, December 30, Chief Wagner and Kay County investigators had talked with Jim McElreath, Virgil Davis, Ruby Herd, Dutch Winchell, and Cecil McFrederick. They gave Wagner and Potter a nearly assembled jigsaw puzzle of their chief suspect. But it was Fern Rogers who filled in the missing pieces.

The day before the funeral, Wagner was talking with Jim McElreath on South Main in Tonkawa, across from Carlton Hotel. McElreath told him what he knew about Earl including: the incident with his wife at the Christmas Eve party; what the two men did that weekend; the five dollars he loaned him; getting kicked out of the dance by the deputy; and that the last thing Earl said to him about "feeling restless," and that he was off to "hijack some bootlegger."

"In fact," McElreath said as he pointed across the street to a green Buick parked in front of the hotel, "there's his car now."

If his car was parked outside the hotel, then it was time to have a talk with Earl Howard.

Inside, Chief Wagner first met with Fern Rogers and asked her what she knew about Earl and his wife. She informed him about Earl's coming and goings during all hours of the night Saturday and Sunday before dawn. On Saturday, Fern explained, Earl got a telegram from his wife in Wichita. He then told her that he was leaving the next day (Sunday) and would be back Sunday night or Monday. But he never returned and Fern was quite surprised when Jeanne drove up in the Buick early Monday morning. She spoke briefly with the young woman who then went upstairs to her room.

Something wasn't right. Earl left town Sunday morning in the Buick, but then his wife returns to Tonkawa driving the

Buick without her husband? It was time to talk to the Missus and get some answers.

But when Chief Wagner spoke with Jeanne in the hallway outside her room, she acted nervous and told Chief Wagner she had no idea where her husband was. She couldn't even suggest where he might be. She wasn't even sure of the last time she saw Earl. Maybe it was at a Christmas party.

He knew she was lying. As unhelpful as she was, Wagner did learn one thing that would help his case: Earl's last name wasn't Howard, it was Quinn, Earl Quinn from Kansas City.

If McElreath was telling the truth about Jeanne Quinn pointing a pistol at her husband, then that might be the gun that killed the Griffith sisters. The other witnesses had reported seeing a small automatic and Fern Rogers knew he owned one. She had seen it in his room.

Jeanne also knew about the gun and she had to know where her husband was. Chief Wagner needed both of them if he was going to solve this case. He arrested her as a material witness. She was taken to the Kay County jail in Newkirk where the cells were on the top floor of an impressive new courthouse recently completed. A few days in there might soften her up.

A records check with authorities in Kansas City revealed that Earl Quinn had already served two terms in prison. In November 1921, he was convicted of check forgery and sentenced to two years in a juvenile prison. The sixteen-year-old served thirteen months and was released in December 1922. Then, in June 1925, he was sentenced to serve five years in the Missouri State Prison for assault with intent to kill. He was released on May 9, 1928. Earl married Jeanne later that year—after they were both arrested for armed robbery. For reasons unknown, that case was eventually dismissed.

Late Tuesday, December 30, County Attorney Bruce Potter boldly announced that ex-convict Earl Quinn from Kansas City was wanted for the murder of Zexie Griffith, and the rape and murder of her sister, Jessie. His name appeared on the front pages of hundreds of newspapers throughout the central United States and he quickly became one of the most hunted men in America.

"This crime was not premeditated," Potter told the Associated Press. "It came through a chance meeting on the highway. The only motives were robbery and [rape]."

Rape was something Earl Quinn knew a lot about. The day before his name was released to the press, a young Muskogee housewife wrote a letter to Chief Wagner which detailed her experience on Thanksgiving Day when she was captured, beaten, and raped under circumstances similar to Jessie Griffith.

> On the morning of November 27, about 4:30, I was held up a mile this side of Tonkawa on my way to Muskogee by a man driving a Buick coupe or roadster with license plate 383-833.
>
> My car doors were both locked and I was told to 'open-up' but instead of doing that I asked what was wanted and who he was. I was told to open the door or I would be shot.
>
> The next thing I knew he broke the glass and when he did that I opened the other door and threw my car keys as far as I could. I thought he was a car thief at first.
>
> He pushed me over to the right side and got under the wheel, but when he saw he could not drive the car he pulled me out. I put up a fight and was almost knocked senseless and the next thing I knew I was in his car and he was driving down a country road. I was criminally attacked [raped] and threatened more than once.

Myrtle Patton's physical description of her assailant matched Earl Quinn who also drove a green Buick coupe with license plate 383-833. Like Virgil Davis and Ruby Herd, he identified himself to her as a federal agent named "Rogers." She further explained in her letter that she had not reported the incident for fear of being publicly humiliated.

Sheriff Cooper made the long drive to Muskogee where Myrtle confirmed that Earl's Missouri prison mug shot was the same man who attacked her. Once in the Buick, she tried to escape by opening the passenger door and flinging herself out. That's when she discovered the door-handle was missing. Her captor saw the terrified look on her face, laughed and said matter-of-factly, "They never get out of here."

They? How many women had he raped and murdered already, Chief Wagner and county prosecutors later wondered.

Earl then parked on a quiet country road a mile or two south of Tonkawa.[8] With a gun to her head and threats to kill her, Earl Quinn raped Myrtle Patton in the small cab of his Buick.

When he finished his sloppy, ugly business, she was scared of what would come next. In her yearning for self-preservation, Myrtle did what some rape victims have been known to do in that situation; she faked it. She pretended she liked it, played to Earl's ego, and asked when she could see him again.

"This will not be the last you'll see of me," Earl Quinn taunted as he dropped her off by her late model, dark colored Chevrolet coupe. It was a near match to the Griffith's coupe, Sheriff Cooper wrote in his notebook.

Myrtle Patton's story, but not her name, was released to newspaper reporters by prosecutor Bruce Potter who wanted to energize the manhunt for Earl Quinn. His capture, Potter predicted for a public crying out for justice, "might be expected at any time."

Four-hundred packets containing Quinn's fingerprints, mugshot, and description were mailed to police in thirty-five states. During January 1931, the reward for his capture steadily

---

[8] Although authorities believed it was the same "old river road" where Jessie and Zexie were murdered, Myrtle could not be certain. She could only say it was one or two miles south of Tonkawa.

grew until it reached nearly $1,800.[9] Throughout the central states of Kansas, Iowa, Missouri, Arkansas, Texas, and Oklahoma nearly one-hundred "Earl Quinn" lookalikes were arrested and released. Sharp-eyed citizens who saw him at this place, that place, over here, and over there far exceeded that number. They were always "positive" it was him.

"For days, the fugitive's arrest was reported hourly in one city or another," Chief Wagner later recalled.

Even J. Edgar Hoover's Bureau of Investigation (BOI)[10] agents were searching for Quinn in Chicago, Denver, St. Louis, and other major cities throughout the Midwest.

The extensive manhunt for Quinn was remarkable considering that Bruce Potter didn't have one shred of physical evidence against him for the double-murder. Although the prosecutor had witnesses, no one actually saw his chief suspect shoot the sisters, or drive away from the scene.

What they did have were some remarkable coincidences that could be construed as circumstantial evidence. Jeanne Quinn was known to have purchased six bullets and six bullets were counted from the crime scene: one to the back of the Chevrolet coupe, three in Zexie, and two in Jessie. The caliber Jeanne purchased was .32, Quinn was known to have a .32 caliber Colt automatic, and three fresh .32 caliber casings were recovered from the crime scene.

Additionally, rape victim Myrtle Patton reported that the passenger side door-handle was missing. When Davis and Herd were kidnapped and released, they told Potter that Quinn let them out from *his* side of the car. After Jeanne was arrested, Wagner impounded the Buick and confirmed that the passenger side door handle had been removed.

---

[9] The 2016 equivalent of $28,600.
[10] It would not be called the FBI until 1935.

Jeanne Quinn

BRUCE POTTER WAS UNDER ENORMOUS pressure to solve the biggest crime in the county's history, and put Quinn away. To get there, he needed more evidence—physical, circumstantial, and witness testimony. However, his desire for more, his need for more, far exceeded the realities of the case.

Before Jeanne Quinn was released from custody on January 4, 1931, Oklahoma and Kansas investigators were able to trace Earl's movements during his first twenty-four hours on the run. His nervous, suspicious behavior made him standout to witnesses wherever he went.

After he murdered Jessie and Zexie at approximately six o'clock in the morning, Earl drove straight to Wichita with $3.10 left in his pocket he borrowed from McElreath, and the $10 bill he stole from Zexie's purse. He met up with Jeanne at her hotel room and told her he was in some kind of trouble. They next went to the Topic Café, where their waitress, Ruth Moore, recalled seeing them before noon. They spent fifty-cents on a single plate of scrambled eggs, bacon, and coffee.

"Quinn was noticeably nervous and ate nothing. He kept watching out of the window and finally changed his seat to a booth where he could not be observed from the street," read a report of Moore's account.

Earl then bought $1.20 worth of gas at a filling station near the café and drove northwest to Hutchinson, Kansas. There, the husband and wife searched the classified ads, found a woman renting out a room, and pretended to strike a deal with her for a long-term agreement. Instead, they stayed one hour and left without paying.

Chief Wagner later speculated that Earl used the rented room ploy as an opportunity to wash-up and "to get rid of any bloodstains or telltale evidence."

After cleaning-up, the two drove around Hutchinson looking-up Jeanne's old boyfriends from whom she tried to borrow money. She was unsuccessful.

Instead of continuing north, to put more distance between them and Oklahoma, they turned around and drove south to Wellington, Kansas, just fifty miles north of Tonkawa. After buying cigarettes and sandwiches around nine o'clock at night, Earl parked his Buick outside the Wellington Santa Fe Railroad Station where Jeanne's bad lying and strange behavior were noted by ticket-seller Bert Emerson. He gave a statement to police.

> About nine-thirty Sunday evening, December 28, a blonde woman wearing a long-seal coat inquired about the fare to Omaha, Nebraska, saying that she wanted to send her mother there. I told her and she thanked me and departed.
>
> At eleven o'clock, the woman came back and asked me for a ticket to Kansas City, Missouri.
>
> 'Isn't your mother going to Omaha?' I asked.
>
> 'No, she's changed her mind. She's going to stop off in Kansas City,' the woman replied.
>
> The ticket was $8.73 and she shoved a ten-dollar bill under the wicket. She appeared to be very nervous and walked off without her change and I had to call her back.

Instead of the woman's mother, a porter observed a man getting on board while the blonde waited until the train pulled out at 11:20 p.m. The porter remembered her because of the expensive seal coat she was wearing.

Jeanne's failure to mooch off her ex-boyfriends created a chain reaction that altered the course of the investigation. When they reached Wellington, the two only had sixty-cents left from McElreath's five-dollars, plus the ten-dollar bill taken from Zexie's purse. For whatever reason Earl decided to make his escape by train, they didn't have enough money for two tickets. Jeanne would have to stay behind. With nowhere left to go, she drove the Buick back to Tonkawa, arriving in the early morning hours. Chief Wagner arrested her later that Monday.

When Bruce Potter, Chief Wagner, Sheriff Cooper, and Deputy County Attorney Ralph Harder tried to interview Jeanne at the courthouse in Newkirk, they quickly discovered that she was really, really, really crazy.

"Her personality is baffling to the psychologist for she is distinctly temperamental, variable as the weather and infinitely more uncertain," Wagner said during his interview with a crime magazine writer. "She blew hot and cold so often in this case that we never knew whether she was with us or against us. One minute she would denounce her husband and promise to aid us in finding him, and the next she would defend him and accuse us of trying to frame him."

Jeanne did blow hot and cold and she could do it faster than anyone else—often within the same sentence, or from one sentence to the next. On the hot side, she wanted her husband with her, even if that meant incarceration; for she needed his support in these difficult times she was going through. Jeanne's hot side also included her temper tantrums directed at Earl for messing around with other women, including the ones police said that he raped.

On the cold side, she wanted to protect her husband from the police who were obviously trying to frame him.

Regardless of Jeanne's rapid emotional swings, Kay County authorities, the Oklahoma State Crime Bureau, and Kansas City special investigators knew that she would eventually lead them to Earl.

After Jeanne was released on January 4, police in several jurisdictions monitored her, making sure she was always within sight. From Newkirk, Jeanne went to Oklahoma City where she lived for a short time before Kanas City detectives physically moved her back to their city where they had the resources to devote twenty-four hour surveillance.

Chief Wagner and his associates were in frequent contact with her. They were convinced she knew where her husband was, but wouldn't tell them. Despite giving up his real name to police, she was still protecting him. As January rolled into February, police were no closer to catching Earl or getting his wife to talk.

But they were patient and as hot and cold as Jeanne Quinn was, they knew it was only a matter of time before she talked again. She just needed a little motivation, something to push her back toward their direction.

That motivation may have come in the form of two more dead women murdered in separate incidents.

Kansas City widow Mamie Houlehan disappeared on January 7, 1931, after she attended the movies alone that night. When his forty-two-year-old mother didn't come home, her son contacted police. She was last seen walking home by herself. Her body was found three days later behind an abandoned house. She had been strangled, raped, and robbed of $10 from her purse. Her diamond engagement ring and gold wedding band were also missing.

On the night of January 25, eighteen-year-old Lucille Price disappeared while she was walking home from the public library in Newton. She journeyed most of the way with her friend, Helen Spriggs, until the two first reached Helen's house. They said good-bye and Lucille set off on her own towards home. Since they were in a quiet, residential area, Lucille had no concern that she might be in danger. With a population of only 11,000, Newton, Kansas, was a small community twenty-seven miles north of Wichita, and thirty-five miles directly east of Hutchinson—two cities Jeanne and Earl were known to be familiar with.

Lucille's body was found fifteen days later in a ditch beside a rarely-used farm road just outside of Furley, Kansas. From her wounds, the coroner speculated she had been punched in the face until unconscious, and then bludgeoned to death by some unknown object. Her jaw was smashed, and her nose was broken in two places. Although most of her clothing had been torn-off, she was not sexually assaulted. Police assumed that her killer couldn't perform when the time came.

With his name already attached to two murders and two rapes, Earl Quinn was a logical suspect for the beating death of young Lucille Price, and the rape and strangulation of Mamie Houlehan. The police had no evidence against him for either murder, but they did fit his criminal behavioral pattern. They interviewed Jeanne on the chance Earl may have known either victim, and that may have gotten her to thinking: Earl was out there and she was by herself. If he was fooling around on her, why was she protecting him?

In late March, she decided to lead police to Earl's gun. It should have been a simple task but since Jeanne Quinn was Jeanne Quinn, she was going to do it the Jeanne Quinn way. This led to the most bizarre and controversial sequence of events in a case destined to have more of both.

According to Chief Wagner's account, Jeanne walked into Bruce Potter's office during the third week of March and dropped a foreign made .38 caliber pistol on his desk.

"Here's Earl's gun," she said triumphantly.

Potter looked at it and shook his head. He wasn't interested in a .38 caliber pistol. She left with a *humph*, but then called him a few days later at one o'clock in the morning.

"Come down to your office. I've got something to show you," she whispered. Not wanting to miss out on anything, Potter played along. When he got to the courthouse he found Jeanne, who by great secrecy and a conspiratorial tone, promised to lead him to Earl's gun. With Jeanne in his car, and the sheriff following behind in his vehicle, Potter drove to a sand bank of the Salt Fork west of Tonkawa. The area had once been a booze cache for Butch and Earl.

With the headlights providing illumination, Jeanne got out, pointed to an area in the sand and said, "Dig there."

Jeanne Quinn

But Potter didn't trust her. It was all too strange. "Oh, I think you'd better do the digging," he suggested.

Jeanne pretended to search, pushing some sand around with her shoe before giving up.

"I'm too nervous to hunt for it," she declared.

In that moment, with her history, Potter was sure that the gun really wasn't there, and they all went back to Newkirk, the county seat. Potter later said he thought this was just one more of Jeanne's bizarre antics.

A few days later, she telephoned Assistant County Attorney Ralph Harder at one o'clock in the morning and with the same air of secrecy, coaxed him out of his house for a long drive to the sand bank.

"Without disclosing the trip she had made with Potter, she took Harder to the same spot, where the same procedure took place with the same negative results," Wagner later said during his magazine interview.

After her third rejection, Jeanne was getting frustrated, but remained determined. She was trying to give them something they had been after her for months about, but they weren't taking her serious. Undaunted, she turned to Chief Wagner who she telephoned on March 25 at her favorite hour—one o'clock in the morning.

"Come down to the police station, Chief. I've got some big news for you; hot stuff," she said over the phone. Wagner already knew about her middle-of-the-night expeditions with Potter and Harder, but he decided to play along anyway. Jeanne's resolve had to mean something. He dressed quickly and dashed over to the Tonkawa police station where he found the twenty-four-year-old waiting for him.

"I listened to the old story under the impression that I was being especially favored," Wagner later recalled. "Arriving at the same spot which had been honored by the visits of the prosecuting attorneys, Mrs. Quinn invited me to dig for the gun. I looked her over and decided I wasn't taking any chances. I didn't care to be caught stooping over in the semi-darkness."

He then told her it was too dark and like Potter and Harder before him, he suggested that she should do the digging.

Again, Jeanne went through the motions of stirring her foot around the sand before giving up in less than thirty seconds. Disgusted, Chief Wagner drove her back to Tonkawa.

As unbalanced as she was, Jeanne had a good reason for not wanting to dig in the sand, and it had nothing to do with booby-traps or ambushes. She didn't want her name attached as the one who found it. After all, she was trying to lead them to *the* gun. She had already made Chief Wagner promise that he would not reveal that *she* was the one who led *him* to the gun.[11] The story, she suggested, was that the prosecutor or police chief found it while searching for evidence in the sand bank known by them as a place where Earl hid his liquor.

After thinking about it for a day or two, Chief Wagner decided to return to the location with one of his junior officers.

"We poked around a few minutes and finally, in almost the precise spot indicated by Mrs. Quinn, I turned up a .32 caliber automatic. There had been fourteen inches of sand over it."

Surprisingly, there was very little rust and the bluing was affected only in spots where grains of sand had adhered to it. As the top men in charge of the entire investigation, Potter, Harder, and Wagner assumed that Earl had buried the gun after he killed the Griffith sisters, and before he drove to Wichita to meet Jeanne. Their theory was that the pistol had been in the ground for three months before it was discovered.

After Wagner gave it a quick cleaning, Assistant County Attorney Ralph Harder took the fatal bullet, gun, and the three empty shell casings found at the scene to Chicago where they were examined by one of the most preeminent ballistics experts in the country. When Captain Seth Wiard completed his examination, the bullet recovered beneath Zexie's hand, and even the three shell casings, were a match to the pistol found in the sand pit.

Now they had the physical evidence they needed to connect Quinn to the murders—but only if they could catch him.

The Arrest

ALTHOUGH THERE WAS A NATIONWIDE manhunt for Earl Quinn, there were only two jurisdictions with an

---

[11] Although she said this was what she intended, they didn't trust her during these late night field trips to the sand bank.

organized effort to capture him: Kay County, and Kansas City. When it was confirmed that his last known whereabouts were in his dominion, Kansas City Police Chief Lewis Siegfried assigned three of his best detectives to track down Earl Quinn and arrest him. Their first order of business was to convince Jeanne Quinn to move from Oklahoma City to Kansas City. If they couldn't find Earl, maybe Earl and Jeanne would find each other, and then they could move in and catch him.

There was just one problem: Jeanne Quinn was Jeanne Quinn, and Jeanne Quinn couldn't stay in one place for very long. She was a freeloader, and lived with whatever friends or relatives would take her in. After detectives hauled her back to Kansas City from Oklahoma City, she lived there a short while then returned to Kay County for a brief time. During the first week of April, she moved back to Kansas City. At some point in her nomadic existence, she even managed to borrow twenty dollars from Chief Wagner.

Just like his wife, Earl may have been doing the same thing. During their manhunt, the three Kansas City detectives assigned to track him down got word that he was in Denver, Detroit, Chicago, Wichita, and then Sioux City, Iowa. On May 13, they were tipped off by one of Jeanne's relatives that she was going to travel by train from Kansas City to Omaha, Nebraska, where she and Earl planned to meet at the Union Station there. Since Jeanne was going, they assumed that this was the real deal. They had rightfully calculated that those two deceitful deadbeats, with their love-hate relationship, just couldn't stay away from each other.

And they were right.

To get to Omaha before Jeannie, the three detectives drove the 200 miles in a private car. They reached the station before her train did, and easily spotted Jeanne when she got off. From there, they followed her to a hotel where she spent the night. The next evening, she took a cab back to the station where she found her husband waiting in the main concourse.

Their reunion was short-lived. Although it is unclear who tipped them off, newspaper reporters were there to record his arrest, which they said was "uneventful."

Earl never saw it coming. Too shocked to resist, he looked around in bewilderment and whispered, "It's alright. I'll come."

Without being told where they were taking him, Quinn was driven back to Kansas City where half-a-dozen more reporters got a good look at him in Chief Siegfried's office on May 16. There, a visibly nervous and fidgety Earl Quinn—his once handsome face now pudgy, his hair, receding, gave dubious answers for why he went on the run. In the mindset of the public, his disappearance immediately after the murders was proof he was guilty. In 1931, it ranked above ballistics.

"Quivering at every step, walking as if he needed a cane to prop up on, well-dressed Earl Quinn was questioned in the Griffith sisters' murder case," the *Daily Oklahoman* reported the next day. "Extremely nervous, exhibiting an appearance of having just ran a mile in the woods with the dogs after him, Quinn talked in a clear voice but in jerks and would venture no information of his own."

He then put on an unconvincing act in which he "seemed to be amazed, puzzled and shocked," that his good name had been linked to this horrible crime. He didn't understand why "the finger of suspicion" was pointed at him because he wasn't even in Oklahoma at the time. He was in Wichita with his wife and friends, and they would provide him with solid alibis.

"Why did you run? Why did you skip?" he was asked by the *Daily Oklahoman* reporter.

After a long hesitation as he thought of his answer, Earl fired back, "I didn't run. I didn't skip. I simply left for Kansas City that night, after having visited Wichita, and the very first that I knew I was being hunted for that job was Monday when my wife called me up."

"Why didn't you come on back and face the music if you had no connection to it?" he was asked.

Earl Quinn with the Kansas City detectives, who captured him, in Omaha.

"Because my wife and other friends in Oklahoma told me that the sentiment was so strong against me that I might be mobbed if they caught me," he replied in a serious tone. "They told me there were policeman on *every* corner of *every* town looking for me and I was convinced that I wouldn't get a square deal then."

"Where have you been all these five months?"

"Oh, here, there, and everywhere," he answered. In his interview with reporters, Earl was smart enough to understand that he would have to overcome the bias associated with a man who went on the run. If he was as innocent as he said, the logical question was why didn't he hire a lawyer and turn himself in? But he didn't, and Earl Quinn had to do what Earl Quinn had been doing his whole life—he lied.

"But they didn't capture me," he said in a smug manner. "I gave myself up. I had notified the police to come and get me, that I was tired of dodging.

"I knew I didn't kill the girls. I never saw them in my life that I know of, and didn't know a thing about the case until the next day, but I would have been a fool to go back to Oklahoma when there was a mob in every town."

Poor Earl. Everyone was out to get him. But his declaration that he voluntarily surrendered opened another line of questioning where he stumbled in his answers.

Would he waive extradition back to Kay County? a reporter asked.

Stunned, Earl didn't know what to say at first, then replied that he would wait until Monday (it was Saturday) to make that decision.

"I want to see what the case is all about," Quinn retorted. "I don't even know what I am being charged with. I don't know a thing about the case. I want to see a transcript of the case and may want to have a hearing on it here Monday. I don't want to be hauled back to Oklahoma without knowing what the whole case is."

A transcript of the case? The case was in the future, not the past. Bruce Potter had only filed murder charges back in January. There first had to be an arraignment, then a preliminary hearing and *then* a trial. For someone who'd been to prison twice, Earl Quinn suddenly got a case of amnesia regarding how the justice system worked.

And his reluctance to waive extradition did not harmonize with his "I gave myself up" claim. A Kansas City lawyer had to point this out to him on Monday. He then gave in and by Wednesday night, May 20, Earl Quinn was secretly transported to the Kay County Jail. Guards, armed with machine guns, had to escort him into the building. Talk of a lynching did circulate throughout the county, but was insignificant. Nevertheless, local lawmen were taking no chances.

The Kansas City authorities agreed to let him go after they questioned him about the murder of Mamie Houlehan. He was also asked about the August 29, 1929, murder of a young couple on a bluff that overlooked the Missouri River. Cliff Drive was a popular place for young lovers to get physical in parked cars. The boy, Paul Odell, was shot in the back of the head. The girl, Ruth Laughlin, was found a block-and-a-half away beaten to death with her clothes torn off. Her killer had smashed her head with a revolver so viciously, the gun broke into pieces that were found by her body. The coroner reported Ruth was not sexually assaulted, despite her near-naked condition—just like Lucille Price seventeen months later.

The killer drove off in Odell's car, which was later found abandoned and wiped clean of fingerprints.

But all they could do was ask him, and all he did was deny having anything to do with the death of Lucille Price; or Mamie Houlehan; or Paul Odell and Ruth Laughlin. Since they couldn't fry him in Kansas or Missouri, they sent him to Oklahoma.

The Trial

BRUCE POTTER WAS FEELING CONFIDENT. When he opened the state's case against Earl Quinn for the rape and murder of Jessie Griffith on September 21, Judge John Burger had given him two small victories. First, he overruled a defense motion for a change-of-venue and second, Myrtle Patton's testimony regarding her rape in a separate incident was ruled admissible. The jury would get to hear all about it.

Even with those advantages, Earl Quinn had something far better—he had James H. Mathers[12]. By 1931, Mathers had

---

[12] In 1933, Mathers was the defense attorney for George "Machine Gun" Kelly and his wife, Kathryn.

replaced the notorious Moman Pruiett[13] as Oklahoma's "most famous criminal defense attorney." Mathers had come to Oklahoma in 1896 and was admitted to the bar two years later. Over the next thirty-three years, he developed his unique legal stratagems during the anything-goes era when prosecution for perjury was never a concern. He learned, early-on, that the guiltiest of men could be freed by heaping affidavits and alibi witnesses on the jury.

James H. Mathers (Courtesy of Oklahoma Historical Society.)

He knew how to play the best of the courtroom from both sides, having served as a former prosecutor. As the county attorney for Carter County, he once shot and killed outlaw and

---

[13] There is a 700 page book that details Moman Pruiett's career as a criminal and criminal defense attorney. The title explains him well: "He Made it Safe to Murder," by Howard Barry.

minor gunslinger, Bill Ballew, during a pistol duel in his own office. He was easily acquitted with the help of his good friend, Sheriff Buck Garrett.[14]

As a star defense attorney, the truth was whatever ol' Jimmie said it was. Object to everything. Scoff at everything. Lie, deny, and counter-attack everything.

In action, Mathers understood the basic principles of being an over-aggressive defense attorney: Why speak when you can yell? Why yell when you can scream? Why scream when you can throw a tantrum right there in the courtroom for thirty minutes before the judge calls a halt to it?

When it came to cross-examinations of prosecution witnesses, Mathers asked loaded questions based on gossip or his own imagination. He was a venomous character assassin who stomped and strutted around before a jury or newsmen with the sanctimonious persona of an agent sent by God.

And when Earl Quinn went on trial for the murder of the Griffith sisters, he had the best damn lawyer in the state.

The little white-haired man, with his black-framed owl glasses, exploded "like a ball of fire" when Potter announced in his opening argument that Myrtle Patton would testify.

"I have talked to a member of the criminal court of appeals and have been advised that no judge in the world would consider letting in this sort of evidence," Mathers began before attacking Myrtle's character. "There isn't a word of truth in this testimony. It is manufactured out of whole cloth. The idea of having some woman, *who plies the streets of this city and highways of this state at midnight,* come in here with her perjury…and no court in the world could erase the poison from the minds of the jury."

According to the *Daily Oklahoman* reporter, "Mathers continued for half-an-hour, citing case after case. His remarks

---

[14] Buck Garrett was one of the most feared, respected, and well-known lawmen in Oklahoma during his time.

resounded with adjectives all ringing with the meaning: 'Absurd, absurd, absurd!'"

Judge Burger ruled against him.

Following his opening arguments, Potter slowly and methodically built his case for the jury beginning with the witnesses who had run-ins with him during the days and hours leading up to the murders. He then connected Earl with the gun that Jeanne had led them to, and called in his expert who connected the fatal bullet and shell-casings to the .32 caliber automatic found in the sand pit.

Although she had led them to his gun, Jeanne had worked her way back to her husband and sat alongside his mother and younger brother during the trial. When her actions were discussed as the one who directed them to the sandbank, she sank in her chair and wept.

On cross-examination, four-hundred spectators, most of them women, watched as Mathers battered prosecution witnesses with contrary facts, alternate theories and possibilities, as well as insinuations disguised as questions that they were either lying or exaggerating their testimony—just as he had done when he called rape victim Myrtle Patton a highway prostitute.

When it came time to present his case, Mathers pursued a strategy that had worked for him in the past: introduce sworn statements and alibi witnesses that placed Earl Quinn in Wichita during the time of the murder. He also proposed two alternate suspects, one of whom was Amos Griffith, Jessie's older brother. Amos was a doughboy on the frontlines during the Great War and was described by newspapers as a "shell-shocked veteran." When he returned from Europe, Amos apparently couldn't get his life together and by 1931, he was an alcoholic drifter.[15] Despite this seemingly far-fetched theory, Mathers called in many of Jessie's friends from Norman who testified she was terrified of her brother.

---

[15] According to newspapers at the time.

To counteract this unlikely scenario, that would have Amos raping and murdering his own sister, the prosecution introduced telegrams and affidavits that he was in New Mexico on December 29. Although he himself had produced affidavits and even telegrams as part of Earl's defense, Mathers publicly alleged that Amos "…arranged to have those telegrams sent after [the murders]."

Mathers further tried to insinuate that Amos was in possession of the .32 automatic before it was found in the sand pit by asking leading questions of a state crime bureau secretary. Potter's objections were sustained and the woman never replied. However, by asking the questions, Mathers was able to reinforce his theory that Amos and his friend, Jim Coleman, were responsible.

Mathers was just as ruthless in his closing arguments when he declared Seth Wiard was a friend of Al Capone's and his $100 per day fee as an expert witness led him to lie in his ballistics report. He then attacked Bruce Potter by declaring that Jim McElreath, a convicted bootlegger, was "the county attorney's friend and sidekick—that politically ambitious county attorney who wants to sail to congress under the momentum of this trial."

The twelve jurors received the case on October 2 and deliberated for the next seventeen hours. During that time, rumors circulated that gangsters from Kansas City were on the way to Newkirk, population 2,135, to assassinate Jeanne Quinn for revealing the location of the pistol. She then telephoned the governor and asked him to send the National Guard to Kay County to protect her. It was a peculiar demand considering she had already threatened to commit suicide if Earl was found guilty.

"She swore she was sincere," the *Daily Oklahoman* reported. But that was just Jeanne Quinn being Jeanne Quinn. When the jury returned with a guilty verdict and a death sentence recommendation, she had a different reaction.

"An audible sigh came from the spectators," Walter Biscup reported for the *Tulsa World*. "Potter smiled. Harder grinned. Quinn's mother threw a protective arm around him while his wife clenched her fists and glared at the jury, visibly furious because they believed the state's circumstantial evidence was strong enough to pluck her man away from life. [She] looked around in a bewildered way and hurried out of court, sobbing out loud."

A short time later, after she had composed herself, Jeanne told the press: "I've done everything a wife could do. I'll help him all I can. Oh what will become of us?"

A well-dressed and carefully groomed Earl Quinn greeted the news with a sour-faced grin. After he was escorted back to his cell, he eagerly gave a statement to the dozen newspaper reporters who followed him.

"They'll never burn me for this. It was a bum rap!" he shouted. "I'm innocent and they're railroading me. I knew I couldn't beat them in their own backyard. I think it was all fixed. I know if I was sitting on a jury, they would have to have more evidence than that to convict me."

Ol' Jimmie Mathers "looked stunned," when he heard the verdict. He agreed with his client and called it a frame-up. He followed standard procedure by immediately asking Judge Burger for a new trial, which was denied several weeks later. Nevertheless, Mathers understood that his real chance to obtain salvation for his client would come with his automatic appeal to a higher court.

"A travesty!" he screamed to reporters outside the courthouse. "There will be fifty reasons why we should have a new trial."

The Griffith family was elated: Earl Quinn was going to the electric chair. "By God that is just fine. That is just what he ought to have," the girls' father told reporters in Potter's office. He was there to congratulate the county attorneys.

But nobody, not even the Griffith family, could outperform Jeanne Quinn. Later that night, doctors were called to her hotel room. "At first, it was thought that she had made good on her promise to commit suicide if her husband was convicted," the *Daily Oklahoman* reported. Physicians said, however, that she "merely fainted from the strain of her ordeal."

Another Trial

WHEN JAMES MATHERS ARGUED QUINN'S appeal in June 1932, he didn't have fifty reasons why Earl should receive a new trial—he had ninety-five. His main points of contention were directed at Judge Burger, who he claimed: failed to grant a change of venue; declined to recuse himself from the case because he was "a bosom friend" of Jeff Griffiths; erred for allowing Myrtle Patton's testimony from a separate incident; and exercised poor control over the sequestered jury. He then blamed all the citizens of Kay County for holding a grudge against his client, who suffered an injustice comparable to Jesus.

> The whole county was inflamed against Quinn. Every man, woman and child was familiar with the case. Sixty-five newspapers were taken from the jury room just before the trial ended.
>
> [The trial] was shot through with bitterness, persecution and malice, and the verdict was in the hearts and minds of the jurors before the trial began.
>
> That was why I didn't send Quinn to the stand; he begged to go. He had no fairer trial than Christ had.

Mathers also raised the valid point that the death pistol was never found on his client. During the September trial, Potter unsuccessfully tried to argue the pistol had been in the sand pit since December. Earl Quinn hid it there after he murdered the Griffith sisters, the prosecutor claimed in his opening arguments. However, this theory was shot down by the county attorney's own witness, a state crime bureau ballistics expert, who declared that the Colt automatic couldn't have been in the sand pit for more than thirty-six hours. This raised serious new questions as to who put it there and who was in possession of it for the three months following the murders.

The Oklahoma Criminal Court of Appeals agreed with Mathers in their decision handed down on November 30, 1932. Earl Quinn, who was sitting on death row in the Oklahoma State Prison at McAlester, would receive a new trial in another county. In reversing the case, the appellate court ruled Judge Burger blundered when he refused to grant a change-of-venue motion. Burger was also in the wrong when he allowed the testimony of Myrtle Patton in her alleged incident that took place one month before the murders.

Quinn was overjoyed when he heard the news and said he had the case "in my hip pocket." He was convicted the first time, he told the *Daily Oklahoman*, because his wife had conspired with Kansas City gangsters to set him up and "get me."

He never explained *why* they wanted to get him.

By the time the second trial began on February 28, 1933, in Enid, the seat of Garfield County, Jeanne Quinn had disappeared. Nobody knew where she was. Also gone was Bruce Potter who declined to run for re-election. The prosecution was led by the new county attorney, Oley B. Martin, his assistant, and Assistant State Attorney General Frank Dudley.

Both sides presented stronger cases. Martin avoided many of the mistakes Potter had made in the first trial, and gave the jury a leaner but more effective version of the state's presentation.

Mathers, on the other hand, came with new arguments. Seven vehicles were seen in the area where the Griffith sisters were killed and his witnesses claimed that none of them were a Buick coupe. Quinn left the area at 4:30 in the morning for

Wichita to reconcile with his wife, and to Kansas City to help care for his dying father.

While he was at his father's bedside, he learned he was sought by Oklahoma authorities for the double-murder and it was his father who told him to, "go away." Five months later, he voluntarily surrendered "because he wanted to see his sick daddy."

Mathers also made the bold claim that Tonkawa Police Chief Charles Wagner was a corrupt cop who permitted Quinn to operate in his area after he paid Wagner a $300 bribe for "protection." This sounded preposterous to those who knew Earl Quinn, a man who was always mooching and borrowing money from others, and could barely scrape a living out of one of the most profitable professions of his time.

After Mathers had called and questioned Earl's alibi witnesses, Quinn himself took the stand to tell the jury what really happened. It was a revealing look into his personality as he issued one denial after another in a long-running narrative in which everyone else was lying—except for him.

On the night of December 27, he did not threaten the deputy at the dance.

He never pulled a gun on Dutch Winchell, who was the one that was drunk that night, not him. He only had "four to five drinks."

He did not pose as a federal officer and force Virgil Davis and Ruby Herd into his car.

He did not force them off the road.

His only mission that night was to retrieve fifteen gallons of alcohol from his hidden cache by the Salt Fork of the Arkansas River.

Afterward, he left Kay County around 4:30 in the morning to deliver the load to his contact in Wichita, where his bootlegging pals testified in court that they saw him before sunrise.

He had never seen the .32 caliber Colt Automatic before, until it was brought into the courtroom.

On cross-examination, an incredulous Assistant State Attorney General Dudley asked him: "Then, all these state witnesses were just giving false information to this jury?"

"That's just what it was," Earl answered. Dudley's hardline questioning continued for ninety-minutes and during that time, "[Quinn] wilted, and his shouting denials grew wild," reported the *Daily Oklahoman*.

This time around, Mathers didn't bother to introduce Amos Griffith as an alternate suspect and he wrapped up his case on March 4, one and one-half days after it began. The prosecution called one rebuttal witness, who stated that at about 5:30 on the Sunday morning the Griffith sisters were killed, he saw a Chevrolet coupe chased on the same stretch of highway by a two-door Buick.

Instead of seventeen, the jury deliberated for just one hour before they were unanimous in their decision: guilty, with a death sentence recommendation.

Earl blamed his wife. "I needed my wife here," he commented as he was being led back to his jail cell. "She could have acquitted me."

He had apparently forgotten about his earlier statement that she had conspired with Kansas City gangsters to set him up.

With a new conviction came a new appeal by Mathers, based, in part, on "newly discovered evidence," and that the court erred when it allowed Clark's testimony on rebuttal and not during the prosecution's chief presentation.

Denied.

Earl Quinn, they said, "was guilty of one of the most heinous crimes in the history of the state."

Quinn's execution date was set for Friday, November 24, 1933.

Like Jesus on the Cross

EARL QUINN WAS IN A forgiving mood. On the morning of November 23, he was moved from the state prison's death row cells in the regular cellblock to the "death cells proper" in the basement of the main prison building, near the electric chair. A narrow corridor which passed by the death cells led to the execution room just a few final steps away. An army blanket hung over the doorway, preventing Quinn from getting a look inside.

A prison barber was summoned and shaved Earl's head and the calf on his left leg. He then traded his convict uniform for a set of civilian clothes. After he paid his debt to society by dying, he was no longer an inmate, and no longer needed to wear prison clothes.

Earl received dozens of special delivery letters all that Thursday, most of them of a Christian nature encouraging him to repent. One letter was from his wife, who he had not heard from in more than a year. Earl refused to tell the nearly one dozen newspaper reporters milling around what she had written, but did say that she had assured him "she didn't plant the gun on me."

It was one of several verbal jabs he took at authorities while reporters milled about, recording his every word. He was bitter, and blamed them for his predicament. Prison officials encouraged him that afternoon to admit that he murdered the Griffith sisters. Stubborn, and refusing to let go of his lies, he did not confess. Instead, he answered their pleas with "I was framed" and "I didn't have a fair trial."

Around four o'clock in the afternoon, Earl was escorted outside and across the grounds to an administration office where he spent a few, final hours with his widowed-mother, Mary, and twelve-year-old brother, Roy. When it came time to leave, he reassured her that he was innocent. Reporters standing by recorded his last words to her—words that may have been more for them than they were for his mother.

"Good-bye mother. I'm not guilty. They'll get the guilty man some time and then two men will burn for this crime."

He shook hands with his brother and gave his mother one last embrace before he was led away. It was the only time there were tears in his eyes. Mary had traveled to McAlester on borrowed money. Sympathetic prisoners in the general population took up a collection to have her son's body shipped back with her on the train.

Outside, he glanced up at the overcast sky as he was led back to the death chamber. That brief walk from the administration building to the execution chamber was his last time outdoors.

At six o'clock that evening, he was fed his last meal, quail on toast. The quail meat was provided by the deputy warden who went hunting that morning.

When he was finished eating, Father John Higgins, Catholic Priest, returned to Quinn's cell and conversed with him in low tones for several hours. Earlier in the day, he had administered the rite of Holy Communion, and heard Quinn's confession.

At midnight, Warden Sam Brown stood in front of Earl's cell and read the death warrant out-loud. As he stood listening to the state's decree that he should die, another prison guard cut a slit in his left pant leg and fastened an electrode to his calf.

"There was no excitement," the *Daily Oklahoman* reported. "Quinn's nerves were under perfect control."

As he strolled the few last yards to the execution room, Father Higgins walked beside him. A flat-bar cage separated him from the one hundred men who had gathered to watch his death. For unknown reasons, prison officials refused to allow Jeff Griffith and two of his sons to witness the execution of the man that had murdered Jessie and Zexie in cold blood.

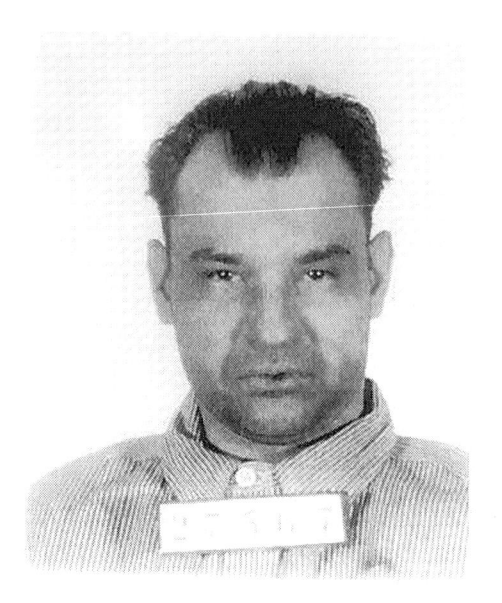

Earl Quinn, no longer the handsome young man he once took pride in.

Before Quinn was strapped into the oak chair, Warden Sam Brown asked him if he had any last words. Earl Quinn, gracious before his death, forgave the men who were about to murder him in cold blood, and pointed out their sins against him.

"I don't hold it against you folks because you have condemned me to death without a fair trial," Quinn began. "I don't even hold it against the jury. Ignorance is not the fault of the ignorant.

"I don't even have malice toward the courts, although they defied all laws in affirming my case.

"I forgive all of you. You loved them girls. You let your desire for revenge overshadow your sense of justice.

"But if Christ on the cross could look down and say 'forgive them for they know not what they do,' who am I to be bitter?"

There it was again: the Christ on the cross metaphor. If he could rise from the dead in three days, it would certainly make a good impression on the one hundred men in that room.

At 12:05 his legs, arms, and chest were strapped into the oak chair built by chief executioner, Roy Owens, in 1915.[16] Owens' men then took a sponge, soaked in salt water, and inserted it inside a leather cap, which was secured on Quinn's head with leather straps. A black hood was then dropped over his face. Another wet sponge was secured against his calf. By 12:07, they were done. Ten seconds later, Warden Brown gave the nod to Owens who was standing by the eight-foot control panel.

Owens returned his nod and pushed the control arm up, and then slowly moved the dial from 600 watts to 2,300, then back down to 1,700 before going back up to 2,300 watts over a forty-two second period. He then turned the dial back and pulled the control arm down.

Five prison physicians used their stethoscopes to check for a heartbeat. Finding none, they pronounced Earl Quinn dead.

It was over.

Earl's body was removed and taken to a hallway where it was covered with a white sheet. With reporters lingering nearby, Father Higgins stood over Earl Quinn and administered the final sacrament of the last rites, Extreme Unction.

Later that day, his body was placed on a train that would take him back to Kansas City from where he came.

---

[16] Owens earned $150 per execution, and during his thirty-two years as executioner for the state, he put to death sixty-six men. He also killed nine other prisoners in various other incidents, including the time they tried to take him hostage. His biography is available on the author's blog, HistoricalCrimeDetective.com.

Epilogue:

EARL QUINN'S SUCCESSFUL APPEAL FROM his first trial was a landmark decision for high profile criminal cases in Oklahoma. District judges thereafter were more apt to grant change of venue motions. It also cautioned them to disallow prosecution witnesses with criminal testimony unrelated to the original indictments.

Jeanne Quinn forever disappeared after her husband's execution and no records regarding her or her life have been located. She apparently left Missouri for there is no one resembling her in the online Missouri death certificate database. Some newspapers and wire services spelled her first name Jean, not Jeanne. No official document recording the correct spelling of her name has been located to date. Since more newspapers spelled her name Jeanne versus Jean, it is believed the former is the correct spelling.

Chapter Five: The Destiny of Luther Jones, 1936

October 17, 1936
Elko, Nevada

LUTHER JONES WAS SO STUPID, he was dangerous. Thirty-six-hours after he drifted into Elko, Nevada, in a hijacked car, the five-time convict was in the county jail facing charges of check forgery, auto theft, armed robbery, and federal kidnapping.

And then there was that angry mob gathering outside that wanted to lynch him on those four counts of first-degree murder he was also looking at. He messed up by killing the wrong people and the locals were raging for vengeance. To keep him alive long enough so he could be executed properly, county lawmen took extraordinary measures and made deals with men who had little patience for justice—the proper kind. Everybody wanted Luther Jones dead. He'd only been out of prison for eight days and now the entire state of Nevada wanted to kill him.

Luther Jones was an idiot.

THAT IDIOT WAS BORN THE only son and youngest of four children to Hugh and Mary Jones in Amboy, Indiana, in 1904. By 1910, his family moved to Marion where his father held menial jobs as a dairyman and street cleaner. Like his dad,

Luther dropped out of school after the eighth grade and went to work.

During his formative years, the tall, skinny boy became an accomplished liar. He didn't do it all the time, but he did it often enough. He did it to get out of trouble and he did it to impress people. He did it because lies were better than the truth.

He also developed a taste for alcohol and fast cars. When he was eighteen, Luther was working in an auto body shop where he took a customer's car for a joy ride that ended with a collision. For that little adventure, Luther earned some time in reform school.

He was out in less than a year and whatever medicine he took, it lasted—for a little while. By 1925, he was still living at home and driving a delivery truck for a wholesale grocery company. These were good years for Luther. He was working hard, stayed out of trouble, and had a sweetheart, Bernice Jackson. She was attracted to his blond hair and blue eyes. The two were married that same year and in 1926, she gave birth to a son, Lester. The following year, on November 23, 1927, the couple had a daughter, Barbaretta.

But in 1928, the old, trouble-making Luther made a comeback after he was arrested and charged with assault and battery. Although nothing came of it, a few months later he was caught with a stolen car and on October 8, sentenced to serve 180-days of hard labor on the state prison farm in Putnam County. He was released after serving five months.

After he got out, his wife gave birth to another son, Kenneth, and in 1929, Luther moved his family into a rented home on South Boot Street in Marion. It was a small, wood-frame house that sat about one-hundred feet from the railroad tracks. Several times a day, they would hear the long, black train engine approach, and feel the ground rumble, and the house vibrate, as the horn blared before it crossed the intersection.

They got used to it.

It wasn't a great place to live, but it was what he could afford. In spite of his record, he had a decent job painting cars in an auto body shop and whether he knew it or not, it was the last good year of his life.

And then he blew it.

Luther couldn't stay straight. He just had to take short cuts. That's how you get ahead in this world. After all, those big-shot stockbrokers were doing it with the buyin' and the sellin' and the this'n and the that'n; and them banks, chargin' folks interest; and those bonds—them weren't no good; and everybody knows the law was takin' money from bootleggers—you read about that all the time.

If them respectable folks were doing it, why not him?

But being a criminal only works out if you are good at it, and Luther wasn't very good at it. On November 26, three days after his daughter's birthday, he was convicted in Fort Wayne, fifty-miles away from home, for doing what he had always done—stealing a car.

This time, he got more time, one to ten years at the Indiana Reformatory in Pendleton. John Dillinger was there serving ten to twenty for robbing a grocery store but hadn't yet made a name for himself. And just like Dillinger, Luther Jones couldn't hold a job or keep his marriage together either. Bernice finally had enough of his lyin' and felonious ways. She took the kids and moved back in with her parents, divorcing Luther in 1930.

When he was paroled in 1931, Luther walked out of prison and into the Great Depression. His wife and kids were gone, and he couldn't find work fixing dents or painting cars. With three prison terms to his name, his name wasn't worth much in Indiana. What he needed, Luther surmised, was a fresh start. He needed to go someplace new and start over with a new name. If he went out west, he could be somebody different. He didn't want to be Luther Jones anymore. Instead, he wanted to be Carl Peters—Carl Peters the cowboy. For a man who'd been surrounded by bricks and bars, going out west to Big Sky country seemed like the thing to do. A man could get a fresh start out there.

To his credit, that's just what he did. Well, that's what Carl Peters did. Carl Peters went to Montana and got a job on a ranch near the tiny town of Belfry, close to the Beartooth Mountains. It was the most beautiful country he'd ever seen. There were ten-mile views that ended with steep hills. There were mountains, and mountain lakes, and mountain streams with lots of fish and wild game. And best of all, the northeastern edge of Yellowstone National Park was at the other end of the county.

Carl Peters, tall, wiry, and strong, worked hard and stayed on with the ranch for two years. It could have lasted longer but Carl Peters was always Luther Jones and Luther Jones started to get big ideas. When things were going good, he thought he could make it better by doing something stupid.

But where Luther Jones stole cars, Carl Peters had his own modus operandi. He had his own little racket and it was foolproof: Carl Peters forged checks. He would go into a store, buy an item, and write the check for five dollars more and pocket the cash and pawn the merchandise. By the time they figured things out, he would be long gone.

When Carl Peters the cowboy wanted a rifle, he went to the Montgomery Ward's store in Red Lodge—the nearest city of any note. There, on May 12, 1934, using the alias Frank Melna, he wrote out a check for $11.05[1] for a new rifle that he turned around and sold to a secondhand dealer.

Checks were great. Carl Peters loved checks. He could give a sales clerk a piece of paper and get back some merchandise and a little cash. Not bad—unless those checks were fakes.

---

[1] The 2016 equivalent of $198. In 1934, one dollar was equivalent to $18 in 2016.

In order to get away with it, he had to be good at it, and cowboy Carl wasn't any good at it. The law soon traced everything back to him. Still using his Montana name, Carl Peters pled guilty to passing a worthless check and on May 24, he was sentenced to one year in the Montana State Prison in downtown Deer Lodge. He served nine-months and was paroled in February 1935.

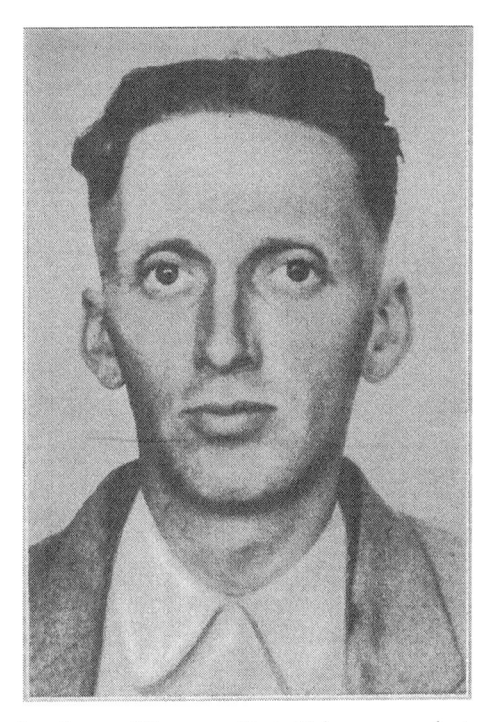

Luther Jones, Montana State Prison mugshot.

February in Montana is a bitter cold place to be, especially when one has no job and no home. Carl stayed warm that winter by moving into a transient camp near Laurel, twenty miles southwest of Billings.

Just like Luther Jones, who always went back to stealing cars, Carl Peters went back to forging checks. Big ones this time—he wasn't messin' around with any small-time stuff. He had nine months in prison to figure it all out.

On Saturday, May 11, 1935, one day less than a year from the great rifle swindle of Red Lodge, Luther Jones using the alias Carl Peters using the alias L.B. Carson met with used-car dealer George Pierce in Billings. After a tall-tale about the life of L.B. Carson, he bought a used-car and a used-truck for $300 and $145 respectively—with a check. Carson even persuaded Pierce to accept one of the checks for five-dollars extra. He needed a little gas and lunch money, after all.

It's unclear how Carl Peters, alias L.B. Carson, was planning on driving both vehicles at the same time, but he ditched the truck and left town in the car. The next day, George Pierce discovered there was no such bank as that listed on the check of the blond-hair, blue-eyed L.B. Carson. The bank, the check, and the buyer's name were all made up.

From Billings, L.B. Carson drove to Laurel, where the next day he bought a wiring harness—with a check. Then, continuing with his bigger-is-better master plan, Carson went to an implement store in Bridger[2] and bought a new $1,400 tractor—with a check. On each transaction, he got five-dollars back in cash.

Carson promised to come back for the tractor, pocketed the ten dollars and drove to Cheyenne, Wyoming, where he continued his shopping spree by buying a lot of furniture—with a check.

There, he made the mistake of hanging around town too long. The police caught up with L.B. Carson and arrested him on Wednesday, May 15. During questioning, Carson confessed that his 'real name' was Carl Peters and he'd been released that February for the same charge he was now facing.

---

[2] Bridger is forty-seven miles south of Laurel by today's roads. After adjusting for inflation, $300, $145, and $1,400 in 1935 is the 2016 equivalent of $5,300, $2,555, and $24,700. Five dollars then is the same as $88 today.

Later that day, the Cheyenne authorities contacted Pierce and told him they had his car. He set off for Cheyenne where he was deputized and permitted to escort Peters back to Montana. The former ranch hand waived extradition and as he drove the stolen car to Billings, Pierce kept his gun pointed at him the whole way. The Cheyenne cops had told the used-car dealer that "Peters is a dangerous man," but when the two had a friendly conversation to pass the time, he found him "to be a gentleman, despite his check-writing shortcomings."

On the road, Carl Peters got to talking about his life back in *Toledo, Ohio,* where he'd stolen a car from the auto body shop he worked at and crashed it, earning a little time in reform school. From *Ohio*, Peters then told how he was busted in *Chicago* on a couple of things.

It was all true, except for the geography and some other minor details.

A few hours after the two men reached Billings on May 17, Carl Peters was standing before Judge Robert Strong—the same judge who'd sentenced him in the last case. "This time, I can't let you off as easily as last," Judge Strong was quoted as saying in a Montana newspaper. He sentenced Carl Peters *from Ohio* to serve two years at Deer Lodge. His crime spree, based on his foolproof idea, his master plan, lasted less than one week.

During the next 514 days while he was in the Montana State Prison, something happened to the soul of Luther Jones. Sure, another prisoner bashed him on the head sending him to the infirmary for a short-time, but that was physical—this was different. This was life changing, and not the good kind. Dispossessed of all his youthful energy and ambitions, he stopped caring. He gave up. He was afflicted with melancholy and in men his age, depression always mutates to anger. He was in his thirties now and looking back at his life was painful. It was so painful that when he was released on October 9, 1936, he started drinking and he didn't stop until he was in the Elko County Jail eight days later.

When he was discharged, the prison gave him a stipend of $15, plus $35 in exchange for all the leather craftwork he did during his stint. He caught a bus to nearby Butte where he met up with a pal from prison named "Scotty." He used some of his release money to buy a quart of cheap whisky. The two started drinking and hopped a freight train to take them to Blackfoot, Idaho, where Luther needed to see someone.

That quart of whisky was the start of a weeklong bender, but they emptied the bottle halfway during the nearly 300-mile trip. That's the thing with benders: there's no use startin' one unless a man can keep it going and they were determined men. In a written statement he later gave, Luther described the fool's journey that brought him to Elko.

"We got halfway to Blackfoot and got off to buy more whiskey; then we went on to Blackfoot and got off to see the mother of a boy who was serving time at Deer Lodge. She insisted on me staying there and seeing if I could get work there.

"I stayed there two days but could not find work and started drinking, staying there two days and kept on drinking and when I left she gave me five dollars. (Scotty had grown tired of their adventure and returned to Billings by this time). I went to Pocatello, Idaho, got more whiskey, run out of money, so I bought a gun with a bogus check,[3] intending to hock it in the next town."

But Luther didn't hock it in the next town—he never planned to hock it in the next town. He kept the little .22 caliber revolver, a type later described as a "Saturday night special." From Pocatello, Luther hitchhiked to Ogden, Utah, where he arrived after business hours on Thursday, October 15.

---

[3] It's unclear where or how he acquired bogus checks so soon after being released from prison. He never volunteered any information regarding this issue.

"It was late in the evening, about 6:30, and I could not sell the gun as everything was closed," he continued in his written statement.

It was a lie.

Luther didn't sell the gun because Luther had a new master plan. With his last dollar, he bought some food and beer, and then went to the Yellow Cab Company office with a story.

"[I] told them I had a date out in the country and wanted to rent a car," his statement continued. "They wanted to rent me a Yellow (yellow colored taxicab) but I told them I didn't want a car with the name on it. So they gave me a sedan and the driver took me about a mile-and-a-half out in the country. When we got there, I told him we wasn't going to stop. I took all of his money but a dollar and made him drive at the point of a .22 special into Nevada."

Luther Jones the car thief, Luther Jones the paper-hanger, was now Luther Jones the armed robber and kidnapper.

Driving northwest out of Ogden, cabbie LeVon Neill took his hijacker[4] on a wide half-circle around Salt Lake. Along the way, Luther made the cabbie stop so he could buy sandwiches—and more whiskey to keep his bender going. For what today might be a three-hour trip, it took them all night and early morning to reach the Nevada border. Just as the Sun was making its slow escape from the horizon, the duo reached Montello, Nevada, a small town just across the state line that had seen better days.

Luther ended their journey there and got rid of Neill by putting him on an east-bound freight train that was just leaving town. "I saw an open box car and I told him to git on it and git out," Luther later wrote in a first-person account. "I seen him leave on the train."

---

[4] Before airplane travel was common, and armed men started commandeering airliners for various purposes, hijacking was the word most often used when an armed criminal took control of a vehicle with the owner/operator driving.

Luther screwed-up when he crossed the border with LeVon Neill. It was the first of many mistakes he made on what would be his last day of freedom. Kidnapping the cab driver was now a federal case and that meant Hoover's men would be after him. Two years ago, those men gunned down Dillinger outside a Chicago movie theater. They never tried to arrest him or stop him or nuthin—just filled him full of lead. Those were the kind of people Luther Jones, son of an Indiana street cleaner, was now up against.

Stupid Luther.

While Neill was making his way back to Ogden, Luther continued driving west. Along the way, he stopped to take-on a frail, gray-haired hitchhiker lumbering along the highway. No one ever knew his name, or where he was from. He was just a nomadic wanderer, going from one place to the next. And lost in that vague cloud of his existence was a metaphor for the trajectory of Luther Jones's destiny—if the next twelve-hours had not occurred.

As they neared Elko, the car battery started giving them trouble. It was a small thing, but it was a small thing that sustained the chain of events that led to one of the worst crimes in Nevada history.

"On the way in, the battery ran down because I had the radio and the heater on all night long," Jones described thirty-six hours later. "We stopped in Elko to get another battery. The man (a local mechanic) wanted a $5 deposit so I offered him a check. He wouldn't take the check so I went to an electric shop."

At a home goods store, Luther paid for a clothing iron—with a check, and got back a few bucks extra, just like old times. Instead of paying five bucks for a deposit, he was able to convince the mechanic to accept one dollar for a new battery. With the hitchhiker still tagging along, Luther continued his journey west out of Elko.

Ten minutes down the road, the Chevrolet went into convulsions and died alongside the highway. While Luther stayed behind to nurse a bottle of whiskey he'd bought in a fancy Elko hotel, the gray-haired hitchhiker got a ride back to town and had the local Chevrolet dealer send out a tow-truck.

Back at the Chevy garage in Elko, the mechanic was able to fix the problem. The bill for towing and repairs came to three dollars. Luther tried to write him a check but was turned down. "He told me to go to the bank so I left and didn't go back. I left the old man at the garage," Luther later reported.

He continued his westward march on foot until he reached the Southern Pacific cattle yard more than a mile west of town. The former cowboy stopped and took an interest in what was going on as men loaded cattle onto railcars. Luther stood by the corrals where his criminal nature took an interest in three men–later identified as Domingo Arrascada, his cousin, Manuel Arrascada, and Otto Heitman–work out a dispute over one of the head Heitman had purchased.

As they worked out the issue, a bad feeling came over Domingo Arrascada. It felt like someone was watching them, someone inside the corral. The feeling was so intense that he turned around to look and saw Luther Jones staring back at him.

"I looked up, and saw a tall, slim man inside the corral a few feet away. He was watching intently," Domingo later said. At the time, he dismissed the blond-haired man as one of the cattle loaders.

Luther *was* watching them. He continued watching as Heitman walked over to talk to Walter Godecke. Together, they stood between a new coupe and a truck to discuss business. They were both successful cattle ranchers from the Carson Valley area of Douglas County, on the California border. Heitman was forty-two-years-old and looked the part of a prosperous cattleman. Godecke was younger, twenty-nine, but was smart, ambitious, and hardworking. They were on a cattle-buying trip throughout Nevada, and Elko was just one of their stops where they purchased livestock from Domingo's cousin, Manuel.

Arrascada was well known in Elko County and lived by North Folk[5]. He came to Nevada in 1904 from the Basque region of Spain and prospered by raising cattle. He was just one of many Basque immigrants that settled in Nevada just before and after the turn of the century. The Basques were opportunists and worked hard; first in mining, then transitioning to raising sheep and cattle.

Throughout the state, it could be said of them that they were a tough and a tight-knit community. Very tough. Very tight-knit.

It was the new coupe that caught Luther's attention. Men who drive new coupes have money, and the two ranchers standing near it looked like they had money. Luther wanted some of that cabbage[6], and he wanted the new coupe. He really liked that coupe. That coupe wouldn't break down on him like that cab driver's old Chevy.

And just like that, Luther walked up to Heitman and Godecke with his little pop gun and told them it was a stick-up. It was an impulsive decision and impulsive criminals usually make stupid mistakes. He hadn't even bothered to look around to see if someone was watching.

"I wanted to know who had the key to the car," Luther later explained. "They said they didn't have no car key. Just then another man walked through the corral gate and seen us, so I told him to get over with the other two."

The third man was Manuel Arrascada. He had seen what was going on, but walked over anyway to see if he could help. Before he did, he took $40 out of his pocket and put it under

---

[5] North Folk is located at the northern end of Elko County, fifty-one miles north of Elko by today's roads. It is now an unincorporated community where only a few houses and buildings remain.

[6] Money.

the seat of his pickup truck. If this was a stick-up, he wasn't about to lose his money.

Walter Godecke & Otto Heitman

Luther was stupefied. He couldn't believe one of them didn't have the key to the new coupe. "I shook them down for the key but they didn't have none. I took the money off them and it wasn't a hell of a lot—about $40 in all."

Now what?

Luther hadn't thought that far ahead. If he could get the key, he could put the men in the new coupe, drive on down the road and then kick 'em out when he got far enough away.

He would have to improvise.

Looking around for the answer, Luther spotted a grove of willow trees near the Humboldt River that ran parallel to the highway and railroad tracks. To get to the trees, Luther ordered the men to march in front of him. The shortest route took them out in the open as they walked across a field adjacent to the river. To reach the grove, the group rounded a bend and Luther spotted a shack that wasn't visible from the cattle yard. The eight-foot by five-foot hut was home for fifty-year-old Johnny Elias, a one-legged pauper who made his living scrounging the city dump for scrap metal and whatever else he could sell.

Now he had four problems to deal with when all he wanted was the keys to the coupe and some money. The shack was the answer. Put 'em in there, tie 'em-up, and get out of town.

"When we got to the shack there was a fourth man there who must have lived in the shack," Luther later explained. "I made all four get in the little shack. I had the man who lived there tie the three I marched over, after having him get some string."

It was small and it was dark. It was like a tomb. A mausoleum.

The hovel was only five-feet high, and the men had to bend over to get inside where there was only room for two, maybe three people. Luther commanded them to get down on their stomachs with their hands behind their backs. He was just going to tie them up and leave, he said. Since Elias was the oldest, the weakest, he was ordered to bind their hands with twine, while Luther kept his gun on him.

When he finished, Luther told the hermit to turn around with his hands behind his back. He was about to tie him up too when Johnny Elias got a bad idea. He spun around and hit Luther.

Luther shot him in the head. Inside the tiny hut, the .22 special roared like a cannon. Elias fell hard. Crashing into two of the men; one of them shouted, "Help! Oh my God—Help!"

Luther kept shooting. At point blank range, he aimed the barrel into the mass of men lying on their stomachs and pulled the trigger five more times. When he heard the 'click-click-

click' of an empty revolver, a wild-eyed, panicked Luther didn't stop there. Shaking with fear, he opened the cylinder, dumped the shells, and one-by-one, loaded six more .22 caliber bullets, closed the chamber, and fired into the men six more times.

"I then shot the three. My mind was blank from there on and I don't remember just what happened," Luther said. "I got some clothes hanging inside the shack and covered them up. None of them was making any noise. I then shut the door and put wood in front of it."

From the shack, the five-time convict and now four-time killer strode back to the highway, where he returned to his slow march west. After walking for twenty or thirty minutes, he hitched a ride with a man who took him twenty-five miles to the next town, Carlin.

He should have kept on going but he didn't. He was still in Elko County and a smart killer would get away from there. He did go to the bus station between 5:30 and six o'clock that night, but was told the bus to Reno didn't leave until 10:30. Instead of trying to hitch a ride out of there, Luther got comfortable. Real comfortable.

First, he went to a beer parlor where he ordered a meal and drank some ale. With food in his belly and alcohol in his blood, Luther felt relaxed enough to visit the barber for a shave. While there, he inquired where he could find some action in Carlin, population 830.

Luther being Luther, he was determined more than ever to keep his bender going—and multiply his money. At Max Sperlich's Saloon, he bought a pint of whiskey and found a card table.

He lost $15 playing poker.

And then his pistol fell out of his coat pocket, hitting the floor with a noticeable thump.

Stupid Luther.

"You are all fixed up," one of the card players said.

"Yeah," Luther answered back with a nervous grin. "I was up trappin' and forgot to take the gun out."

Trappin'? This fella? Dressed the way he is?

It didn't sound right and the stranger didn't look like no trapper. One of the players excused himself and casually made his way out the back door to fetch Night Constable William Thornton. Together, they went to the saloon where they found Luther standing up, looking into a back room. He never saw what was coming.

"I want whatever you got on you," Thornton yelled as he grabbed the stranger's arms.

Panicked, Luther clawed for his gun, but he couldn't quite get his left hand in his pocket. As they struggled, the bartender came around and bashed him over the head with a coffee pot. They took his pistol, and dragged him over to the little city jail where there was another fight after Luther sucker-punched Thornton in the stomach. The two-on-one struggle ended when the constable pulled a weapon and threatened to shoot him unless he got in the cell.

Luther got in the cell.

Over the next twenty-four hours, the story of what happened during the previous twenty-four hours unraveled, and the news echoed across the country. It began with Luther's transport from Carlin to the Elko County Jail inside the courthouse. During the twenty-five-mile drive, he asked Constable Thornton, "Does this state have a gashouse?" He then showed great interest in what was America's first gas chamber as it was described to him.

Gas chamber? That's a peculiar question.

Immediately upon his return to Elko, Luther pled guilty to resisting arrest and was sentenced to 180 days in jail. He was then quickly connected to the bogus check he wrote for the clothing iron and copped to it as well.

And then they started asking him about three men who went missing from the cattle yards sometime around three o'clock yesterday afternoon. He fit the description of a man seen lingering there, and later walking west out of town. Luther held up under intense questioning all that Saturday morning, October 17, but after an FBI agent from Salt Lake City arrived to investigate the interstate kidnapping of an Ogden cab driver, he started to crack.

When arrested in Carlin, Luther gave them an alias, H.S. Kinchabocker, but it didn't hold up for long. Nothing that Luther Jones was keeping secret would hold up for long. They knew just what to say to him.

> *We'll run your fingerprints, your photograph and find out who you really are, he was reminded. LeVon Neill can identify you as the man who kidnapped him with a gun and stole his money and car, he was reminded. Where'd you get that .22 caliber pistol? We can trace it. Those look like prison shoes, where'd you get them? If you cashed a bogus check to get a few bucks, where did you get the money to play cards with in Carlin? We heard you lost $15. Where are Otto Heitman, Walter Godecke, and Manuel Arrascada? they asked. How much money did they have on 'em when you killed them? People saw you, you know. They saw you at the rail yards, and a state trooper saw you walking west out of town around four o'clock yesterday afternoon. We got a posse out looking for the men right now. If you killed them with that little .22 of yours, we'll match the bullets. Did you know Heitman was a county commissioner over there in Gardner County? He had a wife and three kids. Arrascada had a wife and a son. He was Basque, did you know that? You don't want to get them folks after you, they're tough people those Basque.*
>
> *Tell us where the men are...*

By one o'clock that Saturday afternoon, Luther Jones was starting to crack.

Tell us where they are, they pressed.[7]

---

[7] This interrogation, indented and italicized, was constructed by the author based on bits of information within the research, facts known to

"Look around and they might be found," Luther whispered. It wasn't an admission, but it got them started. Without confessing to anything, he then told them about a cabin. Two Elko deputies and the FBI agent went to look for it, and after going to the wrong one, they found the one near the willow grove around three o'clock Saturday afternoon on October 17.

Opening the door, they saw the bodies of four men "all piled up like a lot of kindling," in a space the size of a prison cell, one of the deputies later told a reporter. It was a blood bath; stiff bodies, pale skin, eyes open, grimaced faces, hands tied behind their backs. Each man had been shot multiple times, mostly in the face and head.

They went looking for three dead bodies and found four. They didn't know about the old man, and it would take three days before they figured out who Johnny Elias was: that he'd been born in Iowa in 1875, and had come out west at the turn of the century where he worked in the Nevada mining industry his whole life, and lost his leg in an accident. And that he wasn't fifty-years old, he was sixty-one.

Returning to the jail, the deputies and agent continued their interrogation. By evening, they were able to pry out of him who he was, where he was from, and his time in Montana. Since they had him dead-to-rights on everything else but the killings, he confessed to kidnapping LeVon Neill, stealing his car and all his other crimes. And yes, he was out by the cattle yards yesterday, but he didn't kill them men.

---

the authorities at the time of Jones' arrest, and the investigative methods available to them at the time. Although we may never know what was said during that interrogation, I felt the story called for a logical recreation of what may have occurred. The indented and italicized passages, without quotation marks, is the voice of a nameless interrogator. This is my second notice that this passage, and another one on the following page, should be considered by the reader to be fiction.

As the lawmen pushed him for a confession, news that the killer was in the county jail electrified Elko residents and spread before the evening papers in Reno and Salt Lake City hit the streets.

"Feeling among Elko County ranching people was reported tonight to be approaching violence," the *Reno Evening Gazette* reported Saturday night. "Sheriff's officers kept a keen vigil at the county jail as authorities attempted, in the face of meager evidence, to untangle a motive for one of Nevada's apparently most brutal crimes."

You're in a "tough spot," one of the deputies told him. The mood is running "pretty high" out there on the streets, they told him.

Confess.
We'll match the bullets, they reminded him. We got witnesses, they reminded him. It's better to confess now than be found guilty at trial. Ever seen a man die in the gas chamber? Their skin turns pink. You got three kids back in Indiana? Otto Heitman had three kids.
Confess.

They had him when they started talking about the gas chamber. They let him go to bed that night, but thoughts of the gas chamber kept him awake. He turned it over in his mind; the thought of being strapped to a chair in a room filled with that sodium cyanide they used; it gettin' into yer lungs, chokin' on it, skin turnin' pink.

The gas chamber put the fear in him mighty bad. At two o'clock Sunday morning, Luther Jones the petty criminal was ready to confess to the massacre of four men. He called out to the jailor. He wanted to talk to the chief deputy. And that FBI man.

He told them everything. In a four-page written confession, Luther detailed everything that happened between Deer Lodge to his arrest in Carlin.

He hadn't planned to kill them. He only wanted to tie them up so he could get away.

"It was liquor," Jones wrote. "Liquor is to blame for it all. I was drunk." It was his way of mitigating responsibility for one of the worst crimes in state history.

When he was done, he signed his name to it. The FBI man then told him to sign each page. At 4:30 in the morning, Luther was allowed to go back to bed.

The four victims. The building in the background is not the shack.

By the time he woke up, wild rumors that Elko residents, Arrascada's relatives, and fifty to one hundred men from Carson Valley were going to storm the courthouse had found their way to sheriff's deputies and newspaper reporters. The lynching talk continued for three more days. Twenty-five law enforcement officers from city, county, and state departments were called in to guard the courthouse and filter out into areas where the public gathered. Those assigned to the courthouse positioned themselves inside on every floor, and formed a cordon around the building. Civilians who were employed by the city or county were also deputized and armed to provide reinforcement.

By Sunday night, the atmosphere in Elko, Nevada, was intense—as if the sky could cast down fire instead of rain. Nobody was sure what was going to happen. A gunshot. An angry mob storming the courthouse. One of them green deputies shootin' at shadows.

"There were many rumors last night that there would be a lynching party at midnight," read a special report to the *Reno Evening-Gazette*. "'The party starts at midnight,' was the word passed along."

The next morning, the sheriff called the state prison to request more gas grenades, riot guns, and an armored vehicle to haul the confessed killer out of there if they needed to. That intensity continued Monday and Tuesday before Elko County District Attorney Douglas Castle approached Arrascada's brother and cousins with a plea to put an end to the lynching talk. In exchange, he promised to put Luther Jones on trial and in the gas chamber as soon as possible. With the confession, Castle wanted to try him that week. It was what the Arrascadas wanted to hear, and the Spaniards backed off, but it was a compromise with conditions.

"We have the utmost confidence in our county officers," a high-ranking member of the Spanish Basque community told a reporter. "We know that they will exact justice speedily in this case, but if they don't, I know what will happen."

That same reporter then clarified what the Basque promised to do if things weren't done fast enough. "He indicated in an unmistakable manner that plans are afoot for a 'lynching bee,' in event legal action is delayed."

Since he confessed, everyone expected Luther Jones to plead guilty at his arraignment Monday morning, be sentenced to death in the afternoon, and on his way to Nevada's death row by nightfall. But that's not what happened. Over the next forty-eight hours, Jones retracted his confession, gave investigators a new story, which shifted blame to an unknown accomplice, requested an attorney, and pleaded "not guilty by reason of insanity," he told the judge.

At the time, Nevada law prohibited murder defendants from pleading not guilty by reason of insanity. They could, however, use an insanity claim as part of their regular defense.

"He pleads not guilty," the judge told the court reporter.

Luther's second story had to fit with the known facts in the case. With those restrictions, it sounded preposterous when reported in the *Reno Evening Gazette* Monday, October 19.

> Jones asserted that a partner, whose name he either did not know or would not tell, had shot and killed the four men as the climax of a hold-up planned by Jones and his companion.
>
> The prisoner declared that he and his partner started from Ogden with Reno as their objective. Arriving in Elko, they decided to stage a hold-up to get money, Jones said, and at the Southern Pacific cattle corrals just west of Elko they saw three men standing together. Jones said he had two pistols, one a .32 caliber and the other a .22. The latter weapon, he said, he gave to his partner.
>
> The two men marched the three victims to a cabin a quarter mile distant where the fourth victim lived, the prisoner said. The partner shot down the four men with Jones' gun, then returned the weapon (to Jones). The two then separated, the partner going to Elko to get their automobile and return for Jones, the latter now claims.
>
> On the way to Carlin, Jones says, he lost the .32 caliber pistol. The smaller gun was in his possession when he was arrested.

Furthermore, as part of their agreement, Luther claimed that if one man were caught, he would take the blame for the other. But Luther didn't want to take the blame anymore. "I don't intend to take the rap," Jones told the county sheriff, "when somebody else was with me."

To complicate matters, the attorney assigned to his case didn't want the job. After interviewing Luther in his cell,

Clarence B. Tapscott announced he "flatly refused" to accept the most unwanted job in all of Elko County. He believed Luther was guilty, that the evidence was overwhelming, and "no defense that I could assist in could be presented."

Although he initially said he was willing to face contempt of court charges, the judge convinced Tapscott to change his mind during a privately held conference. Afterward, the new attorney for the most hated man in Nevada retreated to his law office to cobble together some kind of defense.

News that four men were gunned down in a dreary, dirty shack by the river touched a nerve with Americans coast-to-coast. Newspapers from Florida to California, Michigan to Texas, and New York to North Carolina, told the story of an armed desperado, a highway drifter, a hijacker, who wandered into a desert town and valued human life at the price of ten bucks apiece. It was a story that reached his home state of Indiana where it brought shame and sorrow to his family.

It was also a story that in the third week of October 1936, made Luther Jones one of the most infamous men in America.

Luther's decision to fight it out at trial put his life at risk. Locals didn't just want him dead, they wanted him dead *now*. County authorities were quietly advised to get him out of Elko until the trial. The sheriff and district attorney refused, and maintained a heavy guard inside the courthouse.

"Residents here believed Jones placed his own safety in jeopardy by obtaining the delay in his trial," the *Salt Lake Tribune* reported Tuesday morning, October 20. "Aware of the development of lynching sentiment in the frontier area and of the rising tempers of Basque ranchers, one of whose neighbors was among the victims, District Attorney Douglas Castle had hoped to have the trial over and Jones on his way to Carson City Monday night."

But there was always going to be a drawn-out trial. At the time, a little-known state law required defendants facing the death penalty to plead not guilty. The reasoning behind it concluded that since execution was the ultimate penalty, judgement of guilt and recommendation for execution had to come from a jury, not a solitary judge.

An upcoming jury trial put the prosecution in high-gear. Luther's gun, and the bullets taken from the dead men, were sent to the FBI laboratory in Washington DC. On Wednesday, accounts from eyewitnesses made their way into newspapers. James Lynch, a yardmaster for the railroad, identified the tall, gangly defendant as the one he saw marching behind three men over an open field that led to the river. A state trooper saw Luther Jones walking along the highway west of town sometime later. Domingo Arrascada reported he saw him at the cattle yards shortly before the murders. Rancher Wellington Weiland recognized Luther's photograph as a man he saw staring him down inside the bar room of the Commercial Hotel on the morning of the murders. Luther focused his attention on Weiland as he paid Manuel Arrascada $57.50 for the purchase of a bull. Luther was at the hotel bar to buy the whiskey he said he purchased in town. And finally, the sales lady in Pocatello, Idaho, identified a photograph of Luther's gun as the one she sold him. She also sold him twenty feet of rope and a butcher knife.

Charged only in the murder of Walter Godecke, Luther Jones got clobbered during his November trial which was described as "one of the speediest in Nevada judicial history." Although the physical and circumstantial evidence was overwhelming, and there was a signed confession, Tapscott further botched the defense case by: failing to call for a change of venue; allowing ten ranchers to get on the jury when his client had murdered three ranchers; and not securing medical doctors to examine Luther who could then testify his client was insane when he gunned down four men.

However, Tapscott did file a motion to get the confession thrown out. In a hearing called after jury selection, and before the start of the trial on Tuesday, November 17, Luther blamed the confession on smuggled whiskey, fear of a lynch mob, and because he was freezing cold at the time.

"I was told feeling was running pretty high in Elko and I might be lynched," Jones testified. "I was brought to the sheriff's office in my underwear and without my shoes. It was so cold I was glad to make the statement they wanted [so I could] get back to my cell."

On cross-examination, Jones admitted he wasn't forced to sign it, was advised of the consequences, and reviewed each page with the FBI agent who took the confession. He then countered with what was becoming a familiar theme with Jones; he was suffering "the results of intoxication," from a half-pint of whiskey he had kept hidden after his arrest in Carlin.

Drunk in jail? Laughter erupted in the crowded courtroom and the trial judge called for order.

Motion denied.

District Attorney Castle then proceeded with a systematic presentation of his case, which relied on nineteen witnesses to tell the story. This included a firearms expert from the FBI laboratory in Washington DC, who matched the ballistics from seven bullets removed from Godecke to Luther's gun.[8] On cross, Tapscott unsuccessfully tried to get prosecution witnesses to admit they forced Luther to sign the confession.

When it came time to present the defense, Tapscott only called one witness—his own client. He began by questioning Luther about his childhood, wife, and children back in Indiana. They were questions that reminded him of how far he had strayed from what was good, of what he had lost forever, and how he would never again see the people he loved and who loved him.

"Tears flowed freely and he was unable, for a time, to proceed with his testimony as Tapscott questioned him about

---

[8] Investigators found that many of the eleven shots he fired into the three men passed through one man, and into the next.

members of his family," the *Nevada State Journal* told their readers.

When he had composed himself, Luther told a two-prong story that he had suffered brain damage, and that his partner (who now had a name), Bert Wilson, was the one who shot those men. The brain damage had come from sunstroke when he was fourteen, as well as a blow to the head in prison, which had fractured his skull. Those events caused memory lapses and blackouts. His insanity was further aggravated by whiskey.

And he wasn't the one who shot them men, it was Bert Wilson; a man he described as six-feet tall and heavy set, weighing approximately 225 pounds. He was standing ten feet away from the shack when Bert shot them.

The case, which had begun on Monday with a full day of jury selection, was over by 5:10 p.m. Wednesday. Those ten ranchers only needed ten minutes to deliberate before reaching a unanimous decision, which came after a two-hour supper break. They voted twice "to make sure," then called the bailiff.

"Guilty in the first degree, with recommendation of the death penalty," the judgement read.

"Jones showed little visible emotion when the verdict was announced," the *Reno Gazette* stated. "Staring blankly at the packed courtroom, he was led back to his cell."

While the jurors were eating dinner and voting on his fate, deputies discovered a small caliber, automatic pistol in Luther's cell. Carved from soap and colored with ink, the perfect replica had a bolt pushed into where the barrel would be. They also found a matchbox filled with pepper, and two small razor blades. Elko authorities theorized that Luther planned to blow the pepper in a guard's face, obscuring his vision, then threaten him with the replica pistol.

If that didn't work, they figured the razor blades were for suicide. Jones feared the gas chamber and told the sheriff, "He would rather have a mob take him than go [to] the gas house."

He was placed on twenty-four-hour suicide watch until he could be transported to the state prison in Carson City.

The following week, on November 23, the trial judge sentenced Luther Jones to die for the murder of Walter Godecke. His execution was eventually set for January 26, 1937. That date was further carved in stone after his attorney abstained from filing an appeal.

He had sixty-five days left to live.

If there was one thing the thirty-two-year-old excelled at it, it was being a good prisoner—and Luther Jones was a model prisoner, Nevada State Prison Warden William Lewis later told reporters. When the condemned man first arrived, he "cried loudly [and] frequently" in his cell on death row, away from the other inmates.

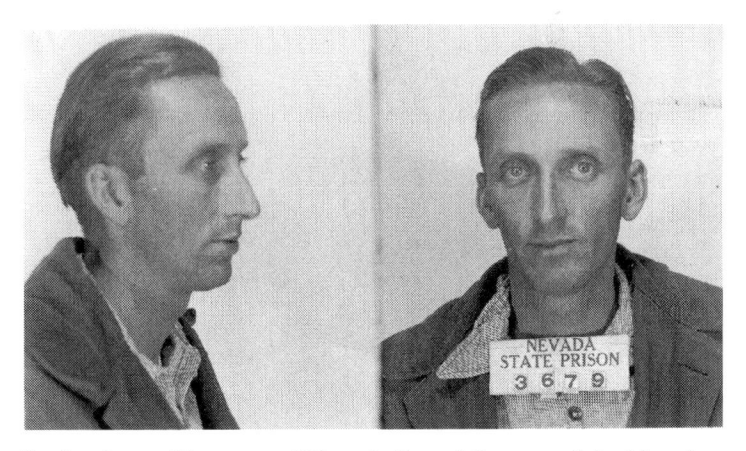

Luther Jones (Courtesy of Nevada State Library and Archives.)

In mid-December, the state pardon and parole board received a petition from Marion, Indiana, with 151 signatures asking for Luther's life to be spared. The passionate request argued that Luther's father, Hugh Jones, was critically ill and that news of his son's death might be fatal.

Since the letter arrived after their December meeting, they could not vote to consider it until they met on January 22, four days before Luther's execution. But the letter was leaked to the press, where it was chewed up and spit-out.

An editorial in a Reno newspaper fired back that Jones was responsible for his predicament and the state could only follow what the law dictated. The editorial then put the blame for Luther's execution back on his parents, when it declared "Jones has been in reformatories and prisons before, and his criminal career may be due to the failure of his childhood training."

At the same time his family and friends back home were gathering signatures for their petition, Luther was learning to accept his fate and turned to religion. He was baptized in the Presbyterian Church and guided through his conversion by Rev. J. L. Harvey.

"He spends most of his time reading the Bible and talking to the ministers who visit him," the warden said three days before the execution. "He seems convinced that he is going to die and hopes for no last-minute reprieve, especially after the state pardon board denied his request for clemency. Since he absorbed all this religion, however, he doesn't seem to mind very much."

In those final weeks, his sister Eva visited with him often, and made a passionate, personal plea for her brother's life before the parole board. She had traveled all the way from Indiana to beg for her brother's life, and to be with Luther in his final days. During their January 22 meeting, they politely but unanimously rejected her request and the Indiana petition.

The death row guards were kind to him, and although Luther never asked for much, they were attentive to whatever they thought he might need. During his last twenty-four hours, Luther was "in good spirits" and seemed "almost unconcerned." For his last meal, he ate a "royal feast," and then spent the late and early morning hours talking and praying with Rev. Harvey. The minister stood beside him when Warden Lewis came to his death row cell at six o'clock in the morning to read the execution warrant. He was then taken on the final walk to the Nevada gashouse, which was merely a rough-cut limestone building the size of a residential car garage. The forty-four witnesses to the execution had to stand outside in the cold, and peer through a small, double-pane glass window.

Before he entered, Warden Lewis gave him a cheery goodbye and asked if he had any last words to which Luther replied: "I would like to take the sheriff with me."

As he was strapped to a heavy-oak chair bolted to the floor, Luther muttered a prayer he had written just for this moment. He was still muttering that prayer when the fifteen sodium cyanide capsules were dropped into a vat with sulfuric acid and water, and a cloud of white, poisonous gas filled the room.

"His face turned scarlet as the gas fogged the double glass windows so that the view of the forty official witnesses was almost obscured," reported the *Nevada State Journal*. "He lunged forward, tugging at the heavy leather straps which securely fastened him to the chair in which he was meeting his doom.

"Then unconsciousness — and his head drooped."

One-hundred and three days after coming to Nevada, Luther Jones was dead.

Epilogue:

LUTHER'S SISTER, EVA, DID NOT wish for her brother to be buried in Indiana, since that would only remind her father of his death and possibly contribute to his own demise. The 1937 newspapers reported a funeral was held at a local funeral home, and that he was buried in the Carson City Cemetery. FindaGrave.com, however, states he was buried in the Nevada State Prison Burial Grounds.

The Nevada State Prison (NSP) Burial grounds are located on a hillside between the Nevada State Prison (closed in 2012), and the Warm Springs Correctional Facility (active prison). The Burial Grounds are not accessible by the public without permission from the Warden.

The NSP Burial Grounds is the resting place of prisoners who died while incarcerated and whose bodies were not claimed by their friends or family. Some of [these] internments are for prisoners who were executed in the United States' first legally sanctioned gas chamber. There are eleven marked graves and the site has the potential for more unmarked graves. The tablet style stone markers were carved by inmates.

On June 28, 1937, 155 days after Luther was the eighth person executed in Nevada's gas chamber, his nine and one-half-year-old daughter Barbaretta died after she was crushed to death by a horse in the barn lot of her grandfather's farm near Swayzee, Indiana, where her mother had moved after the divorce.

"She was standing near the barn when one of the boys led the horse out of the barn and as it turned around it backed into the child crushing her into the barn," the newspaper in Marion reported. "She lived just three hours after the accident, passing away at 6 p.m."

She is buried in Marion, Indiana.

Chapter Six: The Tomato Killer, 1944-45

IT'S HARD TO DROWN IN six-inches of bath water, but on Friday night, December 22, 1944, Laura Fischer was doing just that. She was being helped along by a man she met less than two weeks earlier. In his mid-forties, he was tall, dark, and handsome in the way some men attain as they grow older. But most of all, he had been charming, so damn charming, and in the short-time the redhead knew him, he had seduced her into sharing a room with him at the De Soto Hotel in downtown New Orleans. He rented it on Wednesday the 20th as D.J. Stafford from Chicago. The next day, Laura had checked herself in as "Mrs. D.J. Stafford." A little more than twenty-four hours later, her charismatic Casanova was shoving her face into the bottom of a cast-iron, claw-foot bathtub.[1]

That brief moment before his attack was all the air she had left in her diaphragm. Recognition of what was happening brought panic and panic triggered her adrenaline—both of which required more oxygen. Without any, the CO_2 levels in her blood stream climbed faster than a Nazi V-2 rocket.

It was all over surprisingly fast.

As soon as he figured she was dead, 'Mr. Charming' turned his dead lover over and repositioned her nude body until she was sitting upright in the bath, her head inclined to the left, eyes closed.

---

[1] This version of her death is based on the coroner's report which led to a grand jury indictment. As we discover later, her cause of death baffled the coroner and detectives.

Her murder was necessary, a consequence of what he really set out to do—rob her. He was a man on the run, wanted by police. He needed money and he needed to keep moving. This was how he took care of business. But killing that tomato[2] must have felt good, real good, because soon, the entire country would know how much he liked redheads.

Her body wasn't discovered until 11:00 a.m. on Christmas Eve by a hotel maid.

When investigators arrived that noon, they were perplexed. The only clue they had to go on that the woman may have been murdered was that her "husband" was nowhere to be seen. Hotel employees said he left Friday night around ten o'clock with his suitcase. He told the front desk clerk he and his wife were going to a party that weekend and to not bother cleaning the room.

"We probably won't be back for several days," he said.

Searching through the woman's belongings, Detective-Lieutenant William Grosch found a gold locket with the initials "L.F." One of his men also found $360 sewn into one of her brassieres. But what they didn't find was any identification, correspondence, or a receipt with her name on it. Since she had checked in under an assumed name, they had no idea who she was. It would take four long days before the FBI could match her fingerprints and identify her. Until then, she was the mysterious woman at the center of what the *Times-Picayune* called "the Christmas Bathtub case."

When they did get the report from the FBI, investigators learned twenty-eight-year-old Laura Fischer was born to an Austrian family living in Western Ukraine. She came alone to the United States in 1934. For the next nine years, she endured a quiet, lonely existence in New York City, where she worked as a machine operator for a sportswear manufacturing

---

[2] An affectionate nickname for an attractive woman with red hair during the 1940s.

company. In 1943, she quit her job and left for South Carolina, explaining to her landlord she was moving there to marry an army sergeant. Those marriage plans fell apart and her existence from then to the time of her death was a complete mystery. It was unclear to detectives why or how she came to be in New Orleans in December 1944.

Upon his initial examination of Fischer while she lay in the bathtub, the parish coroner didn't know what to think. There were no marks or bruises on her body; nor were there any signs of a struggle or violence in the room. He labeled her death a "possible homicide" due to "suffocation under water."[3] To cover all the bases, a half-empty drinking glass full of water was preserved for testing. Toxicology results would later show that she was not poisoned, and did not have drugs or alcohol in her system.

The lack of a clear answer baffled investigators. Her cause of death would oscillate between natural causes and homicide—until there was another redhead found under similar circumstances.

And then another one.

Turning their attention to the "husband," Lieutenant Grosch correctly assumed the two weren't married based on his discovery of the $360 sewn into the brassiere. A husband-turned-killer would have known about his wife's secret stash. And although they couldn't be certain, they suspected he had taken everything else of value. Her winter coat was gone, the purse was bare, and no other jewelry besides the locket was found.

Both "Staffords" had listed 4611 Hazel Avenue, Chicago, as their home address on the hotel register. This turned out to be a rooming house, and no one by the name of Stafford had

---

[3] Since there were no marks on her neck, I don't believe she was strangled. It is my personal opinion the coroner possibly meant *smothering under water*, instead of *strangulation*. However, I am not a forensic pathologist, and I wasn't there when it happened so I can't be sure.

lived there in the last two years. But this clue wasn't a total loss; both the address, and the name, did not come out of thin air. They were thinly connected to Mr. Charming, which eventually led to his identification. For now, all they knew about him was that he was in his mid-forties, six-feet tall, 180 pounds, with "piercing, grayish-blue eyes," and a thick head of dark hair. One witness described him as "the Spanish type," while another observer declared he was "exceptionally good-looking."

But they were never going to catch him in New Orleans, or Louisiana, or anywhere near the south. He was long-gone by the time they found Fischer's body. He wasn't a stick around town sort-of guy and after he left the De Soto Hotel, he bought a first-class ticket on a northbound train. Navigating from one major city to the next was part of his strategy. He felt safe in the large crowds of large cities where he could pick-apart new prey.

He wasn't fleeing New Orleans, he was moving to new hunting grounds.

He was a conman, a chiseler, a grifter, a man who lived for the short-cuts, a sugar-tongued sweet-talker with a gift for lies on the fly and charming tomatoes out of their dresses. He was always a big cheese in town on business with a backstory to impress the dames and dudes. He was a two-gun gambler and "a dice game addict." He stayed in swanky but affordable hotels and ate in swanky but affordable restaurants where he always ordered seafood and finished up with a big tip that left a big impression with more people than the waiter.

But one thing about Mr. Charming was more true than any other thing: he was always in character. Always hunting. Always sizing up those dames and dudes. Scouting the angle. Casting verbal lures into the open to start a conversation that would end with tragic consequences.

ON FEBRUARY 7, 1945, A JOHN H. Hanan checked into the Atlantic Hotel in downtown Chicago. He was a big shot horse and cattle trader from Dallas. He immediately began frequenting several downtown bars where he found Blanche Zimmerman, a thirty-eighty-year-old married woman with the requisite red hair and right amount of vulnerability—just like Laura Fischer. He met her in Russell's Silver Bar on the corner of State and Van Buren Streets. It was "a classy place" where a guy could get a drink, meet dames, gamble, throw dice, and watch twenty-six lovely-legged girls on stage.

Blanche Zimmerman

With Blanche at the time was her friend, Lillian Snett, an attractive thirty-five-year-old who had been separated from her husband for six years. He introduced himself, bought drinks, and sweet-talked the ladies into accompanying him to several other taverns where the booze kept coming.

Drunk women and a fun-loving, well-to-do Texan, who wore a wide-brimmed hat and carried two revolvers, was a recipe for an unforgettable Wednesday night.

Hanan was a fun guy who knew how to keep the party going. He was a gambler who understood the odds and his odds of scoring were better if he courted both women. For the rest of that week and all of the next, Hanan telephoned Blanche and Lillian from his 10th floor hotel room asking for dates. Separate dates. Both obliged. Lillian later reported that she went out with him five or six times, mostly to restaurants, where he always ordered seafood. Later, they would hit the bars where Hanan loved to throw dice.

But in the end, he settled on Blanche—and the two impressive diamond rings she wore. She was married to Harry Zimmerman, a department supervisor with the United States Gypsum Company. She had one adult son from a previous marriage who was in the Navy. Blanche and Harry lived with her father over on West 16th Street. She had a part-time job as a telephone operator for Illinois Bell where she always started work at 6 p.m.

Lately, she'd been telling her husband she had to work extra shifts. Those extra shifts often took place in the Silver Bar or the Victoria Tap—but Harry didn't know that. That's when she met the charming Texan. He was so damn charming that Blanche got lost in her infatuation. And on Thursday, February 15, handsome Hanan invited the adventure-seeking housewife to spend the following night at his 10th floor hotel room.

That Friday morning, Blanche saw her skinny, spectacled husband off to his desk job at US Gypsum. Later that afternoon, she called work to say she was feeling ill, and wouldn't be in that night. Then, she put on her best dress, her diamond rings, her mink coat and made her way to the Atlantic Hotel.

Somehow, she was able to reach the elevator without the front desk clerks, the manager, the hotel detective, or bellboys noticing. Lately, that was the story of her life. She just wanted someone to notice her, and Hanan really seemed to notice her.

A few hours later, maid Vera Sequence heard a woman's voice coming from the Texan's room. She made a mental note of it because she knew he checked in alone. As in, there was not a Mrs. Hanan listed in the registry.

Late Saturday morning, February 17, Hanan exited the elevator with luggage in hand, crossed the lobby, walked out of the hotel and hailed a taxi that took him north on Clark Street. Since he was paid up until Sunday, no one at the hotel bothered him. Two hours later, Vera the curious maid ignored a "Do Not Disturb" placard on the door knob and entered the room.

"One minute later, she was racing down the corridor screaming that there was a dead woman in the bathtub," the *American Weekly* newspaper supplement later reported.

When Chicago homicide detectives arrived, they were surprised to discover the bathwater was still warm. This was a fresh kill. But there were no signs of violence in the room or marks on the body. It was as if this naked redhead had just— died. But it was all too much of a coincidence to that case down in New Orleans to be natural causes.

A dead woman in a bathtub with six inches of water, check.

No bruises or cuts, check.

Her coat, hat, and dress were missing, check.

No fingerprints anywhere in the room, check.

The room was rented by a man answering the same description as the one down south, check.

He gave a false name and address, check.

Left hotel before the body was found, check.

Do Not Disturb sign on door, check.

Underwear floating in the bathwater, *huh?*

What the heck did that mean? Did he stuff them in her mouth and hold her head down? And why was he killing tomatoes? And leaving them naked in hotel bathtubs? And taking their clothes?

More importantly, how could they catch this guy before he did it again? To answer that question, Chicago detectives began exploring what they did have: his phone records and handwriting samples from both register books.

The hotel telephone operator logbook led them to Lillian Snett, who gave them the name of the dead woman. Later that Saturday night, Harry Zimmerman walked into the city morgue and confirmed what Snett had told them: it was his wife, Blanche—Blanche Zimmerman.

Although she answered that question, Lillian Snett wasn't exactly honest about her time with John Hanan. She never dated him, she fibbed, he *only* dated Blanche. She never saw them again after she met him on February 7.

They weren't buying it.

It took a lie detector to pry the truth out of her. They dated five or six times, she confessed two days later. She just didn't want police to think she had anything to do with her best friend's murder, which she didn't.

Hanan carried a police revolver in a shoulder holster, and a snub nose .38 in his coat pocket, she included in her account of the last ten days. He also loved to gamble. He was "a dice game addict," she said.

The *Chicago Tribune* started calling him the "two-gun gambler." The *New Orleans Times-Picayune* called him the "bathtub slayer."

But maybe he wasn't a bathtub slayer. They couldn't figure out how Blanche Zimmerman died. If she was drowned in the bathtub, there should be water in her lungs, they reasoned. However, neither Blanche Zimmerman nor Laura Fischer had water in their lungs.

During her autopsy, the Chicago coroner removed Zimmerman's heart and brain and declared both were normal. In spite of this, her death was blamed on alcohol and Benzedrine, which were discovered by a toxicologist. Her niece testified at a coroner's inquest that Blanche sometimes took the popular pills "to pep her up."

In his report, the Chicago coroner ruled the cause of her death was, "Benzedrine intoxication with the presence of alcoholic stimulants."

> ### What they Didn't Know
>
> In most drowning cases, the victim involuntarily swallows or inhales water after their initial supply of oxygen is depleted. This action triggers a laryngospasm (the throat seals tight), which prevents water from entering the stomach and lungs, but also disrupts normal breathing. Lack of oxygen then causes the heart to stop and hypoxia. Water, generally, enters the lungs after the laryngospasm is relaxed, which occurs AFTER death, or between unconsciousness and death.
>
> During World War Two, the War Department commissioned a study to learn what could be done to prevent the drowning deaths of pilots and crewmembers shot down over bodies of water. The study lasted two years and until the findings were published, there was a widely held belief within the medical community that all drowning victims, including Fischer and Zimmerman, should have water present in the lungs.

It was a bold declaration that was unheard of. Died as a direct result of taking Benzedrine? Nobody ever died from Benzedrine. Her heart was normal and the coroner never said it was an overdose. So she took some Benzedrine, so what? Millions and millions of Americans were taking Benzedrine. The US military was giving it to soldiers and pilots. According to the 2007 book, *No Speed Limit: the Highs and Lows of Meth*, by Frank Owen, Benzedrine was a lifestyle drug, and through its over-the-counter, off-label use, it was both America's first anti-depressant and America's first weight-loss pill.

A normal dose of Benzedrine didn't kill people. Some of them died from the crazy stuff they did on Benzedrine, but not from popping a few pills.

Forced to follow the coroner's report, investigators could not say whether Blanche took the pep pills herself, or if they were administered by the killer. Without physical evidence of a homicide, they couldn't charge her lover with murder. Robbery, yes, murder, no.

New Orleans police had the same problem. "Possible homicide" were two words a good defense attorney could exploit to get an acquittal.

But he did it. They knew he did it. They just couldn't figure out how he did it. And if he was going to do it again, he needed to screw it up so they could convict him—whoever *he* was.

The answer to that question walked in off the street about the same time they were trying to figure out how Blanche Zimmerman died. His name was D.J. Stafford and D.J. Stafford was there to tell police who he thought the other D.J. Stafford was.

Mister Charming, the sugar-tongued sweet-talker with a taste for tomatoes, was his ex-employee and escaped convict from the state prison in Jackson, in southern Michigan: Joseph Dunbar Medley. Stafford's suspicion was confirmed by Atlantic and De Soto hotel employees who were shown Medley's prison mugshot. Handwriting samples from the hotel registries were also a match.

By February 25, 1945, Medley's name and photo were in newspapers throughout the country.

JOSEPH MEDLEY WAS BORN IN Philadelphia on July 22, 1901. Although highly intelligent and a fast-learner, he followed the same path as many other boys of his day, quitting school after finishing the eighth-grade. From 1922 to 1924, Medley was employed as a used-car salesman for D.J. Stafford and lived at 4611 Hazel Avenue, the address listed on the De Soto Hotel registry.

Joseph D. Medley

In 1927, Medley was arrested and convicted for obtaining money under false pretenses in Little Rock, Arkansas. He was sentenced to four years but was released in 1929 after serving only twenty months.[4] He broke parole by moving to Michigan where he lied his way into a position as a field representative

---

[4] Little else is known about his life during the 1920s except that in Little Rock, he was married and divorced during that period, and his ex-wife may have had red hair.

with a financing company. He was fired four months later when they learned of his prison record.

Later that year, he was arrested in Lapeer County, Michigan, and charged with larceny by conversion, which involved the theft of an automobile. On December 16, 1929, he was sentenced to serve four to five years at the State Prison in Southern Michigan.

After his release on March 18, 1933, Medley "constantly violated his parole" but was never punished by his Lapeer County parole officer. He stayed in nearby Flint for a few months until he hooked up with prison pals Louis Gonyou and Melvin Brown, who were released that May.

With those three hard cases together, again, it was only a matter of time before they committed a crime that made national headlines.

During the early morning hours of October 31, Medley and his gang kidnapped, assaulted, and robbed the wealthy ex-mayor of Marshall, in Calhoun County, Michigan. Louis Brooks was one of four heirs to the Brooks Rupture Appliance company which manufactured and sold by mail-order a hernia-support device. At one time, it was one of the largest mail-order companies in America with headquarters in Marshall, and offices in New York, London, and Paris.

After they abducted him from his car on a lonely country road, Medley took Brooks to his company offices where he punched and beat the fifty-three-year-old until he opened two safes and handed over $45,000 in municipal bonds, stocks, and jewelry.

While debating what to do with their victim, a fourth gang member, a naïve young man named Lyle Daly, had to talk Medley out of shooting Brooks, as well as from taking him to Chicago, where he wanted to hold the wealthy executive for ransom. Instead, they turned him loose two miles from where his car was left behind on a country road.

Immediately after the robbery, Medley and Gonyou traveled to Chicago where they sold the jewelry for ten cents on the dollar. While there, Melvin Brown and Lyle Daly were identified and arrested in Michigan. Daly started talking and cut a deal with prosecutors.

Their cover blown, Medley and Gonyou went on the run. They first made their way to Little Rock, and then Los Angeles where they unloaded $30,000 in bonds for $7,500. The fence who bought them was arrested when he tried to sell them to legitimate brokers. Police in Los Angeles then traced them to the Brooks robbery, which told them that Medley and Gonyou were in the area.

With the law after them in Los Angeles, they tried to hideout in Tijuana after crossing the border from San Diego. Instead of lying low, the two frequented nightclubs and bars where Gonyou met and seduced a young Mexican woman. Her association with a gringo raised the suspicions of family members who contacted local authorities. Soon, Tijuana police learned his true identity and issued a warrant for his arrest. Tipped off that *la policia* was hunting him, Gonyou tried to cross back into the United States on February 14, 1934. He was arrested at the border by San Diego detectives informed that he was coming.

Although Gonyou never squealed on his partner, Calhoun County sheriff detectives believed Medley was with him in Tijuana, but separated when they learned that Mexican police were closing in on them. Reports then surfaced in Marshall newspapers that Medley crossed the Juarez-El Paso border into Texas and made his way to Dallas where he was believed to have registered at a hotel on February 20, and again in Fort Worth on March 9.

With all eyes on Texas, Marshall investigators were shocked to get a late-night telephone call from Flint police on March 23, advising that they had captured Medley. An anonymous tip led them to the apartment of a local dentist who was making him some false teeth. Taking no chances, sixteen police officers stormed the residence and arrested him.

"When apprehended, the man, who has been described as the brains and ringleader of the participants in the Brooks robbery, had two revolvers in his possession," the *Marshall Evening Chronicle* reported the following day. His capture put an end to what the paper called "the biggest sensation in the criminal annals of Marshall's history."

After he was arrested in November, Daly told police everything he knew, agreed to testify against the others, and in exchange received a five-year sentence. Melvin Brown chose to go to trial and received the harshest sentence of all, forty to sixty years in prison.

On March 30, 1934, Medley and Gonyou pled guilty to kidnapping and robbery and were each sentenced to thirty to sixty-year terms in prison. Gonyou was sent to Marquette while Medley was ordered back to his alma mater, the State Prison of Southern Michigan. He was sent there by request, telling the presiding judge that the dentist, in whose apartment he was captured, was still making him false teeth. It would be too difficult for the dentist to travel to the prison in Marquette, Medley argued.

The judge agreed.

Before he was sentenced, Medley was given a chance to speak. He used his silver-tongue and charm to mitigate his involvement, and shift blame back on the younger, smaller, Lyle Daly. Instead of being the "easily led youth" portrayed by the prosecutor, Medley said "Daly was one of the active instigators of the crime," the *Marshall Chronicle* reported.

"Medley, using impeccable English, although marred somewhat, here and there, by underworld slang, said that the kidnapping had been discussed [casually] but nothing was decided until the actual night of the crime," the newspaper continued.

Joseph Medley the criminal wasn't such a bad guy after all, according to Joseph Medley the charming gentleman.

His desire to return to the Southern Michigan prison had less to do with dental work, and more to do with the fact that it was one of the most corrupt penal institutions in the country. It was a place where high-ranking prison officials colluded with an upper-caste of convicts and "the cons ran the joint."

With nearly 6,000 inmates, Southern Michigan was "the largest prison in the world," Michigan newspapers bragged at the time.

It was also, by default, the world's largest unlicensed casino with the ability to offer prisoners a Sodom and Gomorrah menu of vice, which included: sex with visiting prostitutes, girlfriends, and wives, liquor, drugs, a dozen stills, influence peddling, loan-sharking, kickbacks, bribes, prisoner-owned pawn shops, contraband luxury items, murder-for-hire, and widespread theft of government property. The unholy grail of all the illicit offerings were day passes to the outside, which allowed guarded and unguarded prisoners to visit whorehouses, wives and girlfriends, bars, movie theaters, stay in luxury hotels, and even carry out contract-killings.

With all the wicked comforts of the free world available to them—but none of the responsibilities of making an honest living—no prisoner bothered to escape.

Except for one.

The godfather of the prison crime syndicate was deputy warden Delile C. Pettit. He was hired on as an office clerk in the late 1920s. The attrition of his scandal-plagued superiors paved the way for his promotion to the number two spot by 1933. Over the next twelve years, Pettit slowly built a lucrative criminal fiefdom in which he collected a percentage of all the action.

By 1944, Joseph Medley had used his superior intelligence, charm, and sheer force-of-will to place himself at the center of it all as Pettit's chief inmate clerk.

According to the 2006 book, *States of Violence*, "Medley was one of about fifteen or twenty so-called 'big shots' at Jackson, inmate [capos] who had divided the prison into a series of overlapping rings that organized illicit activities, employed hundreds of other prisoners as gophers, go-betweens, bagmen, lookouts, and dealers, and defended their turfs and monopolies through strategic alliances, elaborate treaty systems, and gangs of enforcers."

Medley, several other prisoners reported in 1945 and 1946, spent much of his time drinking in Pettit's office, and was often "drunk in prison." When he wasn't drunk, he was working his latest scam as Chairman of the Inmate War Bond Drive Committee. Because he was charming, so damn charming, Medley's fundraising efforts with prisoners and guards broke all records and by Saturday, November 25, 1944, he had collected $850. That was the day he asked Lt. Howard Freeland, a seventeen-year veteran of the prison, for a ride into Jackson to gather war bond literature on Monday morning. Freeland told him to get a pass from the deputy warden. Since he was Pettit's clerk, Medley filled out his own twelve-hour pass and had his boss sign-it.

On Monday, November 27, Lt. Freeland and Medley left in a prison-owned vehicle. Freeland first stopped at his own house to change into civilian clothes. When he returned, Medley told his guard that he needed to stop by the home of a prison bookkeeper "who wanted to see him about the prison bond drive."

As Freeland waited downstairs in the accountant's home, Medley went upstairs and changed out of his prison uniform into civilian clothes that were left there by another prisoner. "When he came down all dressed up in a dark-pinstriped suit and overcoat, I asked what the idea was," Freeland later testified before the state attorney general. "[The bookkeeper] said 'when I take him out, I usually dress him up.'"

Against his better judgement, Freeland relented, and dropped Medley off near a bank with instructions to be at the bookkeeper's house by 9:30 p.m.

They never saw him again. Over the next four months, the serial killer with a taste for tomatoes would murder three women.

When Medley didn't arrive, Freeland and the bookkeeper panicked and went straight to the deputy warden's house. Upon hearing that his inmate-clerk had escaped, Pettit's face turned white.

"This is it," he lamented. He knew it was all over with.

Instead of sounding the alarm, the three prison officials drove all over Jackson looking for Medley, hoping he was passed out in a bar or whorehouse. When they couldn't find him, they realized he was gone for good and that's when they remembered the $850[5] collected to buy war bonds. Returning to the prison, they searched Medley's desk and broke open the lockbox.

The money was gone.

And still, the three men said nothing. Word of Medley's escape reached the outside world through the grapevine at two o'clock in the morning on November 28. By then, he had a seventeen-hour head start. Pettit, Freeland testified, ordered him to falsify the escape report.

"I couldn't very well say how he was dressed (in civilian clothes) because I was told to keep my mouth shut," Freeland confessed. "And I didn't object to the clothes at [the bookkeeper's] house because Medley was a pretty good friend of Pettit's and if I didn't play ball I'd be on my way out (of a job)."

By falsifying the escape report, Pettit was attempting to save his own skin. But Medley's escape was about to make national news and lead to an investigation that blew the lid off

---

[5] Other accounts report it was $700.

everything. They all had good reason to be worried about their jobs.

THE END OF NANCY BOYER'S life began with a casual conversation in a Washington D.C. seafood restaurant on February 25.

"This restaurant food is beginning to be more than I can take," remarked a handsome, older man with grayish-blue eyes to a young woman seated next to him. She had struck up a conversation with him by asking if he was enjoying his dinner. "What I wouldn't give for a home-cooked meal," he added.

His name was Larry Fischer and he worked for the government. Except for the fact that he wasn't married, Fischer didn't talk much about his life. It was war time and it was Washington DC. Local residents knew not to ask too many questions. Their friendly chat eventually led to an introduction to the young lady's mother three days later. She prepared an elaborate dinner and the evening ended with all three attending a movie theater before Fischer returned alone to his room at the Roosevelt Hotel.

It had been that easy.

Although Larry Fischer's name bore a striking resemblance to the name of a dead woman found in a hotel bathtub in New Orleans last Christmas, no one seemed to notice and the handsome gentleman spent the next two days in the company of the woman and her daughter. But the trio's new found friendship took a left turn when the woman held a small card party at her house on Friday night, March 2. Among her friends who were invited was Nancy Boyer, an attractive divorcee in her mid-forties. She lived alone on the ninth floor of Washington House, a highbrow apartment building where high-ranking military officers and government employees lived.

Although she didn't work for a living, she was known to be a wealthy woman despite her modest background. Her financial status was something of a mystery, but was believed to have something to do with the high-stakes gambling parties she often held. As the house, hostess, and often the bank for these parties, Nancy earned herself a nice cut of the pot.

Nancy Boyer

Besides the high-stakes poker games, her apparent wealth, and the fact that she lived alone, there was one more reason Larry Fischer was magnetically drawn to Nancy Boyer—she had red hair.

Over the weekend, the two spent nearly every waking moment together. Always a gentleman, and charming, so damn charming, Larry Fischer coaxed his new friend into organizing a high-stakes poker game for Monday night. She got out her little black book, telephoned the ladies in her poker club, and happily announced that several women and one man had agreed to attend.

Fischer was pleased. He had recently pawned two diamond rings and a fur coat after making the rounds through several local shops. The money he got from his ill-gotten gains was all the money he had left. He needed this poker game. He needed to fleece these high-society saps, who were no match for a hardened con like him. The police were looking for him, they knew his name, and they knew he had caught a train to Washington DC. He needed to win big if he was going to put some distance between himself and the law. For the second time in his life, there was a national manhunt in the papers for Joseph Dunbar Medley. His photograph was mixed in with the news of the collapsing German army and the firebombs dropping on Japan. Just that Friday, the night he met Nancy Boyer, news that the New Orleans prosecutor had pushed through a grand jury indictment for the murder of Laura Fischer was published. It was homicide, the authorities there finally decided.

Laura Fischer, Larry Fischer—he picked a bad time to use that name for an alias.

But the cards are a fickle mistress. One night they love you, the next night they don't. And as the group played all night and into the deep morning hours, the cards clearly didn't love Larry Fischer. He learned hard and he learned late that these Washington players were not chumps. Nancy's poker pals, most of them women, were in her contact book for a reason—they were damn good players and they took him to the cleaners.

To keep playing, Fischer had to borrow money from his host. She offered to cash a check for him for ten dollars. He persuaded her to make it twenty-five. When she went to her cash box to get the money, he was quietly impressed with what looked to be more than $300 inside. As he continued playing, he also became impressed with Nancy's diamond and emerald ring. It had been custom-made to her specifications by a prominent New York City jeweler. It was easily worth between $800 and $1,000, he estimated.

When the poker game ended around 5:30 that morning, one of the guests overheard Nancy tell her new male acquaintance to escort one of her lady friends down the street to a taxi-cab stand and make sure she got a ride home.

"And then come back and we'll have breakfast as planned," she was overheard to say. Fischer did as instructed and a watchman for Washington House saw him return at seven o'clock that morning, Tuesday, March 6.

Back inside the apartment, the ambush came fast and deadly. Medley the murderer didn't have time for bathtub romances. He didn't have the time or patience to woo her into some vulnerable position. Just after she had finished setting the table for breakfast, Nancy walked back into the kitchen and was carving a roast when the handsome gambler punched her in the mouth with everything he had.

He wasn't so charming anymore.

And then he tried to strangle her with a scarf, and when that didn't do the job fast enough Medley pulled out his gun and shot her. The first bullet tore off the top part of her left index finger and ended up on the floor beside her. The second two bullets were to the head, above and behind the left ear.

He took her expensive ring and gold watch, got the money out of her cash box, took his check back, and on his way out, picked up her silver fox fur coat. It was a $500 coat, and if it was one thing Joseph Medley the tomato killer knew the value of, it was fur coats.

No one heard the shots. No one saw him leave. And no one called the police·for two days. From Washington House, Medley returned to his hotel, packed his suitcase, and left without paying the bill. Then, like he always did, he took a fast train out of town. The first one he could get was headed to

Pittsburgh. There, on March 8, Medley sold Nancy's $800 ring for the bargain price of $250 to a pawnshop proprietor.

And then he got back on another train heading west.

The day he sold the ring was the same day they found Nancy's body. A friend, who had been trying to telephone her for two days, convinced the apartment manager to check on her. She found Nancy's bloodstained corpse slumped grotesquely against a wall in the kitchen. Splotches of deep crimson discolored the front of her green cocktail dress and seeped to the floor around her. She had that look on her face that murdered victims get—that vacant stare of horror that transmits the fear of her last moments alive to the present of her discovery.

Capital police, long derided for incompetence and cronyism, managed to connect the murder-robbery to Joseph Medley within twenty-four hours. The forty-five-year-old victim held a poker party the night before she was killed. The guests were interviewed, which produced a description of one of the gamblers who was going to share breakfast with Nancy the morning she was last known to be alive.

During a routine check with area pawnshops, a man matching that description had recently sold two diamond rings and a fur coat. A store tag found inside the coat indicated that it had come from Chicago. Searching through recent police bulletins produced one that showed Joseph Dunbar Medley was wanted in Chicago and New Orleans. His photograph was then shown to pawnshop clerks and guests of the Monday night-Tuesday morning poker party. They confirmed it was him.

The tomato killer had struck again.

By Saturday, March 10, Medley's mugshot and the story of his murder spree was on the front pages of hundreds of newspapers throughout the country. He instantly became America's most wanted fugitive, attracting the attention of the Federal Bureau of Investigation. They secured a federal warrant for his arrest and alerted FBI offices across the country. Hunting Medley down became their top priority. Train stations were watched. Pawnshops were checked. His photo was shown to hotel clerks and taxi cab drivers in dozens of cities. Wanted flyers went up in post offices. Detectives with city, county, and state law enforcement agencies were ordered to be on the look-out.

When the escaped convict was named as the chief suspect in the murder of three women, Michigan residents and state leaders began asking uncomfortable questions. What the hell was going on down there in the Jackson prison? Wild rumors of liquor, moonshine stills, drugs, prostitutes, gambling, theft, and corruption made their way to the governor. Michigan Attorney General John R. Dethmers launched a vigorous investigation into the prison, which uncovered all the illegal activities and resulted in the termination of Pettit, Warden Harry Jackson, and six other high-ranking prison officials.

Through his escape, Medley exposed the incompetence and systemic corruption of a penal institution, creating a statewide scandal.

It would not be the last time he did that.

WHEN LADY LUCK LEFT JOSEPH Medley on Friday night, March 5, she left him for good. He was on his own and by himself, he didn't last too long. From Pittsburgh, he had gone to St. Louis where he took a room in the Jefferson Hotel under the name James H. Hanan of Baltimore. He immediately began working his magic on his next target whom he met in the bar of the De Soto Hotel on March 12. Her name was Mabel Mueller and she was an attractive, forty-year-old divorcee and grandmother with platinum blonde hair.

He was done with red heads.

On March 13, the two met-up for lunch inside the cocktail lounge of Hanan's hotel. Seated at the next table, Dr. James H. Elder, a university psychology professor from Washington DC on loan to the war department noticed the couple. Their flirtatious laughter caught his attention. As he sized up the platinum blonde and her handsome companion with dark hair and light-blue eyes, Dr. Elder slowly realized he had seen that man before.

"That fellow over there," he whispered to his companions, "have either of you seen him before?"

No, they hadn't.

"I've seen his face recently," Elder whispered. "It must have been in the newspapers. As I recall, he is somebody wanted by the police."

Devoted to the study of human behavior, his professional colleagues, also psychologists, regarded the man with interest. They took note of his wrinkled gray business suit, his piercing blue eyes, and his charming demeanor. The blonde looked to be having a good time.

Although Dr. Elder made a comment about going to police headquarters, his schedule in St. Louis kept him too busy. But he didn't forget about the blue-eyed man with the blonde-haired woman. When he returned to his home in Arlington, Virginia, on March 17, he went down to his basement and started going through a stack of old newspapers. There, on the front page of the *Washington Star,* was a photograph of the man in St. Louis.

It was him. Those eyes, those piercing blue eyes—even in black and white—were unmistakable.

Doctor Elder contacted the police commissioner who contacted the FBI which contacted their agents in St. Louis. Later that night, Medley's identity was confirmed by Jefferson Hotel staff. He had a room on the seventeenth floor.

They searched Medley's room and found Nancy's silver fox fur coat and purse. It was him and if they were going to stop him, it had to be now. They set up an ambush by taking up positions in the stairwell near the elevator, and in a room adjoining his. Another agent was stationed by the front desk.

Two hours later, shortly after midnight on March 18, Medley and Mueller entered the hotel lobby. By the time the elevator reached the seventeenth floor, agents and officers knew he was coming. When the two stepped off the elevator and made their way down the corridor, Medley was trapped on both sides by men with guns drawn. They knew about the .38 caliber police revolver in the shoulder holster. If he reached for it, they would gun him down right there.

Instead, he surrendered peacefully and confirmed his identity. It was over. The tomato killer was in custody. Medley later said he was going to leave the next morning for the west coast. Every time he left a city, he left behind a dead woman.

They had just saved Mabel Mueller's life.

HAULED BACK TO WASHINGTON DC, Medley's trial began with jury selection on May 28. With about two months to prepare, his lawyers could not construct anything close to an adequate defense that would save him from the electric chair. The evidence against him was overwhelming. The bullets from his revolver matched the two slugs removed from Nancy Boyer's head as well as the one that took off her finger. Her fur coat and handbag were found in his St. Louis hotel room. His handwriting samples matched with pawnshop receipts and hotel registers. Hotel clerks confirmed his identity. The guests at the poker party confirmed his identity. The Washington House night watchman confirmed his identity. Pawnshop proprietors confirmed his identity.

Medley's attorneys, a pair of brothers, first tried to blame the murder on an Indianapolis businessman with whom Nancy had a two-year affair and allegedly feared after he grew tired of her constant nagging for money. Their pot-luck 'someone else defense' also pointed the finger at a mystery woman, who left behind a fingernail at the crime scene. To steer suspicions away from their client, they also tried, and failed, to show that Nancy was alive after Medley left her apartment on March 6.

While the prosecution's case lasted nearly a week with 116 witnesses subpoenaed, the defense took only forty minutes to question ten people. The sugar-tongued sweet talker chose not to testify on his own behalf.

Joseph Dunbar Medley during his trial.

After deliberating for three hours, the jury of nine men and three women came back with their decision: guilty of first-degree murder. His June 26 death sentence announcement was published on the front pages of newspapers throughout the forty-eight states.

Instead of disappearing from the news, his name continued to be mentioned that summer as the man responsible for unraveling the Michigan prison scandal. Six of the seven high-ranking prison officials fired were demanding their jobs back through publicly held hearings. Pettit wisely chose not to participate. It was the second time that year that the country got to learn about the appalling activities going on inside the nation's largest prison, where prisoners were having a good time.

Michigan didn't want its prisoners to have a good time; they were supposed to be having a hard time and none of the six prison officials ever got their jobs back.

When asked about the Southern Michigan prison that summer, Medley called it a "damn sandbox" and said it was "the easiest thing in the world to walk away from."

But that was just the first time one of his escapes provoked an investigation which uncovered misconduct by prison representatives. The second time he got a bunch of people fired began with his escape from the DC Jail on April 3, 1946.

The first account told by guards Hubert Davis and Oscar Sanderlin alleged they were both ambushed and subdued by death row inmates Medley and Earl McFarland, a twenty-four-year-old former Marine sentenced to die for the rape and murder of a young woman. Davis told his supervisors that he was conducting his normal half-hour rounds when Medley, brandishing a .38 caliber revolver, threatened his life if he didn't cooperate. One of the prisoners then called for Sanderlin. The two men overpowered him, took his cell keys, and locked both guards in Medley's cell. The two were further ordered to strip and hand over their uniforms.

"After overpowering their guards," the United Press reported the same day, "Medley and McFarland escaped from jail by making their way down to the ground hand over hand on a rope improvised from bed sheets."

And neither one of them had any idea how Medley got hold of the revolver, and that it was obviously "smuggled in to the prisoners, but they had no idea when or how."

But that's not what really happened. That's not even close to what happened. From the time he was sent there in June the year before to await execution, Medley had been looking for a way to escape. To make his getaway, Medley used the two best tools he had at his disposal: his intelligence, and his charm.

And a can opener.

While his attorneys worked on his appeal, Medley, a celebrity convict by now, observed everything the guards did and how they did it. With his superior memory, he knew exactly which buttons, levers, and keys controlled which doors, cells, and radiators on death row. In a scathing article published in a crime magazine four months after the April escape, it was revealed that Medley reigned as 'the King of the Murderers' Row.'

"A smooth-tongue artist, he lulled guards into a state of naïve good-fellowship with helpful suggestions on how to run the place," author James Booth wrote. "So thoroughly, in fact, did he command Death Row, later testimony showed, that whenever a guard was in doubt as to which key fitted what lock, he let the killer correct his faulty memory. Medley would tell the morning screw (guard) to use key No. 37-A to let the prisoners out for breakfast, and say 'pull No. 14 switch' when asking for more heat."

His knowledge was much in demand by his new keepers: city police officers reassigned to replace jail guards fired after the escape of eight prisoners in late 1945. This move, thought to be an improvement, proved to be a mistake. The quality of men serving on the district's police force was no better than those who were replaced. Sanderlin and Davis were a couple of crumbs who benefitted from the manpower shortage caused by World War II and miracled their way into jobs as police officers. Tasked with working the midnight shift on Murderers' Row, the two halfwits quickly became acquainted with what had by then become a nightly ritual for Medley and McFarland: 'the Death House Card Club.'

"It was Medley who launched the Death House Card Club, a chummy little four-cornered affair comprised of himself and McFarland and whatever two police guards were on duty after midnight," the crime magazine exposé continued. Although Medley and McFarland were supposed to be locked into their cells by nine o'clock, they were let out for their nightly game of rummy, which took place in a small recreation room near the death cells. A few hours into the game, Sanderlin complained of feeling sick.

"Why don't you go in my bunk and lie down for a while," Medley suggested. "You wouldn't be the first guard to do it."

Sanderlin, oblivious to the Hansel and Gretel trap he was walking into, took Medley up on the offer with appreciation. The card game continued with just Davis and the two condemned prisoners. Medley kept a careful eye on the officer. He knew his habits. For nine months, he had observed and took mental note of everything.

Everything.

"He was a sleepy guy," Medley later said. "He always got drowsy late in the morning."

At four o'clock, Officer Davis fell asleep in the middle of the card game, just like Medley knew he would. The two cons quietly overpowered him, liberated him from his uniform, and threw him into McFarland's cell. During the melee, Medley went over to his cell and shut the door on Sanderlin. Startled, the officer was given another opportunity to validate his stupidity.

"Sanderlin, by his own account, obediently passed his wallet and uniform through the bars, helping the killers' escape, despite the fact that the murderers had no firearms to force him to strip and that the bars, which couldn't keep the prisoners in, at least could kept them out," the exposé reported.[6]

---

[6] Sanderlin later testified that Medley and McFarland threatened him with an unseen gun and knife. He claimed he was awake when they shut

The rest was easy. In police uniforms, Medley and McFarland grabbed some dirty sheets from the laundry room and made their way to the roof by cutting through a copper ventilator with the can opener Medley had charmed from a prison guard earlier that year. Before leaving, the tomato killer, "picked up the telephone and reported to the jail switchboard that everything was 'okay' in the death house—a routine which guards were supposed to follow every hour."

From the roof, the two fastened the sheets into a sixty-foot rope, which stopped about ten to fifteen feet from ground level. Forced to drop the rest of the way, Medley sprained his ankle in the fall. McFarland, a young, ex-marine, easily made it. The two split up and while McFarland made his way into the city, Medley limped a few blocks east to the bank of the Anacostia River. There, he crawled inside an eighteen-inch wide drainage pipe to wait for the pain to ease and night to come.

An alert police officer found him seven hours later. McFarland fared better, but was captured in Knoxville, Tennessee, after eight days on the run.

News of the early morning escape of two death row inmates flashed across the wire services and appeared in thousands of newspapers nationwide. A photographer, standing by at the jail, snapped a picture of a wet, dirty, disheveled Medley handcuffed to an officer. Always the charmer, he gave reporters a snappy quote for their readers.

"You can't hate a guy for trying," he said with a grin. "I'm just glad no one got hurt. But I'll tell you this—I'll try again, if I get the chance, and you can stick that in your pipe and smoke it."

---

his door, and that he then saw them attack and gag Davis and shouted at them to stop. His account was discredited by Medley and McFarland.

The drainage pipe where Medley was found.

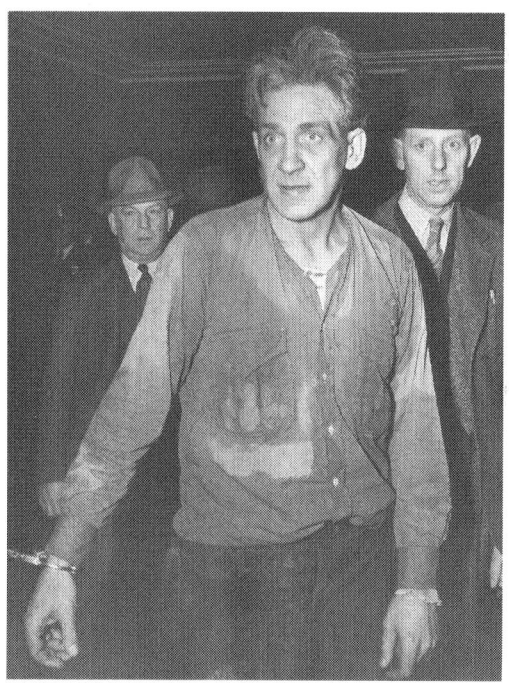

Medley shortly after he was recaptured.

After suffering the national embarrassment of having two condemned prisoners escape, the United States Congress[7] launched an investigation which uncovered lax conditions, drinking, gambling, contraband smuggling, and corrupt guards colluding with gang leaders who orchestrated their criminal operations from behind bars.

Retribution came swiftly. Howard B. Gill, the district penal superintendent, got fired. Claude O. Botkin, another jail superintendent, got fired. Sanderlin and Davis definitely got fired.

And Joseph Medley got to die. Two weeks after his escape, on April 17, the United States Court of Appeals affirmed his death sentence. Despite an April 30 execution date, his new lawyers continued a hopeless fight, giving their client another eight months to live. Their legal maneuvers included a bid for the United States Supreme Court to hear their appeal, which was rejected, and a plea for executive clemency from President Harry S. Truman, which was ignored.

When those tactics failed, they tried to get a stay-of-execution order through a lunacy petition after three psychiatrists declared Medley "was a chronic, alcoholic paranoiac and legally insane," the *Washington Post* reported. This diagnosis came less than one week before his December 20 execution. During his last seventy-two hours, the 'our client is too insane to be executed' petition was rejected by the DC district court, the US Court of Appeals, and the US Supreme Court.

His last days on earth were pure hell—offering a preview to his afterlife. As his lawyers went from court to court, Medley was plagued with the most important question of all: *will I live, or will I die?* He refused to eat, and barely slept during a nerve-breaking time in which his own execution was delayed by two hours as the Supreme Court considered his petition.

---

[7] The US Congress governed the capital until 1973.

By the time he was strapped into the District of Columbia's electric chair at 12:44 p.m. on December 20, 1946, he wasn't handsome anymore. He looked old. He looked as if he had been ground down to the nub. Over the last eight-months, the thought of dying had bled forty-five pounds from his body, and his hair was more gray than it was black. After losing twenty-five percent of himself, his skin sagged and the creases across the blue-white pallor of his face communicated his "haggard, fear-ridden hulk," and that he "aged ten years in appearance."

Even his own Catholic priest, who guided Medley's return to religion in his final days, acknowledged his transformation from the once vain and proud man he was, to the one who was about to answer for his sins. "The strain of waiting for death became more and more apparent on him as the execution drew near," Father David O'Connor told a *Washington Post* reporter. "He was highly nervous, but in his last days he appeared to be someone resigned to his fate." His passage to the after-life may have taken a detour if he had confessed his sins, but always the gambler, Medley stubbornly played the cards he always had by protesting his innocence to the very end. From the time he walked into the death chamber to the moment he was hit with 2,200 volts of electricity, Medley could be seen clutching a rosary and uttering a death prayer.

Even to the very end, he was trying to charm his way into getting more than he ever gave anyone else.

Chapter Seven: A Soft Touch, 1955

That Morning

ON THE MORNING OF JANUARY 19, 1955, business was slow at Lamb's Conoco Station in San Angelo, Texas. Inside, behind the tempered-glass windows, owner Henry Lamb, his wife Bessie, and their attendant, John Ramirez, kept warm by an old heater. As they often did, they took stock of all who drove by the business located on the corner of Koenigheim Street and Beauregard Avenue, the busiest intersection in their city of 55,000.[1]

Across the wide street of Koenigheim, about 150 feet to the west, the Lamb's had an open view into the driveway and two-car garage of the Ralph Harris mansion. Most folks called it a mansion, some called it a "stately-home," and one newspaper described 303 West Beauregard as "a showplace."

Sitting back far from the avenue, with "a half-block wide lawn," the two-story red-brick mansion[2] was crowned with a unique, green-tiled roof. Just like the Conoco station, it occupied a strategic corner of the two most important streets in town. Despite the conspicuous location of the home, the two-car garage and driveway on the east side were partially camouflaged behind a white picket fence covered in vines, a few trees, and some shrubs. The Lambs had the best view to see family members coming and going.

---

[1] Estimated population based on splitting the difference between 1950 and 1960 Census records.

[2] The house is gone, replaced by a bank.

On the west and south sides of the property, towering elms, standing like giant sentinels, lined the two sidewalks, and cast welcomed shade from the west Texas sun. The house faced north, and beyond that wide lawn and Beauregard Avenue, was a place where life began: a maternity hospital.

The Harris family, a wealthy and influential name in San Angelo, as well as Tom Green and Coke counties for more than a century, would never call the house a mansion. It was home. Mansion was a pretentious word for a religious family that prospered through banking, ranching, and oil. Hard work, brains, and good timing made them wealthy, but it also kept them down-to-earth and well respected.

In those days, it was a big house for one person. Ralph Harris died in 1943, and now it was just his widow, Sadie Gwin Harris, who lived there. In her eighties, Sadie had a stroke a few months earlier, and she was spending more of her time in Shannon Hospital than she was at home. By necessity, the hospital had become her nursing home. Long-term care facilities, suitable for someone in her position, were still a decade or two away.

Visiting her as often as she could was her oldest daughter, Helen Harris Weaver. She and her husband, Harry Weaver, an architect with a small measure of national notoriety, had arrived in San Angelo the night before following a six-day trip to Houston to file their income taxes and visit with her daughter's family. Married in 1938, this was the second time for both of them. Semi-retired now, they settled down on the family ranch in neighboring Coke County, where they resided in a $50,000[3] house Weaver designed that was special enough to have its own name: *Butterfield Peak Lodge*. It straddles the top of a wide-hill that overlooks the Colorado River Valley, and was known throughout both counties. Every Easter, the

---

[3] $50,000 in 1948 or 1949, when they likely began construction, is the 2016 equivalent of $500,000.

Weavers invited the entire congregation of San Angelo's Emmanuel Episcopal Church for a special service and Sunrise Breakfast. Her grandfather, Leasial, was a founding member.

With Mrs. Harris's poor health, Henry Lamb and his wife had seen a lot of Helen and Harry Weaver recently. He knew the family well enough to send his employee over there and without being told, bring one of the cars back to the station to be serviced. The only problem was, which one to pick from the four that were over there that morning.

The one nearest the road was Helen's 1954 Chevrolet 210 four-door, which came in sixteen colors that year. She chose "Surf Green," a light-green pastel that reflected her own warm and friendly personality. The '54 was her everyday car she used to get around her Coke County ranch, go grocery shopping in nearby Robert Lee, and to make the twenty-mile drive to San Angelo to see her mother.

Parked further into the driveway, was Harry's 1952 Chevrolet. Its beige color, "Beach Ivory," may have reflected his and Helen's post-retirement passion as active members of the state societies for both archeology and paleontology. As much as he loved Texas, Harry had no use for ranching. However, their emotional connection to the land they cherished, and their desire to uncover the mysteries that lay beneath it, provided them with an important element for a happy marriage: spending time together and building memories while participating in activities they both enjoyed.

Two other cars, parked inside the garage, were rarely driven. The fancy black Cadillac was supposed to be Helen's town car, but Harry never took to it. He didn't like the automatic transmission. The blue Buick was Sadie's car. Although it was kept-up, it rarely left the garage.

Lamb was in the middle of telling his wife his idea for servicing one of the four cars, when they spotted the heavy-set Weaver emerge from the house at approximately 8:30 that January morning without his coat on. With a purpose to his step, Weaver opened the passenger door on the '54, grabbed some papers and a camera from the glove compartment, and transferred them to his car. Returning to his wife's vehicle, he opened the trunk, removed an old-style carpenter's box, saw, and some other tools, and placed them in the trunk of his older Chevy.

Returning once again to Helen's car, he pulled the trunk lid down; shaking it to make sure the latch had caught. He then reached into his pocket and fiddled with a key ring, and used the rear chrome bumper to bend the key ring back into shape.

When he was finished, Weaver opened the driver's side door, stuck the key into the '54's ignition, and slammed the door loud enough for Lamb and his wife to hear. The architect then hustled back into the house. Lamb could see Weaver had left the trunk open on his car, and figured he'd gone to fetch something, and would be right back. He should. On cold-mornings, without fail, Weaver would start the engine on his wife's car, slide the heater knob to the right, and let it run, just so Helen would be more comfortable when she drove.

But when the blonde, fifty-one-year-old emerged from the house at approximately 8:44 a.m., wearing a red coat with matching purse slung over her shoulder, Lamb and his wife figured ol' Harry must have forgot. She didn't have time for her husband to warm-up her car. It was brisk outside, but not cold, and they continued watching as she opened the door, sat down and before she could close it, Mrs. Weaver disappeared behind a brief flash of orange and a titanic burst of thick, yellow smoke.

It was the loudest god-damn sound Henry Lamb had ever heard in his life. An invisible force of energy seemed to roll right through his building and everything in it. He could feel it in his head, and pass through his chest and innards. The floor was moving. The walls were moving. The glass shook violently: miraculously, it held together.

"Lamb looked on in stunned horror as the Chevrolet seemed to fly apart," crime writer Bill Cox later wrote. The station owner could see objects soaring up into the air, arcing out in a 360-degree radius, propelled by a force that carried them up to one block away. One of those pieces landed in front of his filling station. It was a windshield wiper-arm.

He wasn't the only one who saw airborne debris. Hylton Buster, a used-car salesman, closing a deal on his lot behind the Harris home, said he saw "hoods[4] and fenders and pieces of automobile...going up in the air like a whirlwind."

Helen Weaver's car.

---

[4] The hood on all 1954 Chevrolet cars is actually two pieces welded together at the center, and the split is covered by a chrome strip that runs the entire length of the hood. The author speculates this is the reason why Hylton Buster uses the plural "hoods."

"Other witnesses in the neighborhood who looked up as the loud boom shook buildings saw pieces of the front part of the car in the air above the house tops," Cox wrote.

They were all emanating out from one central point—what was left of Mrs. Weaver's Sea Foam Green Chevrolet. Floating above the wreckage, climbing slowly, a giant ball of smoke was just beginning to peel back on itself, forming a mushroom cloud. Henry Lamb called the police. And then, with all the strength and speed he could muster, the fifty-four-year-old took off running across the street.

The explosion that blew-apart Mrs. Weaver's Chevrolet was heard a mile away and shook buildings within a fifteen-block area.

"We felt it in the *Standard-Times* building four blocks away and we're sound proof," staff reporter Grady Hill exclaimed to an Associated Press man.

Two blocks west on Beauregard, a secretary working inside the courthouse–an impressive granite block structure with a full row of colonnades from one end to the other–said the blast "rocked the building."

Across the street from the Harris mansion, the maternity hospital fared worse. "Windows in the Clinic Hospital were broken by the terrific concussion," Cox wrote.

No one was closer to the blast than Harry Weaver himself. He later said he felt "the call of nature," and abandoned his tradition of starting the car. Meeting his wife at the top of the stairs, she asked for the keys, and was told they were already in the ignition. Ten seconds later, he was standing in a second-floor bathroom when he heard the roaring explosion and felt the blast as it caved in the nearby bedroom windows, blowing a thousand pieces of glass out across the room. Outside, he heard his wife of nineteen-years scream "two or three times."

Henry Lamb was the first man to reach the mangled, smoking car that was missing most of the front end. "She was inside, slumped over, and gasping," he later told the *San Angelo Standard-Times*.

Hylton Buster, neighbor Sewell Kenley, and a doctor arrived just behind Lamb.

"Her clothes were blown practically off and her face was an ashy gray," Buster later said. "She groaned three or four times."

Looking up from the car, the small group saw a confused Harry Weaver running out of the house. He was holding his stomach, and his zipper was down.

"He then went to the car and put a hand on his wife's shoulder and said, 'mummy, what happened?' He then asked someone to get a sheet," Buster continued.

Helen Harris Weaver (Courtesy of Tess Keehn).

When he looked at his wife he saw what the coroner would later report were thirty-nine puncture wounds. Her red coat, blouse, and face were covered in blood and black soot, and like Buster said, were nearly blown off. This was improper. Helen wouldn't want this. At her husband's suggestion, neighbor Kenley ran into the Harris house and retrieved a sheet. Believing his wife was dead, and wanting to preserve her modesty, Harry Weaver tenderly placed the large white cloth over her. It seemed like the thing to do for a man who didn't know what to do.

"Mr. Weaver was more or less in a state of shock," Dr. R.E. Capshaw told the local paper. His office was next to Lamb's station.

Within minutes of the blast, an ambulance had arrived, carefully removed Helen Harris Weaver from the car, and transported her to nearby Shannon Hospital where her death certificate reported she died at 9:10 a.m.

Box 20a on the form described those last twenty-six minutes in one word: "Homicide."

First Response

MRS. WEAVER'S MURDER WAS HEARD by nearly everyone in San Angelo, including most members of several branches of local law enforcement. Arriving within minutes of each other were San Angelo Police Chief Clarence Lowe, and Tom Green County Sheriff Cecil Turner. Leading the investigation for local police were Detective Sergeants Lee Braziel, and William "Dub" Gunn. They were supported that morning by several dozen uniformed officers, deputies, and highway patrolmen. Also joining them was the newly elected District Attorney Aubrey Stokes. Only thirty-three-years-old, Stokes was eager to prove his mettle among a cadre of experienced lawmen.

Even with a platoon of officers there, it was barely enough to contain the enormous throng of people gathering from all directions. They heard the earth-moving eruption, and by observing the long plume of smoke reaching for the atmosphere, easily found their way to the blast site.

"Hundreds of persons from downtown offices were on the scene soon after the explosion was heard," the *Standard-Times* reported later that day. "Police were promptly instructed to keep the crowds from near the wreckage, a difficult job at best. Later, the area was roped off to keep sightseers from touching what might develop into important evidence."

From the beginning, they knew it was a bomb. "It was obvious to lawmen that an explosive, probably rigged to go off when the motor was started, had torn the Chevrolet asunder," Cox wrote in his article. But what they didn't know was if there were *more* bombs. They only had to look at the victim's car to get an idea of what could happen to them if they were careless with the other vehicles.

"The front part of the car looked like its insides had been scooped out. The hood was gone, fenders ripped off," the *Abilene-Reporter News* described later that day. Parts of the intake-manifold were found in the trunk of Weaver's Chevrolet—the trunk he'd left open before running inside to answer nature's call. The radiator was blown forward, barely hanging by a piece of metal.

Inside the car, the damage was jaw dropping. The engine cowl, which supports the windshield, dashboard, and instrument panel, resembled a crushed beer can. The steering wheel was bent in half, across the horizontal center, and was now two half-circles at a ninety-degree angle.

On the front seat, a large, circular bloodstain told its own story.

Their first concern was for Weaver's Chevrolet. Though the trunk had taken a direct hit from a manifold, they weren't worried about the back of the car. The bomb, if there was one, was probably wired to the generator. Although his detectives and officers were smart, capable men, Chief Lowe wasn't about to ask them to dismantle a bomb. The Texas Department of Public Safety had specialists for that. After assessing the situation, Chief Lowe contacted Texas Ranger Ralph Rohatsch in Austin and informed him of the bombing death. Rohatsch, who was in the state capitol on other business, replied he would fly down there that afternoon, bringing a team of experts with him.

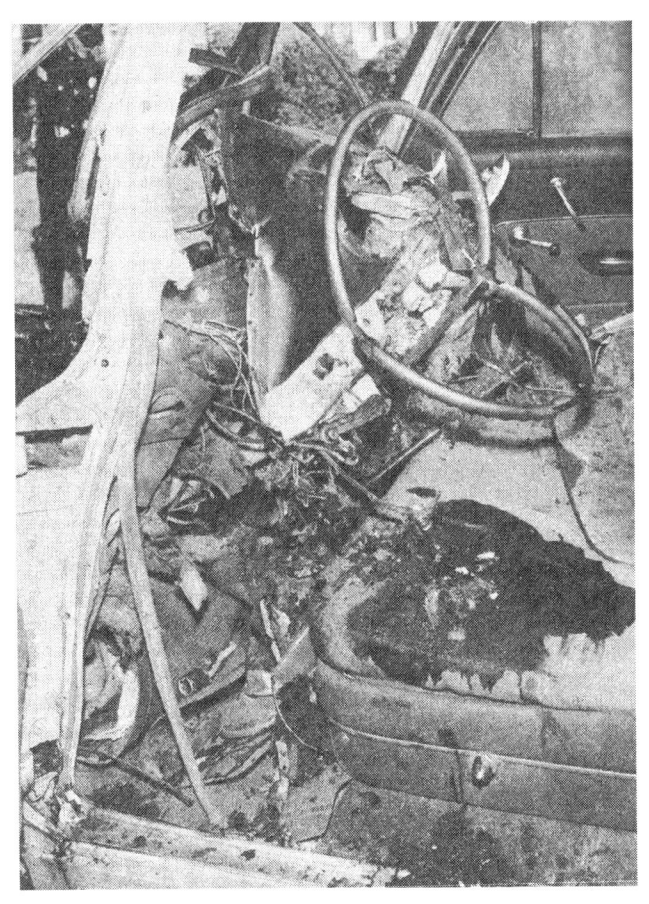

Interior view of Helen Weaver's car.

But they wouldn't arrive for a couple of more hours, hours that Chief Lowe needed to keep the investigation moving forward. While San Angelo detectives Braziel and Gunn examined what was left of "the death car," Lowe, District Attorney Stokes, and Sheriff Turner sidled up to have a talk with Harry Weaver.

The big question on everyone's mind: why would anyone want to kill Helen Harris Weaver? They didn't have to wait long. Weaver told Braziel who did it. "Get ahold of Ralph Rohatsch, a Texas Ranger. He knows about this and he can pin it on the son-in-law.

Pin it on the son-in-law?

Their conversation began on the front lawn of the Harris mansion, then continued later that evening in the law office of a former district attorney. Stokes was there, along with the sheriff and the lead detectives. Still in shock, Weaver did his best to answer their questions. Whether he knew it or not, this was the beginning of a long and dark road for him.

According to crime writer Bill Cox, some of those questions included retracing Harry and Helen's activities for the last week. Weaver began by explaining that they left *Butterfield Peak Lodge* six days earlier in the '54, and traveled to Houston where Helen, or "Mommy" as he always called her, visited with her daughter and three grandchildren, one of them a newborn. Weaver, who made his architectural career in Houston, used his time there to file the couple's annual taxes with his accountant, as well as to tend to several rental properties he owned.

On Tuesday, January 18, the pair left Houston early that morning and after driving approximately 400 miles, arrived in San Angelo early that evening.

"When did anyone last use the car?" Chief Lowe asked.

"She drove it last night," Weaver answered. "We...returned home about 5:30 p.m. yesterday. Later, we went downtown to the Cactus Hotel for dinner. We went in separate cars because Mommy was going to visit her mother after dinner, and I had other business."

Weaver further explained that he arrived home before his wife. As the first one to pull into the driveway, Weaver made sure to give his wife plenty of room to park behind him. She got home a few minutes after he did, and they went to bed between 8:30 and 9:00 o'clock that night.

Harry Weaver

On the day his wife was killed, Weaver was asked several times who he thought was responsible. He was always fast and confident in his answers—maybe a little too fast: "Find out where Harry Washburn has been in the last twenty-four hours," a reporter heard him say.

Harry Leonard Washburn.[5] The investigators and newspaper reporters in both San Angelo and Houston knew about Harry L. Washburn. The unemployed thirty-eight-year-old was Mrs. Weaver's former son-in-law, and father to her two grandchildren in which he was, currently, the custodial parent.

Harry L. Washburn, a big galoot with champagne tastes on a Coca-Cola budget, was also the man who broke into their ranch house four years previously and threatened to murder both Helen and Harry as part of a cockamamie scheme to get his wife back. He also demanded a check for $20,000[6] and, if it wasn't too much trouble, he wanted to be put in charge of *Butterfield Peak Lodge*, the ranch, and everything that came with it.

A lot of people suspected Harry Washburn and even a San Angelo newspaper reporter told Texas Ranger Ralph Rohatsch they should check out his alibi for last night. The ranger had arrived mid-afternoon with bomb, fingerprint, and chemistry experts. After careful examination, they quickly determined there were no explosive devices in the other three cars at the Harris mansion. They also checked the residence, and in the days to come, would inspect the ranch house in Coke County. None were found.

But their search for clues wasn't a total loss. San Angelo detectives earlier that day had found a clean, copper wire near the ignition switch, speculated it had been used by the bomber, and was most likely connected to the generator. When Mrs. Weaver turned the key, KA-BOOM; but even the demolition expert from Austin could not be sure how it was detonated. The one thing he did know, based on the smell that

---

[5] Harry Leonard Washburn should not be confused with the public servant Harry L. Washburn of Houston who served as Harris County Auditor for many years and for whom the Washburn Tunnel there is named after.

[6] The 2016 equivalent of $185,000, when adjusted for inflation.

lingered, the bomb was nitroglycerin-based dynamite; the kind any adult could buy in a farm supply store, where they were required to show identification and sign a logbook.

"A bomb, possibly composed of nitroglycerin, was discharged near the left side of the engine block," the *San Angelo Standard-Times* reported the following day. When Helen sat down and turned the key, she was facing the bomb.

Although Harry Weaver gave out the name of his top suspect, District Attorney Aubrey Stokes had another name in mind. It was the name of the man who stood to gain the most from Helen's death.

Harry Weaver.

The Media

NEWS THAT A TEXAS SOCIALITE was killed by a car bomb was as explosive as the nitro-gel dynamite. The story was on the front pages of major newspapers such as the *Chicago Tribune*, *Kansas City Times*, the *Detroit Free Press*, the *Oregon Statesman*, *the Reno Gazette*, the *Arizona Republic*, *The Tennessean*, the *Daily Oklahoman*, and *the Des Moines Register*, to name a few.

Across the country, over 1,000 dailies in both medium and small markets ran the story along with a photograph of either Helen Harris Weaver, or, if they were lucky, a then famous picture of the blown-out engine compartment, with a hatless, coatless Harry Weaver in the background. Photo captions of Helen's Chevrolet referred to it as "the death car," the name by which it forever became known.

In Texas, nearly every single daily newspaper, including Dallas, Houston, El Paso, Austin and all the way down to *The Paris News*, ran it as a front-page story. But nowhere was the story bigger than in San Angelo, where: "Newsmen were tested to the maximum to separate fact from fiction, proof from speculation," the paper later reported.

Indeed, the event fired-up the imagination and excitement of nearly every San Angelo resident old enough to know what was going on. Wild rumors about the Dallas underworld, or shadowy strangers catching a flight out of town that morning, or of Harry Weaver hiring contract killers, mixed in with the cold winds from the north and cast a chilling effect over the city.

As fictional as the rumors sounded, one of the last Texans killed by a car bomb was the wife of Herbert "The Cat" Noble, the "numbers racket kingpin" of Dallas[7]. And there *were* strangers on a plane leaving San Angelo that morning, but they were later cleared by the Texas Rangers. And if Harry did kill his wife for the money, he wouldn't be the first or the last man to do so. Even with her family's wealth behind her, Helen was a self-accomplished woman. She not only saved the family fortune, she added to its wealth.

"San Angelo was rumor laden with reports of doubtful accuracy. The *Standard-Times* began receiving calls from newspapers throughout the country, as well as inquiries from the British press, indicating the widespread national and international interest in the case," the paper later recounted.

The British press? Blimey. If the British press was calling San Angelo, Texas, along with reporters from coast-to-coast, then there was one thing Mrs. Helen Weaver's killer may have learned a little too late: You bloody 'ell don't kill someone with a car bomb. The widespread reporting on radio and television, as well as in the newspapers, should have scared 'Mr. Dynamite' into realizing that killing a well-loved, Texas socialite with a car bomb was a really bad idea.

Really bad.

With so much national and international attention on San Angelo, the killer's choice to use dynamite to blow-up a

---

[7] More information about the interesting life of Noble, and his wife's murder, can be found on my blog, HistoricalCrimeDetective.com. A link to the relevant page is at the end of this book.

grandmother from a prominent family meant one thing and one thing only: that the media and lawmen were never going to let it rest. It would be solved.

Helen Harris Weaver, 1903-1955

IF THE CAR BOMB WAS the *how*, which puzzled investigators, the *why* did as well. Why kill Helen Weaver? What was the motive? The lawmen, like most folks in the area, were familiar with Helen and the Harris family. The fifty-one-year-old mother of two was the granddaughter of Leasial B. Harris who moved to Texas in 1832 as a boy and witnessed the Battle of San Jacinto from a distance.

He was the first rancher in Tom Green County to fence his land in with barbed wire—controversial at the time. His ranching operation prospered during the cattle rush years from 1866 to the 1890s. He used part of his wealth to found the Concho National Bank, build the San Angelo Hotel, and was later named president of the First National Bank of San Angelo.

Born in 1903, Helen was the oldest of four children of Ralph and Sadie Harris. Ralph, the youngest of eight children, inherited his father's love of ranching and head for business. Their fortune increased when oil was discovered beneath their thousands of acres of grassland in 1923. When Ralph died in 1943, Helen assumed control of the family business.

Helen's mind was a force of its own. In 1921, she was the valedictorian of her high school class, and was offered scholarships to every leading university in the state. She attended the University of Texas for a brief time, but left during her sophomore year to marry her high school sweetheart, Harvey "Hicks" Allen. The couple had two daughters, Sadie Gwin in 1924, and Helen in 1927.

That marriage ended with a divorce during the early 1930s. With two kids to care for, a thirty-year-old Helen headed back to school and graduated from Incarnate Word College in San Antonio with a bachelor of art's degree in 1938. Before she could enter the teaching profession, her ultimate goal, she was swept-off-her feet by Harry Weaver, thirteen years her senior. He was also recently divorced, and father to two adult children. The two married soon after she graduated college and with Helen's children, settled in Houston where Harry rebuilt his architectural career following the great depression.

When Helen assumed control of the family estate in 1943, it was her opportunity to show that she could be more than a homemaker, mother, and college graduate.

"She was admired as a shrewd businesswoman, more than adept in the competitive business of ranching. It was said she could guess the weight of livestock within a few pounds," writer Bill Cox wrote in his magazine article. "Her business sense was demonstrated in the early 1950s when, seeing a drought coming on, she sold her livestock and leased her ranch land at $1 an acre until the worst was over, averting disaster that struck many ranchers in the area."

She continued in the ranching business, but not in Texas. In South Dakota, she leased land, bought cattle, and carried on for several more years. By the time of her death, she was out of the ranching business altogether.

After the war, Harry, fifty-eight-years-old then, began looking forward to an early retirement, or semi-retirement at best. He wanted to spend more time with his wife, and explore his interest in archeology, geology, and paleontology. Later, he would team up with other semi-adventurous men on mining expeditions throughout the southwest, searching for the hot new metal everyone was talking about: uranium. Within their plans for retirement was the construction of their dream home on their 14,000 acre ranch in Coke County.

There was just one thing standing in his way: Helen's unmarried daughter, Helen Allen, or "Little Helen," as she was often referred to by family and friends.

According to the memoirs of Little Helen's daughter from her second marriage, her mother attended the University of Texas but dropped out after one semester. Maybe two.

"My aunt [Sadie Gwin] followed in her mother's [Mrs. Helen Weaver] footsteps, and excelled academically. My mother did not," Tess Keehn writes in her book, *Alchemical Inheritance*. "Even though she was highly intelligent, Helen just couldn't be bothered with higher education. She didn't find a career either, which would have been nearly impossible in those times."

Quitting her freshman year wouldn't seem unusual in the 1940s, and Keehn states that women of privilege from that era were expected to marry and start their own families. After all, the victim herself had once put her education on hold to get married. Unfortunately, nineteen-year-old "Little Helen" showed "no signs of snagging a husband and settling into her own family life."

Keehn later speculates in her book that before Helen and Harry could retire to what would become *Butterfield Peak Lodge*, they felt obligated to help the youngest daughter find a husband. They chose poorly.

Enter: Harry Leonard Washburn

HARRY LEONARD WASHBURN WAS OPERATING a photography studio in the same building as Harry Weaver when he was introduced to "Little Helen" Allen. Tall, spectacled, and mildly handsome, he looked far more respectable than he really was. He was friendly, outgoing and had the charming personality of a politician. Or, as Keehn writes, that of a sociopath.

Born in 1916, the thirty-year-old was eleven and one half-years older than his future wife. He grew up in a large family where his father, through two marriages, conceived eleven children according to public records. Those same records report that Harry himself married young, fathered a daughter in 1938[8], and divorced long before he married the young, attractive Little Helen from the rich family in May 1947.

It was an odd pairing. The best that could be said of it is: Washburn had ambition but no brains, and Helen had brains but no ambition.

Harry Leonard Washburn

"Aunt Sadie Gwin told me that everyone in the family was aware that the man (Washburn) came from the 'wrong side of the tracks,' but that they graciously accepted him anyway. Mother later told us that she was forced to marry the man and never really wanted to," Tess Keehn writes in her book. "The wedding portrait that hangs on my wall certainly bears witness to my mother's reluctance—a beautiful young woman in a stunning satin gown with flowers all around, but no joy in the

---

[8] Please see Epilogue for more information.

eyes of the bride and a resolute expression on her face. There is a severity to her stiffness, certain darkness to her demeanor."

For Washburn, the marriage was his passport to riches and glory. He ran for Harris County Commissioner in 1948 and 1950, losing both times. By then, he'd given up photography and started a "wholesale appliance" business, but most of their income came from the $250[9] check Mrs. Weaver sent each month. He was smart enough to impregnate his young wife, who gave birth to a son in November 1948, and a daughter during the summer of 1950.[10] Not long after her grandchildren were born, Helen and Harry Weaver left Houston and settled into *Butterfield Peak Lodge* near the town of Robert Lee.

Washburn, a man who believed himself to be greater than he really was, entitled to more than he deserved, was a horrible husband, and horrible father, according to Keehn.

"I have a very vague memory of my mother talking of a time when Washburn tied my sister to her bed with the bologna sandwich she had declined at lunch, having been told she would be staying there until she ate the food that was offered. Maybe parenting should require a license," Keehn relates.

On December 14, 1950, Helen filed for divorce, putting Washburn in danger of losing his income stream. He counter-attacked by hiring the most famous, most successful attorney in all of Texas: Percy Foreman.

"There is no better trial lawyer than me," Foreman once asserted before he died in 1988. In a 1969 *Time* magazine article, he claimed that of 1,500 death penalty cases he had handled, fewer than half ever went to trial, and of those that

---

[9] The 2016 equivalent of $2,500.
[10] Their half-sister, Tess Keehn, did not release their names in her book, *Alchemical Inheritance*, and I am following her example.

did, he lost only fifty-three. Of those fifty-three, only one client was executed.

In addition to defending the South's most high-profile criminals of that era, one that eventually included James Earl Ray, his 1988 obituary from the *Washington Post* reports "he kept an active file of an average of 2,200 divorce cases' during a practice that spread across half a century."

Foreman, known for his theatrics in and out of the courtroom, made sure that his client's side of the story made its way into newspapers. "My mother's divorce from Harry Washburn was as messy as they come, with slanderous newspaper accounts—fed to the press by Washburn—of accusations of misdeeds," Keehn writes in her book.

As the divorce grew contentious, Washburn privately blamed Harry Weaver for setting his twenty-three-old wife against him, and for his dismal performance in the wholesale appliance business. The man was a well-known architect through-out Houston; of course he used his influence and connections to run him into the ground. With Weaver working against him and his marriage, Washburn's dreams of wealth, status, and respect were slipping away. When her daughter filed for divorce, Mrs. Weaver stopped sending the $250 checks. After all, that money was for the benefit and welfare of her grandchildren, not her son-in-law.

But Washburn didn't see it that way.

By the spring of 1951, Washburn's stress over his lifestyle adjustment fueled a rage inside that literally drove him 390 miles from Houston to *Butterfield Peak Lodge* where he confronted the Weaver's directly. At two o'clock in the morning on April 23, the couple was asleep in their bedroom when they were suddenly awakened as the light was turned on. Weaver later said that as their eyes adjusted to the light, they could see their son-in-law standing at the end of the bed with a pistol in each hand, and a knife in his belt.

"Get out of bed. You're going to write a letter for me," Weaver later quoted Washburn. "He looked at my wife with the gun and said, 'You are going to write a check for me for $20,000, and then some other checks.' He said, 'Mrs. Weaver, I ought to kill you now the way you stopped giving me that $250 a month.'"

The astonished couple put on their robes and Helen sat down at her vanity desk. Washburn thrust a typewritten letter toward Harry. "Read it out loud," he said, and turning to Mrs. Weaver, added, "You take it down in your own handwriting."

Part of the letter set the context for what Washburn wanted everyone to later believe was a murder-suicide. "I'm going to kill Poppy (Harry Weaver) because he had to do something about Harry (Washburn)," Helen was ordered to write. She was also killing her husband, according to Washburn's letter, because she discovered "he was a communist."

At one point Washburn raised the Venetian blind of the bedroom and said, "I'll look to see if my men are still out there. If anything happens to me they will come in and kill you."

Over the next hour, Mrs. Weaver took down the text of Washburn's letter. "Hurry it up, or I'll kill you both," he threatened at intervals. She was going as slow as she possibly could while her husband tried to pacify their would-be killer.

Even though she was known for her broad vocabulary, was class valedictorian, and a college graduate, she wasn't very good at spelling that night—this was her tip-off to family and investigators that she was forced to write the suicide note, Keehn wrote.

Near the end of the letter, after "Mrs. Weaver" explains her motivation for the murder-suicide, she urges her daughter to reconcile with Washburn.

"Harry is a good boy. He just became a little confused," she copied from Washburn's letter. Her dying wish, before she was to 'commit suicide,' was for her daughter to get back together with "good boy" Harry, and live together on her

14,000-acre ranch that Washburn would manage—for a high salary, of course.

Eventually, with his wife's help, Weaver was able to dissuade Washburn from killing them both with a promise of $5,000 soon, and $500 a month[11]. Weaver also pointed out to Washburn the one thing that never occurred to him as he typed that letter and then drove eight hours from Houston to Coke County. "...after Mrs. Weaver is -- after we are dead, you won't be able to cash any check anymore and they will suspect you [of the killing]."

Weaver's logic kept them alive. He also projected a demeanor in which it may have seemed like old times to Washburn, before his wife left him. He further played to that sentiment by asking Washburn to come live with them, and repeated his offer of financial support.

"I had to do something," he later said. "I discussed giving him $5,000 cash and $500 a month. He agreed to it. He said, 'now you folks aren't going to be sore at me?' With a couple of guns on me, I couldn't afford to be sore."

After he was offered $5,000, Washburn put one gun on the table, along with his knife, and put the other pistol in his pocket. "Then he shook hands with me," Weaver said. "I don't know what for."

Taking his original letter with him, Washburn promised to come back and kill them both if they didn't pay him the money or if they went to the police. "If either one of you tell a soul I have been out here I will come back and kill you both," Washburn was quoted as saying. He then "signaled to his henchman" that he was coming out.

There were no henchmen. He was alone.[12]

---

[11] The equivalent of $46,155 and $4,615 in 2016, when adjusted for inflation.

[12] Accounts of this 1951 incident vary slightly according to different sources, which include wire services, local newspapers, crime magazines, and court documents. The account as narrated above is a compilation of all four, told as accurately as the author could discern from his research and

A few days later, the Weavers reported the incident to the Coke County Sheriff's Department. Since Washburn lived outside their jurisdiction, Ranger Ralph Rohatsch was brought into the investigation. Two months later, Washburn was indicted by a Coke County grand jury for attempted burglary, extortion, and assault with intent to kill. He was arrested, booked, and released on bail.

Percy Foreman was able to keep the case out of the courtroom long enough to wear down the Weavers, who, after one year, "no longer cared to pursue the matter," due to "unwanted publicity." On March 3, 1952, the charges were dismissed.

Helen's divorce had become final the previous July, and since she was awarded custody of the children, the Weavers might have believed the worst was over.

Far from it.

The Gambit

LITTLE HELEN REMARRIED QUICKLY AND she married well. Her new husband was a petroleum engineer and his work soon forced the newlyweds to leave Texas. However, the marriage complicated her custodial rights as the couple resided first in North Dakota, and then Montana. According to Keehn's memoirs, when Washburn found out where they were living, he drove to Montana to exercise his visitation privileges. He then took the children back to Houston where he petitioned the court for full-custody.

Everyone on the Harris side understood that this was a ploy by Washburn to milk more money out of the Weavers, but matriarch Helen Weaver in particular. After they got the charges against Washburn dismissed in 1952, attorneys for each side came together to sign a peace treaty. In exchange for

---

authenticating sources.

a $5,000 one-time payment[13], Washburn agreed to "waive any and all rights" against the estate his ex-wife would eventually inherit. They hoped the settlement would make him go away. Permanently.

Wishful thinking. Washburn was never going to go away. He had a lifestyle to uphold and the Weavers were going to pay for it. He was driving a new Ford, and living in a "well-to-do" section of Houston where houses were priced in the $30,000 to $40,000 range[14]. The waiver may have blocked access through his ex-wife, but he was shrewd, and cunning, and most of all, he was unstoppable. Within months of getting his cash pay-out, he went for the kids.

In response to his latest ploy, the Harris-Weaver family made a decision and counter-attacked with a gambit of their own. Instead of fighting him for custody, they would give him the children, but no money to raise them. Zip. Zero. As the owner of a failing wholesale appliance business, Washburn would just have to work and financially support his kids on his own.

With that strategy, the Washburn kids were just pawns in a grown-up game of chess.

Keehn writes:

> Washburn eventually figured out they were living out of state. At some point, he went to Montana to pick up the two children for a visit and never returned them. Mother got legal advice that produced very little in the way of legal recourse. My parents and everyone else in the family agreed that this was just one of Washburn's manipulations aimed at getting money from the family. My father told me that my mother consulted with her mother and her mother's attorney in San Angelo. They all agreed that giving Washburn full responsibility for the children

---

[13] It was widely reported that the settlement was $30,000, but this is incorrect. The actual amount was $5,000 cash, and an unspecified property settlement.

[14] The same as $277,000 to $370,000 in 2016, when adjusted for inflation.

would be a way to call his bluff - as long as no one gave him any money….

The thinking was that, if no one gave him any more money, Washburn would eventually tire of the struggles of parenting and return custody to my mother. But it seems that Washburn just farmed the children out to his sister, his neighbors, and whomever else he could find to watch them…. My father emphasized the reluctance with which my mother agreed to this plan to call his bluff.

In March 1953, Harry L. Washburn, a man with little to no actual income, became the primary custodian for his children.

In contrast to what Keehn wrote, his neighbors described him as a good father. "He used to wash and iron the children's clothes and devoted practically all of his time to taking care of them," a woman told a *Houston Chronicle* reporter, days after the 1955 blast.

All of his time? If he was spending all of his time taking care of the children, how was he making a living? Where was the money coming from? That's what the nosy neighbor wanted to know as well.

"The one thing we sometimes wondered about," she said, "was how he made his money. He never said and yet you know he had to have money to live."

When told that Washburn described himself as a building contractor,[15] "this neighbor [said] there was never any outward indication that he was working," the *Chronicle* reported.

On one occasion, the neighbor added, the question of adopting one of the children was raised. She quoted Washburn as replying, "No. Never. I'm going to keep those children together and with me just as long as I possibly can."

Washburn's determination reveals that the Harris-Weaver family underestimated their adversary. The plan was to give

---

[15] At the time of this interview in January 1955, Washburn was trying to establish himself as a building contractor.

him the kids, but no money, and wait for him to surrender. In theory, it made sense. It was logical and practical.

It was a bad plan. It was a logical plan for an emotional situation. From the start, it was doomed to fail because it didn't take into account the human factor that children are children, not pawns; and it didn't take into account Washburn was a highly-skilled manipulator who wasn't afraid to bully and intimidate Helen Harris Weaver into sending him money.

Money that was for the children, of course.

Helen Harris Weaver loved her grandchildren more than she wanted to triumph over their father and between 1953 and 1955 she discreetly and indiscreetly funneled money to Washburn.

But where Helen would turn the spigot on, Harry Weaver would turn it off. Helen would turn it on, Harry would turn it off. On, off. On, off. And when Harry would turn it off, Harry Leonard Washburn would get angry—not, normal person angry; it was more like abnormal-obsessive person angry.

The Prime Suspect

January 20, 1955

HARRY WEAVER KILLED HIS WIFE. By the time he drank his coffee the next morning, the chubby, Pennsylvania-born architect was in the legal cross hairs of Tom Green County District Attorney Aubrey Stokes.

The young prosecutor made that decision upon learning that Washburn never left his house the night before the blast. Washburn was the first name on everyone's mind—from Sheriff Turner to Stokes to Ranger Rohatsch to newspaper reporters from San Angelo to Houston. He was such a hot suspect that Rohatsch flew to Houston later that evening, January 19. Described in newspapers as "a 38-year-old Houston businessman," Washburn and his two children were escorted to the Harris County Sheriff's Office, where he was questioned for two hours. The former son-in-law denied having anything to do with Mrs. Weaver's death; declared he was at his home all night, and that he was driving his daughter to school—private school, of course,—when the explosion occurred nearly 400 miles away.

During the closed-door, no attorneys allowed interview, showman Percy Foreman paced up and down the hallways and remarked to newsmen, as if he were in charge, "They are welcome to question him….at a decent time and at his home."

Miranda v Arizona was eleven years in the future. They didn't have to do anything the slick-back-haired lawyer said. They did give him the courtesy of ordering the press not to release his client's name, however.

At midnight, Washburn and his children were driven home by four Texas Rangers. Although they were letting him go, he wasn't completely crossed-off their suspect list.

"He will probably be questioned again," Rohatsch said during a telephone interview with the *San Angelo Standard-Times* the following morning, January 20. He told the local paper he was going to stick around Houston, likely to try and verify Washburn's alibi, but then he made a comment that indicated the direction the investigation was about to turn.

"I think you have more suspects in San Angelo than we have in Houston."

San Angelo? Harry Weaver was in San Angelo.

In newspaper reports published later that Thursday and throughout the weekend, there were subtle indications that Stokes and company had focused their attention on Weaver: who was seen near the car shortly before the blast; who put the key in the ignition; and who didn't start the car like he normally did.

The prosecutor held a 9:30 a.m. meeting with all available family members to discuss the case "in a search for further clues to Mrs. Weaver's death," the *Standard-Times* reported. What he really wanted—was access. Later that afternoon, the entire investigative team of city, county, and state officers went to *Butterfield Peak Lodge* to "search for more bomb-traps."

It was a polite way of saying they were looking for evidence: copper wire, nitro-gel based dynamite, detonators, those kinds of things. However, something happened out there that day that told Weaver he was their prime suspect. Since Sheriff Turner reported that they found "nothing out of the ordinary," perhaps it was their line of questioning or the way in which they searched for "bomb traps."

Although Harry Weaver had many friends in San Angelo, primarily through the Emmanuel Episcopal Church, he was still something of an outsider. Helen was the hometown girl, the class valedictorian, third-generation heir to the oil and ranching fortune of a prominent local family. Rumors began. Innuendos. Whispers about a friendship with another woman. Not just any woman, this one ran a local tavern. She was a sultry, sexy vixen with heavy-set bedroom eyes and a perpetual half-smirk as if she knew the man she was talking to was thinking something dirty for which she neither approved, nor disapproved.

And the cold Texas wind that blows through the Concho Valley carried those whispers to the ears of Aubrey Stokes and investigators.

The next day, Friday, January 21, Stokes and company backed away from Harry and the Harris family as the deeply depressed man buried his wife. Several hundred people attended Helen's funeral held at the Emmanuel Episcopal Church, at two o'clock that afternoon. An hour-and-half-later, the entire case took a wild detour when a nut job from Ardmore, Oklahoma, telephoned Weaver at the Harris mansion demanding $3,000 in exchange for a photograph of the man who killed his wife. After a week of cat and mouse games with the extortionist, he was eventually arrested and hauled back to Texas where he was wanted on other warrants.

But Stokes didn't back away too far. The grand jury, which was in session that week and recessed by the explosion, would be recalled the following day. Weaver, the maid, and most of Helen's immediate family were "asked" to attend. Also called, and noted in the newspaper, were witnesses Henry Lamb, the detectives, Sheriff Turner, and at the very end of the list, where folks would remember it, was a name that raised eyebrows from San Angelo to Houston: "Mrs. Helen Adams, owner of Helen's Lounge in San Angelo."

What did she have to do with case?

Stokes. He was pushing buttons.

From that moment forward, Weaver was seldom without his lawyers, the local firm of Runge, Hardeman, Foy, and Smith. Carl Runge was his point man.

"Tension ran high at the courthouse as Weaver and members of the family [waited in] the grand jury reception room on the third floor of the building," the *Standard-Times* reported. A composed Weaver entered the courtroom at 9:10 a.m., then left five minutes later to confer with two of his attorneys at the far end of the hallway. One hour later, he re-entered after a brief conference with Sgt. Lee Braziel and Ranger Rohatsch. He left the courthouse at noon, telling investigators where they could find him if needed.

But later that day, Helen's will was filed at the courthouse along with an application for probate. Harry Weaver and Helen's two daughters inherited her entire estate. Specifically, Weaver was left about fifty acres near the west boundary of San Angelo, seventy-two acres near the Concho River south and east of San Angelo, eleven acres in Harris County, 120 acres in Kendall County and all his wife's interest in her properties in Arizona and Arkansas.

She also left him the best piece of the pie, *Butterfield Peak Lodge,* (but not the 14,000-acre ranch) on one condition: that he make that place his permanent residence within sixty days.

Although he was about to receive a good portion of her estate, Weaver had amassed his own small fortune and certainly didn't need his wife's wealth. Evidence was found in

Helen's own will where she stated, for the record, that she had made "a settlement with my husband and have paid him in full for [his personal money used to build the residence and improve the property] located in Coke County, on the ranch that is my separate property."

And in reality Weaver was better off financially if she were alive, not dead.

But that didn't matter to Stokes. When queried outside the grand jury room for comment, he would only tell reporters that he and the investigators were working the case day and night. After Helen's will was filed, his mood became more adversarial. Asked the same question later that evening, Stokes gave a cryptic remark that cranked up the gossip mill and reverberated in newspapers across the country.

Two people, he said, questioned in this case, had declined, upon advice of counsel, to take a lie detector test. "The requests were made outside the grand jury room," the *Standard-Times* added.

Ka-boom. Two sentences gave birth to a thousand rumors and exponentially multiplied the number of people throughout the country who thought Harry Weaver did it.

There were only two people it could be: Harry Weaver, and Helen Adams—the woman that made wives worry.

The inheritance, the love affair, it all added up to motive, in Stokes' crockpot mind. Those two ingredients, mixed in with all that business around the 'death car' that morning, were heating up his imagination. By Sunday night, he had dropped the subtleties. Feeling confident, he made a bold but ambiguous statement to United and Associated Press reporters.

"We have some pretty strong evidence," the AP reported him as saying the following day. "We have made a great deal of progress."

They left out the rest of what he said, but their competitor released a more thorough account of his proclamation.

"I think the man who did it is right here in San Angelo, [and the] suspect knows we're after him," read a United Press dispatch late that night. Stokes then explained that his investigative team had gathered a lot of circumstantial evidence, but needed more to make an arrest.

"We want to have enough to make it a good case whenever we present it to the grand jury," he added.

He explained the investigative team had been "picking up pieces" and were trying to fit them together. "Then we stumbled onto something good."

His brashness continued when he greeted reporters gathered outside his office on Monday morning.

"This is so ticklish that I can't say anything without giving away my case," Stokes replied to a reporter's question. "The way it looks now, it's just a matter of time before an arrest is made.

"The end is near."

Stokes finished the impromptu press conference by reporting that his plans for the day included interviewing witnesses, meeting with investigators, and getting a copy of Mrs. Helen Weaver's will from 1949. The one filed on Saturday was from 1953, and revoked all previous wills. The '49 will was inside her safety deposit box at the First National Bank. The thirty-three-year-old wanted that document so bad, he ordered a locksmith to break into the box. Before that could happen, the key was produced.

Harry Weaver, meanwhile, was going about his normal routine, one of his lawyers reported, or at least he was trying to. He was one of several architects working on a new design for the Coke County Courthouse. He was also an unpaid building consultant for the United States Navy, advising them on how to best maximize space. There was unfinished work ahead of him and all-the-while, he was aware of what many in San Angelo were saying about him. He took comfort in the more than one hundred letters of support he received from friends and acquaintances scattered across the country.

Runge and the rest of his legal team were astounded by Stokes' claims and the zealous nature of his attacks on their client known to many as a soft, caring man who didn't drink or smoke. Or chase women. If he was going to put their client on trial in the court of public opinion, they were going to knock Stokes off his bully pulpit with the same tool he was using—the newspapers. Harry Weaver was going to tell his story.

"On Tuesday [January 25], the *Houston Press*[16], it's curiosity fired by Stokes' hints at a solution, sent Jack Donahue to San Angelo," read an article in *Front Page Detective* published a few months later. "Donahue is one of the top crime reporters in the country, but his regular job was city editor at the *Press*."

Still wearing his tan and blue-striped pajamas, Weaver invited the veteran reporter up to the couple's bedroom where he was standing when the car bomb blew apart the windows and he heard his wife scream for help.

"I didn't kill her," Weaver said with a wavering voice. "You don't kill someone you love like I loved Mommy."

To Donahue, the chubby man with deep blue eyes looked more like a British pub owner than he did a killer.

"The walls of the small room were not as blue as Harry Weaver's eyes," Donahue wrote. "He pushed shell-rimmed bifocals up on the bridge of a nose that is the most noticeable feature of a round and friendly face. District Attorney Aubrey Stokes and Sheriff Cecil Turner have made it clear that this man is their chief suspect.

"I sat and talked with Harry Weaver for more than two hours. Talked in the room from which he says he looked last Wednesday, where his wife was dying in billowing smoke and twisted metal."

---

[16] This is not the same *Houston Press* newspaper that exists today.

He described the worst day of his life in detail. "She was screaming, 'Help, Harry, Harry!' I don't know how I got down the stairs and to the car. Her lips were moving and I kept telling her I would get help.

"I was frantic. I would run toward the service station across the street and then back to her. I didn't know what to do. And then—I knew she was dead. My Mommy was gone," he said as he pushed his hand through his thinning, gray hair. "Can anyone make anything of that—that a man is shocked and bewildered because his wife is dying in front of him?"

The memory of it all was too much. Without saying a word, Weaver got up, filled a glass of water from the adjacent bathroom, returned, and sat down.

"His face quivered and his deep-set eyes were moist behind his thick lenses," Donahue wrote in his notebook. He wisely chose not to say anything, and patiently waited for the broken man to speak first.

"Let me tell you about that morning," Weaver began again with a soft voice. "Mommy was going to the hospital to see her mother and then to the beauty shop. We were talking…I was going to get some coffee, but I happened to think, 'Why don't I get those tools out of the back of Mommy's Chevrolet so they won't be bouncing around and annoying her.'

"I hadn't taken them out of the car trunk when I got out the luggage Tuesday night when we got home from Houston. I took them out and put them in my Chevrolet that was parked in front of Mommy's car.

"I had broken the key ring to her Chevrolet and I hammered it together on a back bumper. I opened her car and took some stuff out of the glove compartment—a camera and some things—and threw them in my car. I was going to take it all to the ranch."

Weaver told Donahue what witness Lamb saw—that he put the key in the ignition, was overcome by the urge to use the bathroom, went back inside and was upstairs standing in front of the toilet when it happened.

"That's when I heard the explosion. It blew out these windows and I ran to them and could see all the smoke out there—and Mommy under the wheel...

"I was thinking of Mommy, and who could have done this, and I tried to tell the officers about the fellow in Houston who had threatened Mommy. But none of them seemed to understand," Weaver said.

To Donahue, Weaver "appeared bewildered" by how Stokes and company were handling the investigation. His attorney, Carl Runge, was succinct and candid with his opinion on the matter.

"They just flubbed this thing from the very beginning," he told Donahue in a separate interview.

Weaver then surprised readers by announcing that police officials wanted him to take a lie detector test the same day his wife was killed.

"I said I would, but then I remembered that all the kids were coming in and all the folks," Weaver said. "I couldn't get away to go to Austin for the test right then. So I said I would take one later."

Later, at Saturday's grand jury hearing, they asked him again to take the test. "I was going to do it, but my lawyer told me not to do it."

Earl Smith, the attorney that advised him against it, explained why. "Stokes told me Harry was a suspect," he said. "I didn't want Harry cross-examined and given tests when he was a suspect."

Donahue couldn't resist asking the one question that was on most people's minds, which had nothing to do with the case: *why did he call his wife 'Mommy?'*

"I met her in San Antonio at a cocktail party." he began. "It was just after the depression. I was an architect, but I was actually doing carpenter work on a job outside San Antonio, and was glad to do it.

"We talked at the party. She was there with some oilman, I remember, but I got her telephone number, and next day I made arrangements to come to town and I called her house.

"A little girl answered the phone and said, 'Mommy's not at home'

"'Who is Mommy?' I asked, and the little girl told me, 'Mommy is in school.'"

This was a happy memory, the first during the entire interview, Weaver smiled and his blue eyes sparkled as he recalled how he met his wife.

"Helen was taking her degree—that's the school the little girl meant. After that, we always laughed about my surprise that she had children and that one of them had answered the phone. And I always called her 'Mommy' after that."

While Donahue was interviewing a pajama-clad broken-down old man, across town, Stokes was peacocking for reporters during a press conference held in his office.

"I know the killer of Helen Harris Weaver and he knows we know him!" he said in a confident, loud voice. "I told him in front of his lawyer that he is the number one suspect. He is walking the streets of San Angelo. We have picked up some stuff, certain types of evidence. I'll show it the first time in court. This murder was well planned. The murderer is intelligent and has covered his tracks well."

But Stokes had a hard time keeping it together when hit with a barrage of questions. "Stokes refused to give a motive and got irritated when newsmen tried to press him," the United Press reporter scribbled in his notebook. The prosecutor ended the interview by promising more to come on Friday (January 28) when he presented his case to the grand jury.

Texas Ranger Ralph Rohatsch was in a better mood when reporters caught up with him later that Tuesday. "I'm smiling and that's more than I could say on my return from Houston," Rohatsch said. "I haven't slept for three days."

Donahue's story was published the following day, January 26, in Houston and El Paso, with the title: **"EXCLUSIVE: 'I Didn't Murder My Wife'–Weaver."** Two other stories about the case were also published that day. The article **"Officers Know Bomb Killer!"** by Charles E. Webb for the United Press was an account of Stokes' day-before press conference; and the third piece of news was a press release from Weaver's attorneys announcing a $10,000[17] reward for information leading to the killer. Harry, her children, and son-in-law Dr. Ed Blackburn, had grown weary of what they saw as Stokes' incompetence and misguided focus.

"The family of Mr. and Mrs. Harry E. Weaver of San Angelo, Texas, offers a reward of $10,000 for information leading to the arrest and final conviction of the person or persons responsible for her death by bombing on January 19, 1955," the announcement read. "Address all replies to Harry E. Weaver, San Angelo, Texas."

It was signed by Weaver, Helen's daughters Sadie and Helen, and Sadie's husband, Ed Blackburn, MD.

When he heard about the reward later that day, Stokes came unglued. He took it personal, and by the statement he released, seemed to fear he was losing control.

> As the offer now stands, it does in no way help or aid in the prosecution of this case. On the contrary, it will hinder the prosecution of the real murderer and tend to defeat justice.
>
> If this offer is made in good faith, the money should be put in escrow and paid on the condition that the information be sent directly to the district attorney's office. For in every criminal case, information should be sent to the prosecuting attorneys, and not to the defense attorneys. Information or evidence that would help lead to the final conviction in this case might be lost forever unless given to the district attorney's office.

---

[17] The 2016 equivalent of $89,554, when adjusted for inflation.

His last paragraph repeated three times what was on his mind most: *give it to me, not them*. And his last sentence seemed to indicate his belief that Weaver would ultimately destroy or tamper with any evidence he was presented.

Judging by some of the other publicized comments, not everyone at the courthouse was on board with his 'get Harry Weaver campaign.' The assistant district attorney, Justin Kever, thought the reward was a great idea, and would help the investigation. "Someone might now come forward with information we don't already have," he told the San Angelo newspaper. Sheriff Cecil Turner thought it would result in "10,000 bum steers, but, then again, somebody could come up with a solution."

Come up with a solution? Didn't Stokes have all the answers?

While Donahue's Wednesday, January 26 "exclusive" washed some of the mud off Weaver, he didn't address the lurid aspect of the case readers wanted to know more about: Helen Adams. But the veteran crime reporter knew his job, and knew he couldn't leave San Angelo without interviewing the town's most feared mantrap and recent divorcée.

"Helen Adams is a tall, slender, dark-haired tavern keeper with $3,000 worth of diamonds on her fingers and she drives a green Cadillac," Donahue's January 27 story began. He was exaggerating about the diamonds, but was trying to add a little color to his article about the local business owner hyped to the status of femme fatale. "Ten years ago, she must have been a knockout. She must be a year or so past forty now, but every masculine head turns when she walks on high heels across the tavern floor with a cold beer and a glass."

Before she was the owner of a barely profitable drinking establishment, she was the owner of an unprofitable record store where Harry often shopped. She still had 12,000 records in her garage she was trying to unload.

"Casually," she answered when asked how well she knew him. "He used to come into my music store downtown a couple of years ago. He liked old records, some of them twenty-years old. He liked Bing Crosby best of all. He was always wanting something like, *I'll Take You Home Again, Kathleen*, or *Sweet Leilani*, you know, old songs. He never wanted to pay more than a quarter for a record. He was a pretty shrewd bargainer. He wanted to get for twenty-five cents records that were twenty-five years old. But he was a perfect gentleman."

As for the grand jury, she would not repeat what she was asked or what she told the district attorney, but her passive expression indicated it was much ado about nothing. Instead of the 'sultry vixen,' the 'femme fatale,' and the 'other woman' created by gossip and semi-endorsed by Stokes' pursuit of Weaver, Donahue's article portrayed her as a colorful but innocent character swept up in a Texas-sized drama. Helen Adams was an attractive, divorced, forty-something-year-old woman who was the mother of a thirteen-year-old boy, trying to scratch out a living by serving drinks to airmen from the local Air Force base, who only had cash two or three days out of the month, and then wanted credit.

From *Helen's Lounge*, Donahue next interviewed Henry Lamb and the Harris maid, Sue Davis. Both of them described Harry and Helen as an exceedingly happy and loving couple.

"I never leave home without kissing my wife good-bye; neither did Harry Weaver," Lamb said.

Davis, who knew the intimate details of their life, told Donahue: "They always got along good together. They were always in good humor."

On the same day Donahue's second article was published, the wire services released a follow-up story on Weaver who granted a second interview to discuss the reward. Questioned in the office of his attorneys, Weaver was thinking of what his wife would say about his predicament: "If Mommy was here, she'd give these people (Stokes and company) hell," he told reporters. "I sure did love her. I don't know of ever failing to kiss Mommy once."

During the interview, Weaver shocked reporters when he theorized that the bomb may have been meant for him, not his wife. "It was natural for me to go to the hospital that day. I hadn't gone with her for four or five days," he said. Even now, he told reporters, "He couldn't discount the possibility that his life was in danger."

His life wasn't in any immediate danger, but he was right about one thing: the bomb *was* meant for him, not Helen.

The Arrest

THE $10,000 REWARD LOOSENED THE lips of a couple of Houston ne'er-do-wells who knew the score and started talking. On Thursday afternoon, one of them contacted Henry K. Thompson, a Houston Police Department burglary and theft detective, who took his statement. His accomplice was picked-up later that evening and verified his partner's account. A third man, mentioned in their reports but who wasn't involved in the case, was arrested on a street near his home at 8:30 p.m. Friday.

With three men in custody and sworn affidavits, the detective's commanding officer, Captain Cecil Priest, telephoned Aubrey Stokes and Ranger Rohatsch at their Houston hotel to inform them they had cracked the case. Stokes and Rohatsch were in town working with the Harris County Sheriff's Department to investigate leads and execute search warrants on local property owned by Weaver. They were looking for bomb-making materials, including the store where he purchased the dynamite. They also were there to question a Houston schoolteacher who was acquainted with Mrs. Weaver four years prior. Reporting on the woman, it was clear from the *El Paso Post* article Stokes and Rohatsch were hoping to find signs of an illicit love affair.

There was no affair, not with her and not with Helen Adams. When Stokes stood inside the police station and read the affidavits, the realization that he had been wrong all that time did not register on his face.

"Mr. Stokes read the affidavits and stated as far as he is concerned, it was enough to file murder charges," Detective Thompson wrote in his report. Within those sworn statements, the three men had pointed the finger at a fourth man—the only man with a motive to kill Harry Weaver. In the weeks to come, more witnesses, unwilling co-conspirators, and the physical evidence against him was "appallingly conclusive," a crime magazine writer would later state.

Stokes and Rohatsch quickly questioned the three connoisseurs of cheap alcohol in custody and when satisfied with their verbal statements, Stokes phoned a judge in San Angelo who telegraphed two arrest warrants back to Houston. At approximately 2:30 in the morning on Saturday, January 29, Stokes, Rohatsch, Thompson, and five other Houston detectives left police headquarters at 61 Reisner Street, drove seven miles west to a high-class Houston neighborhood, and parked in front of 43 West Broad Oaks Drive. After detectives surrounded the house, Rohatsch knocked on the front door. One minute later, a pajama and bathrobe clad Harry Leonard Washburn walked out onto the overhead porch and called down, "Who is it?"

"Harry, this is Ralph. Get up and open the door," Rohatsch yelled back.

"Okay, I'll let you in," Washburn replied in a calm voice. After allowing the officers into his pinewood-paneled breakfast room, he appeared nervous and asked, "What's it about?"

"We have a warrant for you Harry," Rohatsch replied. "You'll have to come with us."

Washburn was allowed to get dressed and to telephone a neighbor, the wife of a doctor whom he was friends with, to come over and watch his still-sleeping children. During the car ride back to headquarters, he was silent, and refused to answer any questions.

According to the *Houston Chronicle* and wire reports, Washburn said very little when greeted by beat reporters at police headquarters. He referred them to his attorney, Percy Foreman, repeated his previous alibi that he was taking his daughter to "private school" at the time of the explosion, and told them, "You know more about this than I do."

When he saw the two men who fingered him, his face grew stern as he proclaimed, "I am an innocent man. I have nothing else to say until I have talked with my attorney."

A short-while later, the *Houston Post* reporter found a more talkative Washburn, who said he liked Mrs. Weaver and had no motive to kill her, but that he had an "intense dislike" for her husband.

"I wouldn't want to kill her. Why, only last summer, I got an anonymous letter in the mail from San Angelo. It contained five $100 bills for my two children," Washburn said. "I'm pretty sure from the handwriting that it was from Mrs. Weaver, their grandmother. If I had still wanted to kill a Weaver, it would have been Harry and not Helen."

Still? If that was an admission for his 1951 home invasion case, he quickly recovered, called it a misunderstanding, and said his visit to the ranch was at Mrs. Weaver's request. She wanted to discuss patching up his marriage to Little Helen, but her husband came home, got angry, and threw him out. The later settlement was an agreement for him not to sue the Weavers for filing a false police report.

When Washburn was arrested early Saturday morning, Stokes also had a warrant for his Houston friend and associate, John Carlton "Carl" Heninger, a forty-five-year-old unemployed carpenter's helper, who was picked up Friday night on the streets of Houston. Heninger was the third man to point the finger at Washburn, but had very little to do with the case and was eventually released. His estranged wife, a one-time female wrestler whose professional name was "Nature Girl," knew more about it than he did.

Both men were driven to Austin, put on board a Texas Department of Public Safety airplane, and flown to San Angelo, where a highway patrol car was waiting for them. When they reached the courthouse on Beauregard Avenue, just a block-and-a-half-away from the blast site, a throng of onlookers and reporters swarmed the vehicle as it approached the rear entrance.

With detectives taking positions on both sides of their suspects, one of them yelled to his colleagues "Hurry up and get these men inside," as newsmen rushed towards them. Rohatsch tried to pacify the roar of questions and flash-bulb popping photographers as if he were talking to children begging for candy.

"Just a minute and I'll let you get your pictures," he told them.

Harry Washburn, center, shortly after he was returned to San Angelo. From left to right, District Attorney Aubrey Stokes, Washburn, and Texas Ranger Ralph Rohatsch.

When they were allowed inside the booking room, Washburn was the first to speak.

"Hi Joe," he called out to Joe Dominic, a former employee of his photography business, now working for the *Standard-Times* in San Angelo. Dominic's colleague, reporter Ed Freitag, was there to capture in words a description of the man who was, at that moment: the most famous murderer in America; and the most famous to have ever killed the wrong person; and probably the dumbest; and the biggest sucker of all since he was repeatedly conned out of his money by a couple of deadbeat barflies he hired to be his hitmen.

"Washburn was handcuffed, a suede sports jacket hung loosely over his shoulders," Freitag wrote. He described him as "a better than average-looking man" who stood nearly six-feet tall. He was wearing brown pants with a white-button shirt "heavily stained with perspiration," which was odd since it was January. "[His] glasses gave him a wide-eyed appearance. He alternately grinned and looked grim as the flash-gasses of the cameras snapped around him."

When reporters caught up with Harry Weaver at *Butterfield Peak Lodge*, his lawyer Carl Runge had already given him the news. Unable to reach him by telephone, he drove there as fast as he could at nine o'clock that morning. He was still in good spirits when asked for comment.

"That's wonderful! Wonderful!" Weaver said with a half-smile. "I suspected Washburn did it. I was the intended victim. Washburn wanted me out of the way. I was a man. He couldn't handle me. If he could have killed me, he would have bullied Mrs. Weaver out of all the money she had. I am positive that was the reason."

Then, Weaver's deep blue eyes glistened with tears, and his chubby face dropped as he was hit with the realization that Washburn's arrest wouldn't bring back 'Mommy.'

"I feel sorry for Washburn," he said, his voice choking on the words.

"The smile was a disturbing one," a Houston correspondent wrote in his notebook as Weaver walked away. "Sorrow for his slain wife still looked out of his somber [blue] eyes, still tinged his voice. There is no bitterness in Harry Weaver's heart, although he is a lonely, tragic figure."

Weaver may not have had any bitterness, but his lawyers sure did. Attorney Earl Smith made it a point to tell the reporter that "during the dark days when he was described as the number one suspect" the broken man was consoled by the hundreds of letters from friends and supporters across the country.

"They were letters written by people who knew that Harry Weaver couldn't have killed his wife," Smith said. "This has been a terrible ordeal for the man." Weaver's attorney then remarked that he "hoped" District Attorney Stokes would make a public apology to his client.

But the crotchety, short-fused Stokes would do no such thing. Instead, he developed a case of amnesia, and swam backwards like a crawfish. It began late Friday night, after he had read the affidavits and before Washburn was arrested, when he answered a *Houston Post* reporter's question about Harry Weaver's suspect status with the snide remark, "Weaver named himself as the number one suspect. We consider him a suspect—not the number one suspect."

Weaver named himself the number one suspect because Stokes had named him the Number 1 suspect—on Tuesday. Stokes' sudden reversal was published in the Saturday morning edition of the *Houston Post*. They were too late to get the scoop on Washburn's arrest, which went to the *Chronicle*, an afternoon paper. Stokes' attempt to rewrite history pissed-off the *Post*, which called him "the suspect switching District Attorney," the following day.

The *Houston Chronicle* called him out as well. "Stokes, reminded by a reporter that he had named Weaver as the key suspect in the presence of three other newsmen, replied: 'I said at the time that we had two suspects, and that Weaver was one of them.'"

Not true. His exact quote from Tuesday, published by several different sources, was, "I told him in front of his lawyer that he is the number one suspect."

In spite of this, Stokes did make it clear to reporters that not only was Harry Weaver cleared from suspicion, he was the intended victim.

"It was a mistake killing, no doubt about it," Stokes said. "There are two more [people] we have to get before this is wrapped up."

"Do the charges filed against Washburn and Heninger clear Weaver as a suspect?" a reporter asked when the group was in the Tom Green County Courthouse.

"Yes," Stokes said in flat tone.

"Completely?"

"I'm not speaking for my office, but in my mind, it does," Stokes answered. When pressed further on the Weaver issues, Stokes got "piqued," told reporters to draw their own conclusions, and abruptly ended the press conference.

Although Heninger never should have been arrested in the first place, Stokes was more or less right when he said there were still two more people they had "to get." When Washburn was arrested that Saturday, they only knew about twenty-five percent of the facts. They were still trying to figure out who planted the bomb, how, and when. Did it happen in Houston, or was it done in San Angelo? It would take another ten days for the entire story to unravel.

The Big Con

IT WAS A STORY THAT BEGAN ten months earlier. By March of 1954, Washburn's wholesale appliance business was going bankrupt and he was $114,000 in the red. Since gaining full custody of his two children the year before, he was starting to realize that his gamble wasn't paying off like he thought it would. And the manipulation tactics that used to work on Helen Harris Weaver weren't having the same effect. She may have sent him a check here and there, but it wasn't like it the old days—before his wife left him. By early 1954, he had come to understand that this new Helen, the resolute Helen, wasn't going to pay out like the old Helen who he described as "a soft touch." It was as if she was fortified by something or someone, and he had a good idea who was doing the fortifying: Harry Weaver.

If he got rid of Harry Weaver, Washburn estimated that a scared and intimidated Helen would pay him off with $20,000 in two weeks and $100,000 by the end of the year. But it wasn't just about the money, it was also about revenge. Although Weaver had introduced him to Little Helen, he ruined it with his meddling and wouldn't make his stepdaughter come back to him. Then, he double-crossed him by going to police on top of breaking his promise to pay him $500 every month. And Harry Weaver was the reason why his custody scheme had backfired on him. A check here and there wasn't enough. He had the kids. *Her* grandkids. Helen should be sending him a fat check every damn month.

But she wasn't.

Get rid of Harry Weaver, and he could keep his lifestyle. However, because of that whole messy business back in '51, he knew the cops would suspect him. He couldn't do it. He would have to get someone else to do it, and in March of 1954, Harry Leonard Washburn started looking for someone to go to San Angelo and kill Harry Weaver.

In the last days of that month, he called his old friend, Ray Fife, and invited him to come over to his fancy house in his fancy neighborhood. Although their friendship went back twenty-five years, Fife hadn't seen or spoke to Washburn in nearly ten years. The down-on-his luck taxi driver gladly accepted. After they "talked over old times," Washburn got right to the point.

"He [said] had a party he wanted me to kill," Fife later told Detective Thompson. "He said the party was Mr. Harry E. Weaver."

Taken aback, Fife said, "I don't do things like that, Harry."

"Well, if you don't do it, how about getting me someone to do it?"

"Well, I'll look around," Fife replied half-heartedly.

On the third day after their conversation, Washburn went looking for Fife to see if he had found a killer.

Yes, he found one. On April 1, the most appropriate day of all, Fife introduced Washburn to forty-five-year-old John McKinnon, a down-on-his-luck unemployed heating and air conditioning repairman. Or, maybe he worked in construction. Or, he was a cabinetmaker. His occupation seemed to change with every news story. But what is known about him is that in April 1954, McKinnon was broke and living with Carl and Adela Heninger. Ten years younger than her husband, Adela was an attractive, muscled young woman with dark, curly hair who recently ended a career as a professional wrestler known to her fans as "Nature Girl."

Fife introduced McKinnon to Washburn in front of the *Houston Chronicle* building. "Harry here has a deal for the two of us," Fife told his friend.

"What do you mean by deal?" McKinnon asked.

"I want you to knock off a man by the name of Harry Weaver who lives in San Angelo," Washburn said. He and McKinnon left Fife and continued walking, with Washburn doing most of the talking.

The next day, Fife and McKinnon met at The Princess, a Houston hamburger joint. There, they discussed how they were going milk Harry Washburn like a cow. "I knew all the time we would not do it," Fife later said.

Karma.

Two days later, the trio met again. Fife was now 'on the job,' or so Washburn thought. He told his contract killing team that with Harry Weaver out of the way, his "children would receive $20,000," and that he (Washburn) could spend the money as he pleased. He promised both men $5,000 when the job was done.

"He said if I listened to him, I'd be driving a Cadillac," McKinnon told authorities.

Washburn met up with the pair again in mid-April and handed them the keys to a rental car, $450[18] in cash for expenses and an order to kill Weaver.

Instead of going to San Angelo, the thrill-seeking duo went on a sixteen-day drinking and partying spree with stops in Del Rio, Texas, and Nuevo Laredo, Mexico, where they spent Washburn's money on gambling, drinking, and prostitutes. They did get down to business when they struck-up a conversation with a Mexican cabinetmaker who said a pistolero could be hired for $1,500. On their return trip to Houston, they partied in the gulf shore city of Galveston until they ran out of money.

When they got home on May 3, McKinnon told Washburn they were unable to get to Weaver "because too many people were around every time they saw him." Washburn "swallowed the story," with some difficulty. Then, Fife handed over the keys to a rental car that had 2,430 more miles on it then it did when they left town. If they had driven from Houston to New York City, they still would need to drive another 800 miles to put the same number of miles on the car.

When Washburn returned the vehicle, he couldn't or wouldn't pay the entire bill. Rental car employee Vernon Thompson was reprimanded by his boss, Walter Cruse, for renting the car to a loser. Cruse later said the final payment had to be settled "off the books," and Washburn was put on the company's blacklist.

---

[18] The 2016 equivalent of $4,020. One dollar in 1955 is the equivalent of nine dollars in 2016.

In his affidavit to police, McKinnon said, "We never went close to Weaver. We didn't intend to do any murder. We were just carrying Washburn along for his money. We figured we had a good live sucker."

Two days after they returned to Houston, McKinnon continued, Washburn ordered them to meet him at 5:30 in the morning at the corner of Post Oak Road and Memorial Drive. When they got there, Washburn told them to follow him.

Pulling his car some fifty yards off the road, he opened the trunk and handed Fife and McKinnon a double-barreled shotgun, a .22 caliber pistol, and a knife.

"Get him this time. Here's the artillery," Washburn ordered.

Then, he opened his wallet and handed over $90 in cash and told McKinnon, who was to be the actual triggerman, to use both the shotgun and pistol, "and then cut his throat to make damn sure he was dead."

After leaving the guns at Heninger's apartment, the undeadly duo took a bus to San Antonio, where they rented a hotel room and watched the Yankees versus Washington baseball game on television. The next day, Fife and McKinnon took another bus to San Angelo where they again rented a hotel room, took a long nap, went to a movie, and telephoned Washburn to inform him they couldn't get to Weaver because the weather was bad, and it was raining too hard, and there were too many people at the ranch. Then, because they had nothing to lose by asking, they told Washburn they needed him to Western Union $40 to San Antonio where they were headed. He sent it, and they spent it. McKinnon kept the San Angelo bus ticket to prove to Washburn they'd been there.

When they got back to Houston, they learned that Carl's attractive wife, Adela, needed $10 to buy clothes for her new job outside of the pervert-infested female wrestling circuit. McKinnon, living there at the time with his wife, gave the shotgun to Carl who pawned it. Working as a barmaid, Adela got her new clothes and by then, she had also gotten to know Harry Leonard Washburn.

The following month, June 1954, Washburn was desperate to get the job done. He had already filed for bankruptcy on his appliance business and needed Mrs. Weaver's money if he was going to keep the lifestyle he'd grown accustomed to. And the kids. Them too.

For the third and final "mission," Washburn talked Heninger into loaning out his car for the trip to San Angelo. Fife and McKinnon were given cash and guns and told to call him from Del Rio when Harry Weaver was dead. Details about this trip are unclear, but the opportunistic playboys who outsmarted a master manipulator knew it was their last excursion. Together, with Adela and Carl, the four went on a little vacation to Galveston, and then on to Del Rio, where McKinnon said he placed a collect call to Washburn's home, but he was not there at the time.

When Fife got back to Houston, he said he told Washburn "he had better forget about it."

"I already have," Washburn replied in a flat tone.

That wasn't true, of course. In April, while Fife and McKinnon were off gallivanting all over Texas and Mexico racking up the miles in a rented car, Washburn was also seducing Adela Heninger: to kill, not for sex. Money was sexier then sex.

Washburn went to the bar where she worked and told her that he would receive $20,000 in ten days if Weaver were killed.

"Weaver is a hard touch. Mrs. Weaver is a soft touch," Washburn told her. "If I can get rid of Weaver, his wife would pay-off to keep her family from harm."

But the $20,000 was just the beginning. "He had an overall sum of $100,000 in mind in the extortion-after-murder," Adela later told police.

Adela "Nature Girl" Heninger gives her statement to Houston Detective Henry Thompson.

Washburn's master plan was for Adela to use her feminine charms to lure Weaver to Houston, where he or one of his hapless hitmen could shoot him. Feeling the sociopathic style pressure Washburn was known to possess, Adela relented to Washburn's persistent demands and telephoned Weaver at his ranch.[19] According to her statement to police, Weaver refused

---

[19] Cox wrote in his magazine article that Adela, at Washburn's suggestion, telephone Weaver and tell him that she was "a young divorcee looking for a good time." Adela later said in court that she never got around to making that phone call by herself. It was only after Washburn insisted and stood next to her, that she finally called Weaver.

to travel to Houston to see her, but agreed to become her pen pal.

After failing to get him to come to Houston, Washburn then proposed that Adela engage Weaver about his gun-collecting hobby, and suggest to him that he invite her up to the ranch to show her how to shoot a rifle. Since Weaver wouldn't come to Houston, the killer would have to go *Butterfield Peak Lodge*.

"The plot, as Washburn outlined it to [Adela], was this: She would go to the Weaver ranch on the pretext of seeing Weaver's gun collection. She was to lure him into the yard to try some of the guns in target practice and then 'accidentally' shoot him," Cox explained in his magazine article.

She refused.

Prior to her telephone call, Washburn had given her a piece of scrap paper with Weaver's name and telephone number scribbled on it. She later turned this over to police.

Hers, Fife's, and McKinnon's statements were enough to get Washburn arrested, but since they weren't actually connected to the bomb that killed Helen Weaver, investigators didn't have all the pieces to the puzzle when Washburn was arrested. They did, however, tell police where to look for those pieces, which then led to the arrest of the last member of Washburn's motley crew of down-and-outers and no-kill contract-killers. His name was Andrew Nelson and he was a career criminal with the requisite lantern jaw, bushy eyebrows, boxer's nose, and deeply lined face that made him look-like "Bad Man Number Three" out of Hollywood central casting.

And by the time he was done talking, he had painted Washburn's hand red.

His incredible story took police on a trail that ran from Houston to San Angelo and back again with evidence and witnesses scattered in between to fill in all the gaps. When they had it all figured out, the evidence against Washburn was so overwhelming, his legendary lawyer quit the case.

According to Nelson, Washburn contacted him in April 1954—the same month he was talking to Fife, McKinnon, and Adela Heninger—to inquire, "if he knew of anyone he could get to kill a man," a court document reported. Nelson replied, "he didn't know of anyone since he had been out of contact with the criminal element for several years by then."

Four months later, in August, Washburn hinted to Nelson that he wanted him to do the job. "I want a man in West Texas killed," Nelson quoted him as saying. Although he never gave Fife and McKinnon an explanation for why he wanted Harry Weaver dead, he told Nelson that he blamed the man for breaking up his family and for ruining his appliance business.

Nelson said he wasn't interested.

But murder wasn't the only thing Washburn found useful in Nelson. In desperate need of money, Washburn arranged to have his friend burglarize the home of his neighbor, the young doctor and his wife, while Washburn served them dinner at his house. A 1959 article in *Master Detective* magazine was one of the few periodicals to reveal this insight into Washburn's deteriorating financial situation by the Fall of 1954.

"This burglary," Nelson said, "was set up by Washburn."

Never afraid to bite the hands that fed him, the couple had helped Washburn out financially in the past. The young doctor's wife was also the same one he telephoned to look after his children the night he was arrested.

"While they were dining there [on the evening of October 5, 1954], Nelson was looting their home," Pat Clausen wrote in his article. "This statement received curious corroboration when the doctor's wife (later) recognized as her own a purse which Mrs. Nelson was carrying. The $42 handbag had been stolen the night she and her husband dined with Washburn. Nelson admitted giving the bag to his wife as a gift."

Always persistent, always pushing toward his goal of turning the money tap back on, Washburn contacted Nelson again in November, four days after he bailed the forty-five-year-old out of jail for some unspecified offense. He offered him the same deal he offered Fife, McKinnon, and 'Nature Girl': $10,000.

"[He wanted me] to go out to Robert Lee and shoot a man named Weaver on his ranch home at his ranch house," Nelson later told a prosecutor.

Andrew Nelson

Again, he refused.

Washburn didn't give up. On December 29, he telephoned Nelson to inquire if he knew where he could get some "nitrogel or dynamite."

Nelson didn't know.

Without Nelson's help, Washburn found a supplier in Rosenberg, Texas, thirty-three miles southwest of Houston. On January 13, he again called Nelson and "asked him if he wanted to go for a ride." Washburn didn't explain their destination or purpose until Nelson was in the car.

By this time, Washburn had sunk low enough to resort to check fraud. "Washburn had been 'kiting' checks at Houston markets for some weeks before Mrs. Weaver was killed," Clausen wrote. "He would cash a check at one market and when it bounced, he would cash a check at another market to pay it off."

With some of this money, they drove to Rosenberg that Thursday morning and stopped at a combination service station and supply store.

"Is this the place that sells dynamite?" Washburn brazenly asked an attendant.

No, it wasn't, the young man answered. He wanted the Southern Sale and Transportation Company, and directed the two men in the 1952 black and red trim Ford on how to get there, he later recalled to investigators.

At that store, a twenty-six-year-old employee said he sold a case of one-hundred sticks of dynamite, fifty blasting caps, and copper wire to two men he later identified as Washburn and Nelson. The sales clerk said he had to drive five miles out-of-town to the store's magazine to get the dynamite. When he returned, the two were parked across the street at the local Dairy Queen. He loaded the dynamite in the trunk of their 1952 or 1953 black and red Ford.

At the Dairy Queen, waitress Billie Rogers recalled serving them hot dogs. They were there for more than an hour.

"He was real friendly," she said of Washburn. "Bought a hot dog and put chili sauce on it. He smeared some of the sauce on his hands and it tickled me the way he joked about it. 'This is the bestest messiest hot dog I ever ate,' is what he said."

She also remembered the car he was in: a black and red Ford.

Harry L. Washburn. Bless his heart[20]. He just had to make a memorable impression wherever he went.

Back in Houston, Nelson then said they experimented with the dynamite in an undeveloped, wooded area near Washburn's home. After several unsuccessful attempts, they eventually were able to explode seven or eight blasting caps wired to the car's generator.

Nelson then described to the officers how Washburn had taken ten dynamite caps, one stick of dynamite and hooked the explosive to the car's generator with sixty-feet of wire.

"He started the ignition of his car and the dynamite blew up," Nelson said. "By this time, I figured he wanted the dynamite for something else than blowing up tree stumps like he told me earlier."

When investigators went to the area, they found the blast site, as well as copper wire Washburn had carelessly left behind. They also spoke with a seventy-five-year-old man who lived nearby in a small cabin. During the approximate time Nelson said they were there, he recalled seeing two men near a black and red car with the hood up while he was out gathering firewood. He greeted Washburn, shook hands with him and asked if they were having car trouble. When told everything was fine and they were just out squirrel hunting, the elderly man left.

Shortly after he returned to his home, he heard a loud noise, "like a big firecracker."

The wire at the test site was consistent with wire found inside Washburn's garage, as well as the wire found near Mrs. Weaver's 1954 Chevrolet.

---

[20] In Texas, "Bless his/her heart," is a well-known, passive-aggressive phrase used to insult someone.

Two days later, on January 15, Washburn advanced the car bomb idea to his old hitman he still believed in, John McKinnon.

He turned him down flat.

"I'll do it myself then," Washburn snapped.

On the morning of January 18, Washburn telephoned Nelson and asked if he and his wife would babysit his children while he went on a date later that day. Nelson agreed and he and his wife were picked-up by Washburn and taken to his house. He last saw Washburn driving away at two o'clock that afternoon. Not long after he left, the milkman came by the house to collect on Washburn's bill. Vernon Brady later identified Nelson as the man who answered the door, and paid him $25 in cash. He then left a quart of chocolate milk for Washburn's children as a gift. Nelson's wife confirmed her husband's account and added that she later cooked supper for the children, her husband, and herself, and then settled into a long night waiting for Washburn to come home.

The distance between Houston and San Angelo traveling the highways of that era is approximately 400 miles. Depending on how fast he was driving, if Washburn left Houston sometime after two o'clock, he would have made it to San Angelo between nine and ten that night. According to one witness, that's likely when Washburn reached his destination.

A man, similar in appearance to Washburn and driving a black and red Ford with out-of-county license plates, was seen at a San Angelo gas station between 9:30 and 10:00 p.m. Sgt. Bobby Clayton, an airman on the local air force base working part-time as an attendant, told authorities that the gentleman wasn't interested in full service.

"Don't bother with the windshield," he told Clayton. "I'm in a hurry."

Although Clayton wouldn't make a positive identification, he said Washburn "resembled" the individual who purchased gasoline that night.

Not long after the man drove off, Henry Lamb was closing-up his service station across town. A street light on the corner gave a relatively clear view into the Harris home's driveway, and when he locked up at ten o'clock that night, he saw no one or nothing suspicious. He may not have seen a man underneath Mrs. Weaver's car, but he also said he never saw her or her husband arrive home that night either.

Although Lamb may not have seen Washburn, and the gas station attendant couldn't positively identify him, there was one person that night who did and could.

To make it home in time to take his children to school, Washburn had to drive as fast as he possibly could. In 1955, without an interstate, all the main roads back to Houston were two lane highways that cut through the center of every city that lay in between. Washburn was just seventy miles from Houston when fate intervened and evidence was produced that fractured his alibi.

He ran a red light in Columbus City and got a ticket.

Poor Washburn. Bless his heart. He was so hell-bent on killing Harry Weaver he never thought about how to cover his tracks.

Deputy Sheriff E.V. Ginn gave him the ticket at four o'clock on the morning of January 19. "He was headed west toward Houston when I chased him down," Ginn told investigators on February 3, 1955. I was going seventy-five or eighty miles-an-hour when I stopped him."

When Washburn finally pulled-over, they were outside city limits, and Ginn couldn't issue him a ticket for speeding, the deputy explained. He did, however, cite him for running the red light. He told the man from Houston that he could return later to Columbus City and face the judge in traffic court, or he could pay the five-dollar fine right there. Washburn paid, and signed his name to a receipt.

His real name.

Bless his heart. The receipt was later presented to investigators, and handwriting experts matched the signature to Washburn.

But since Harry L. Washburn was Harry L. Washburn, he had to dig his own grave deeper that day. Nelson told police he next saw Washburn at seven o'clock that morning wearing his pajamas, sitting on the side of his bed. He then took his children to school, and Mrs. Nelson home.

Washburn returned to his house, picked-up Nelson, and was driving around Houston when they heard a radio news report Mrs. Helen Weaver had been killed by a car bomb.

"My God! That's the wrong one," Washburn screamed.

"Harry, is that your job?" Nelson asked.

"Yes."

"How did you do it?"

"I took a dozen sticks of dynamite and put it in a sack and put on the back of the motor," Washburn answered.

"Harry, that's murder, you better play it cool," Nelson replied.

"I better get me a job digging ditches," Washburn said.

After Fife, McKinnon, Heninger, his soon-to-be ex-wife Adela, and Nelson came forward, the authorities found the witnesses in Rosenberg, San Angelo, Columbus City, and in Houston where a barber came forward to say he overheard Fife, McKinnon, and Washburn discussing their plans to kill Harry Weaver. His claim was in addition to the milkman, the elderly cabin dweller, Mrs. Nelson, and even Washburn's own children, who confirmed the Nelsons had spent the night at their house. They also recovered the shotgun and .22 caliber pistol from two different pawn shops, and matched the serial numbers to store records where Washburn had purchased the weapons and signed his name. His real name. They also found he had used his real name when he sent Fife and McKinnon the $40 money order by Western Union to San Antonio, which corroborated their account.

On the same day newspapers reported Nelson was talking to police, Percy Foreman announced he was quitting the case. His client was indigent and faced an impressive array of witnesses and scientific evidence that was "appallingly conclusive," Clausen wrote in his 1959 crime magazine article. But Foreman being Foreman exited with a good excuse.

"If the case were tried in Houston, I would take it," he told reporters on February 3. "But I can't take the time away from my practice for an extended trial in San Angelo."

He then publicly attacked the man-of-the-hour and principal witness against Washburn, Andrew Nelson. He pointed to Nelson's long rap sheet, the conspiracy to murder charges he was facing, and declared the man was lying in order to gain his freedom and get his hands on the reward money.

"Every motive of greed and gain—cash and liberty—is at stake, and I know of no more compelling reason for false testimony," Foreman told reporters. "A man faced with a life term will seek to curry favor with the law—to trade someone else's liberty for his own."

He was wrong about everything in his statement except for one thing: Nelson's past was an issue and did become a huge problem for the prosecution who mishandled him completely. Nelson's twenty-eight-year criminal record dated back to 1927 and revealed he had served time for armed robbery, embezzlement, auto theft, and post office burglary on twelve convictions. In 1934, Nelson was sentenced to life-in-prison as a habitual criminal on the armed robbery charge. He was given a conditional parole on July 5, 1944, by then Governor Coke Stevenson.

When police arrested him on February 2, it was with a warrant for the $7,400 burglary of a supermarket. That charge alone revoked his conditional parole and sent him back to prison for life in May 1955. By then, he was indicted, along with Washburn, for murder with malice, conspiracy to commit murder, and aiding in the commission of a murder. Both pleaded not guilty.

"I think this is just another way to put the pressure on me to testify against Washburn in the Weaver case," Nelson said on May 17 when he was hauled back to prison. "All of this will come out and finally show who the guilty parties are."

His wife was also a reluctant witness and would soon leave town.

Although Washburn's trial was scheduled to begin on April 25 in San Angelo, the prosecution sought a continuance when Adela, or "Nature Girl" as the newspapers preferred to call her, was stalled from testifying because she was six months pregnant with her future husband's baby and living in Illinois. The judge denied that request, but was forced to grant one for a different reason.

The day before the trial was to begin, Stokes was admitted to the hospital with severe stomach cramps. "...Stokes, a World War II Navy veteran who had suffered with a stomach ulcer since his service days, was stricken...and admitted to the hospital," Bill Cox explained in his 1965 article[21]. "A doctor said he would be unable to participate in the trial."

The trial was postponed until his condition improved. But when their second attempt at prosecution came in September, more witnesses had gone missing, including Adela's ex-husband, Carl Heninger, and Andrew's wife, Katherine, also known as Alice Kate McCoy. Ten days before the trial was to start, she was arrested in Roswell, New Mexico, on a fugitive warrant for perjury. Somewhere in between, she gave different accounts of when she looked after the Washburn children while their father was making a midnight run to San Angelo.

---

[21] *Master Detective* magazine, one of the oldest and most respected crime magazines of a bygone era, published two different articles about the Washburn/Weaver case: one by Pat Clausen in 1959, and another, more thorough account in 1965 ,by writer Bill Cox. See Sources, Chapter Seven, for more information.

However, her arrest didn't matter because the second attempt to prosecute Washburn was also doomed.

Out of a potential pool of 250 prospective jurors, only nine thought to be impartial were seated. After questioning another eighty-two Tom Green County residents, the prosecution and the defense couldn't find the last three jurors they needed.[22] Stokes found a way out when he made the unusual decision to have the trial moved to Waco, in McClennan County. There, District Attorney Tom Moore said he read about the six-day selection process in newspapers and noted to himself that it was Stokes who was turning down most of the potential jurors. He telephoned his colleague and pitched an offer to move the trial to his 54th District. Stokes agreed.

"I never knew a DA that didn't seek and enjoy publicity and I was one of them," Moore said in an undated internet video posted on Vimeo.com. "And I said [to Stokes over the telephone] 'you wanna send that case down here?' He said, 'I'll try.' And he did."

Washburn's court-appointed defense attorneys, C.S. Farmer, Clifton Tupper, and Clyde Vinson argued against it, claiming their client, who was denied bail, had been in jail long enough. The judge ruled in Stokes' favor, and after a week of wrangling back and forth with McClennan County District Attorney Tom Moore, the trial was scheduled to begin Monday, December 5, in Waco. Although it was his case, Stokes was second chair. Not only had he successfully moved the trial, he also shifted his burden.

And in Waco, the second biggest development of the entire case was made public on Tuesday, December 6, when local television station KWTX broadcast the proceedings live to a local audience for the first time in United States history. Presiding Judge Drummond W. Bartlett said he agreed to the request by news director Bill Stinson because "telecasting is

---

[22] If successful, it would have been the first time in county history a trial included female jurors.

the coming thing and TV should be allowed in courtrooms provided it does not distract from court proceedings."

The arrangement, which was agreed to by prosecutors and defense attorneys, came with some conditions: that the station only use one camera, and that it be placed out-of-sight from the jurors. He also forbade KWTX from running commercials during its live broadcast—he didn't want them profiting from such a controversial event. Stinson eagerly agreed and the result was non-stop, unedited, gavel-to-gavel coverage, in which they didn't even pause for station identification during the trial.

Waco residents were glued to their television sets.

"From Dec. 6-9, 1955, as the story goes, one could have 'shot a cannon down Austin Avenue [in Waco] . . . and not hurt a soul' because the normally frenzied Christmas shoppers were all inside watching the trial," reports a 2010 online article from the *Waco Tribune*.

When asked if he objected to the camera in the courtroom, Washburn called it "a fine thing," and said, "Naw, let it go all over the world."

He had no shame.

"The only special accommodations made for the broadcasters was boosting the lighting from 50-watt bulbs to 100-watt bulbs and hiding three microphones among the furnishings: the witness stand, judge's bench and prosecutor's table," the *Tribune* continued in its 2010 report. "During the four-day trial, the station lost out of $10,000 in potential advertising revenue."

But that didn't matter to station founder and Texas broadcasting legend Milford Nelson "Buddy" Bostick. It was his idea to broadcast the trial, despite the revenue loss. On air for less than a year, the worldwide publicity of the first televised murder trial put the small Waco station in the headlines.

"It became a civics lesson for school classes and it garnered the fledgling station headlines in newspapers from New York City to London," Bostick said in a 2012 interview when he was ninety-four-years-old. "It was all over the nation: Station in Waco, Texas, broadcasts the first murder trial!"[23]

The station received hundreds of telephone calls supporting their coverage, as well as 1400 letters and postcards. Out of those, only four were against it.

The Washburn trial in Waco was the first live televised murder trial in the United States. The arrow is pointing toward Washburn. (Photo credit: Library of Congress.)

---

[23] This was the first live telecast of a murder trial. Two years before, Oklahoma City's WKY-TV, now KFOR, broadcast selected edited portions of the December 1953 trial of Billy Eugene Manley. Manley, an eighteen-year-old escapee from Missouri's infamous Boonville Reformatory, shot and killed Oklahoma State Trooper Johnnie Whittle on September 14. Manley was convicted of manslaughter and sentenced to serve sixty-five years. He was paroled in 1972.

One of those letters may have been from Georgia Supreme Court Judge William Henry Duckworth who sharply criticized the live coverage when he stated that it turned Washburn's trial into a "bull-fight," and "thwarted the essence of justice."

Judge Bartlett laughed at this criticism, and replied, "That's water off my back, just like a duck's. When Fulton used a steamboat, he was jeered, but the steamboat is accepted now. They just don't understand—if they understood how this is being handled, they wouldn't object."

As exciting as this development was to Waco viewers, they realized with the first witness that Helen Weaver's murder was both sad and horrendous. During five and one-half hours of testimony, her husband told the jurors in graphic detail what the bomb did to his wife.

"There was a terrific explosion," Weaver began. "She just had time to get to the car . . . As quickly as I could I got to a window and looked out. I saw an immense cloud of smoke like an atomic bomb . . . I rushed down the stairs."

"Did you see your wife when you got out there?" Moore asked.

"Yes. She was sunk down in the seat of the car."

"Just describe what you saw."

Weaver took a deep breath, wiped perspiration from his temple and began.

"She was leaning on one side—a dead stare on her face. Her intestines were hanging out. Her knee looked like someone had chopped it with a hatchet, little bones were showing in her ankle. She was full of holes."

Weaver paused and looked at Washburn sitting at the counsel table. "The dead stare on her face was terrible," he murmured.

"Could you tell if she was alive or dead?" Moore asked.

"I was sure she was dead."

"What was the condition of the automobile?"

"Just shattered to pieces…I haven't described all the terrible things…" Weaver said, his voice trailing off to a whisper before regaining strength. "People came running from everywhere. A man asked me what happened. I said, 'I guess a bomb exploded.'

"He said 'Do you have any idea who done it?'

"I said 'yes, my son-in-law. He threatened to kill us.'"

Weaver said an ambulance came and took his wife away. He never saw her again. She died at the hospital a few minutes after arriving.

"She was so horribly mutilated I didn't want to see her," Weaver whispered.

Washburn had no expression. His dark hair was cut short, and he had lost weight since his arrest ten months earlier.

His cohort, Andrew Nelson, didn't have much to express either. When called to testify on Wednesday, December 8, his attorney informed the judge and prosecutor that since his client was still under indictment, he had advised Nelson to plead the Fifth Amendment. Moore offered him immunity from prosecution on the spot, but it was never put in writing and Judge Bartlett never formally approved of the spontaneous deal. Nelson was smart enough not to take Moore at his word, and refused to answer any questions.

Unfortunately, Judge Bartlett allowed Moore to question Nelson in front of the jury, despite several objections from Washburn's attorneys. Since Nelson was pleading the fifth, Moore's questions were loaded with accusations for which the defense could not counter.

It was a costly mistake—one they wouldn't realize until much later.

But on the night of Friday, December 9, Moore, Stokes, and Weaver were unconcerned when they celebrated Washburn's conviction. After three hours and twenty-five minutes of deliberation, the jury filed back into the courtroom at 6:25 that evening.

"Washburn sat wide-eyed and tense during a three-minute interval after the jury first filed into the box," *The Waco News-Tribune* reported. They had neglected to fill-out the back of the jury ballots. Judge Bartlett gave them time to correct this omission and Washburn's eyes never strayed from the ten men and two women who controlled his fate.

Guilty of murder with malice: life sentence.

To the surprise of reporters, Washburn accepted the verdict with good humor, but couldn't resist taking several jabs at his adversary, Aubrey Stokes.

"I feel sure the verdict will be reversed and I will be vindicated ultimately," Washburn told a large gathering of reporters from all over the state. "The verdict is definitely a surprise."

"Aside from a few verbal shots at the Tom Green County District Attorney, Washburn expressed no bitterness at the verdict," the Waco paper reported. "He said the trial should have been conducted at San Angelo with Stokes as prosecutor."

"He's the man who originated the whole thing and if he doesn't have guts enough to try it, he shouldn't be DA," Washburn said. "I don't know whether Stokes is an attorney or not. If he is, he must have missed something in school," Washburn said.

Stokes either didn't hear him, or never replied, and the two shook hands. "See, I told you I wouldn't be mad at you," Washburn told him.

Washburn was right. The conviction was overturned by the Texas Court of Criminal Appeals on October 3, 1956. The trial judge erred when he did not formally approve the immunity from prosecution offer Moore pronounced verbally in the courtroom. Without that, there was no deal and Nelson had been wise to keep his mouth shut. When Moore was finished with Nelson, Washburn's attorneys requested that the DA's examination, which ran twenty-one pages, be excluded from jury consideration. Overruled. They then asked for a mistrial. Again, overruled.

Judge Bartlett should have considered their request to retire the jury during Moore's examination more carefully. His decision contradicted a black and white trial procedure statute, as well as case law.

Washburn's attorneys outlined the problem in their appeal.

> Appellant objected to the state asking [Nelson] any questions in the presence of the jury on the ground that it was by innuendo placing matters in the record that it could not show by him directly….
>
> Among such questions he was asked about the purchase of dynamite, while accompanied by the appellant, their testing of it by exploding a portion of it by the use of electric wires attached to an automobile, and as to electric wire picked up at the scene of the test as well as photographs showing damage to trees as a result of the test.
>
> None of the questions were answered by the witness, Nelson. Such questioning covered twenty-one pages of the statement of facts and was in detail as to names, dates, and places. By these fact-laden questions, the state was permitted to plant, in the jury's mind, full details as to how they claimed this crime was committed; and yet the only substantive evidence which they were producing was the answer of the witness who refused to answer on the ground that such answers might tend to incriminate him, which of course was no evidence at all.

And they were right. Moore appealed the ruling but lost. Washburn got a second trial, and Moore never got a second chance. Washburn's second trial was moved to Dallas, where prosecutors asked for the death sentence. This time, Nelson was compelled to testify against his old friend. "[Nelson] related he had been offered immunity by the state and threatened with pressure against any eventual parole on old sentences he was serving if he did not testify," a court filing later stated.

On June 19, 1957, Washburn was again found guilty but instead of life in prison, the jury recommended the parole-eligible ninety-nine years. With good behavior, he could get out of prison in fifteen years. Washburn, who had expected to be released on bail shortly after his 1955 arrest, and expected to be found not guilty later that December, was baffled the jury could find him guilty a second time.

"If they thought I was guilty, they should have given me the electric chair," he told newsmen. "But I really thought they were going to turn me loose. I'm still innocent of this thing. I had nothing to do with it."

And like many convicted murder defendants throughout history, Washburn claimed to know the truth; only he knew it, but other people were preventing him from telling it.

"When I get out of this, I'll tell the whole story. I wanted to testify at trial but my lawyers told me it wasn't necessary." After dramatically wiping his eyes with a handkerchief when asked about his children, the forty-one-year-old vowed, "to keep fighting."

Instead of going to prison, he sat in the Dallas jail for another eighteen months while his new attorney argued his appeal on that conviction. He lost. Petitions for a rehearing were also shot down. Twice. It was time to pay for his sins.

On January 3, 1959, Texas Ranger Ralph Rohatsch and Tom Green County Sheriff Cecil Turner were given the privilege of escorting a pudgy, pale, older-looking Washburn to the state prison in Huntsville. He was then quickly transferred to Eastham Prison, [24] a state prison farm in rural Houston County, where he was obliged to work in the fields.

Washburn's legal saga was far from over, however, and over the next fifteen years, he filed numerous appeals,

---

[24] Eastham Unit is where Clyde Barrow served time from 1930 to 1932. There, he killed an inmate who had sexually assaulted him on prior occasions. He also convinced another prisoner to chop off two of his toes to escape grueling work on the prison farm.

sentence reductions, and *habeas corpus* petitions in state and federal court. Among his many allegations were violation of his constitutional rights, witness tampering and suppression, and because they found evidence[25] in his garage. He also claimed, incorrectly, that arresting officers didn't have a warrant when they arrested him, and they later abused him while in custody.

"He said a Ranger tried to make him swallow 'conscious pills,' and sat outside his cell telling him he was going to 'Old Sparky,' the electric chair," the Associated Press reported in July 1967.

Apparently, the verbal abuse was quite traumatic to Washburn.

He was unsuccessful with every one of his court actions with one notable exception that included a twist. At one hearing, his Dallas trial judge gave time-served credit for approximately three of the four years he was incarcerated from his arrest to the day he was carted off to prison. When his lawyers tried to get the remaining year applied to his sentence, they not only lost, but the Texas Court of Criminal Appeals ruled the Dallas judge erred in granting him time served for a six-month period in 1957, between his first appeal and second trial.

But it was all math that didn't matter and paperwork that filled the file of prisoner 149130. On April 19, 1974, after serving fifteen years, three months, and sixteen days in state prison, and a total of nineteen years, two months, and twenty-one days behind bars, fifty-eight-year-old Harry Leonard Washburn was released from prison.

As a free man, Washburn remarried and relocated to rural Upshur County, two hundred miles north of Houston, and became a building contractor, the same line of work he said he

---

[25] The evidence they found was copper wire, which was consistent with copper wire found at the crime scene and in the woods where Washburn and Nelson tested the bomb.

was in just before he was arrested. According to his prison records outlined briefly in a public information disclosure sheet obtained by the author, Washburn was sent back to prison on March 28, 1978, for an unspecified parole violation. He was released one month later.

On the last day of the last year of the 1970s, Washburn suffered a fatal heart attack at his home in Gilmer. He was dead before he reached the hospital. He was sixty-three years old. He is buried in Houston National Cemetery with a flat-marker military headstone.

Epilogue

The $10,000 Reward

DISTRIBUTION OF THE HARRIS-WEAVER $10,000 reward for information leading to the arrest and conviction of Helen Harris Weaver's killer was delayed until after Washburn was sent to prison. In June 1959, Weaver's attorneys asked a federal judge to decide on the matter, and submitted a list of fifty applicants. Among those included were Houston Police Captain Cecil Priest, Detective Henry K. Thompson, and Inspector Tom Eubanks. Texas Rangers Eddie Oliver and Ralph Rohatsch also applied, as well as Andrew Nelson, John McKinnis, Adela Heninger, and Charlie Brown, the elderly property owner who witnessed Nelson and Washburn experimenting with dynamite in the woods near his home.

The fifty names were quickly cut-in half and after a long review, US District Judge Joe Ingraham announced his decision just before Christmas 1960. The reward was distributed to thirteen people and included: Detective Thompson, $2,918; John McKinnis, Ray Fife, and E.Y. Ginn, $850 each; Captain Priest, Inspector Eubanks, $450; Rangers Oliver, and Rohatsch, $450 each; Dairy Queen waitress Billie

Rogers, Andrew Nelson, pawn shop owner Charles Sobrov, $450 each; and Charles Brown, the elderly property owner, who was black, received the smallest portion, $250. The balance of $1,132 went to client attorneys. At that time, lawmen were eligible to receive reward money.

Harry E. Weaver

On December 29, 1969, Washburn's brother, Frank, filed two $3 million lawsuits each against Weaver and Percy Foreman, alleging they conspired together to set-up his brother.

"Both suits allege Weaver entered into a conspiracy against Harry L. Washburn and that Weaver and Foreman entered into an agreement under which Foreman would see that Harry L. Washburn remained in prison until after Weaver's death," read a Houston-based Associated Press report. The article further states that Frank suffered great mental, physical and emotional suffering," because of this conspiracy. Foreman laughed when he heard the news and said it was ironic since he had just received a Christmas card from his old client thanking him for his help and wishing him a Merry Christmas.

There is not another report of this lawsuit and it was apparently laughed out of court.

With this exception, Harry Weaver lived a quiet life after Washburn finally went to prison in 1959. He remarried, to a woman named Florence, and died from a stroke on April 16, 1970. He was eighty-three years old. He is buried in Houston's Forest Park Lawndale Cemetery. His death record reports Weaver was living in Houston at the time he died and that his general physician, Dr. Abbe A Ledbetter, had been attending to him since February 18, 1964. This would seem to indicate Weaver had moved to Houston just prior to that time.

Helen Harris Allen Willcockson

Washburn's second wife died on May 30, 1981, from a self-inflicted gunshot wound to the head. Her long struggle with major depression and bipolar disorder is detailed in her daughter's book, *Alchemical Inheritance*. Tess Keehn also wrote about her grandmother's murder, the fallout, her own struggles to find her way in life, and the loss of the family fortune in the 1980s. Some of the facts surrounding her grandmother's death reported in her book do not match those presented by this author, but I believe those differences are inconsequential. For more information about the Harris family, I encourage you to purchase her eBook, which is available through Google Play, Amazon and BalboaPress.com.

District Attorney Tom Moore, Jr.

Tom Moore Jr. left the prosecutor's office in 1958. Nine years later, he entered politics and served in the Texas state legislature from 1967 to 1973. He is (at the time of publication) ninety-eight years old and recently retired from the Waco firm of Giles and Giles, where he specialized in criminal defense and estate planning according to their website. The only reason I mention him, here in the Epilogue, is because of an outrageous allegation he makes in an online video stating that Harry Weaver and Harry Washburn conspired together to marry the Harris women.

Video: https://vimeo.com/41586119

"What had happened was, Harry Washburn and…Weaver were in Houston and met a wealthy widow and her daughter—the people from San Angelo—and they set out to court these ladies and *did* marry them. And Weaver, the architect, of course moved to San Angelo with mama and Washburn and daughter lived in Houston."

His bizarre claim is contradictory to the known facts. Weaver met his wife in 1936, while working on a construction job in San Antonio, where she was attending Incarnate Word College. The two were married in 1938, shortly after she graduated. The 1940 federal census reports they lived at 705 Drew Street in Houston with Helen's two daughters, Sadie, fifteen, and Helen, twelve. The Weavers did not immediately move to San Angelo, as Moore stated. Instead, they lived in Houston for approximately nine or ten years before moving to *Butterfield Peak Lodge* in Coke County, near the town of Robert Lee.

Washburn was already married in 1938 and his wife, Mickey Mae, gave birth to their daughter, Harriet Louise, on October 24 of that year. They divorced the following year and according to the 1940 US Census records, the high school dropout was "single," and working as a salesman in "retail merchandise and grocery." He lived at home with his mother and younger brother, James.

For Moore's statement to be true, the two men conspired together for Washburn to marry Little Helen when she was just ten or eleven years old in 1938. There is no documented evidence that Washburn and Little Helen knew each other until they were introduced by Weaver in 1946. According to Weaver's testimony, and information provided by Tess Keehn in her book, *Alchemical Inheritance*, Weaver and Washburn first met after Washburn left the military and opened a photography studio in a building Weaver was either renovating, or where his architectural firm was located.

I strongly disagree with Moore's statement. The author attempted to interview Moore by inquiring through his former law firm, Giles and Giles. My request was forwarded to Tom's personal email account, which is monitored now by his wife, Robbie, a generous and lovely woman, who agreed to pass along my questions about those statements to her husband. Unfortunately, he was unable to remember anything related to what he said on that video, or the events that led him to make that statement.

In spite of my disagreement with Tom Moore on this issue, it is worth noting that he is well thought of in Waco, where he volunteered with the Meals on Wheels program for more than a decade, and never bothered to bill his clients. "He says if people are going to pay, they will pay," his wife Robbie told a *Waco Herald-Press* reporter in 2009. Only forty-percent of them ever paid for his services, the article states. He also distinguished himself as a state representative and member of the "Dirty Thirty," which fought against powerful and corrupt state politicians. You can read more about Tom Moore Jr. on Wikipedia.

Aubrey Stokes

Stokes left public office and together with local attorney Tom Webb, entered private practice specializing in personal injury cases under the banner Webb & Stokes. Today, that law firm is now known as Webb, Stokes & Sparks. Their website is online. Dog bite cases are one of their specialties. Aubrey Stokes died in 1990 at the age of sixty-nine. Some people theorize that Stokes suspected Washburn from the beginning, but publicly cast guilt toward Weaver to put the real killer at ease. The author disagrees with this theory.

Andrew Nelson

Andrew Nelson's wife, Katherine, died in her Dallas hotel room on June 30, 1957, just six-days after her husband testified against Washburn. Her parole from prison, where she was serving time on perjury charges, occurred just days before the trial began. It is unclear if her parole and her husband's testimony are related. On the night she died, the forty-year-old telephoned the front desk from her room to complain that she could not breathe. Hotel employees called for an ambulance but she died before she could reach the hospital. An autopsy revealed she died from a collapsed lung. Her husband was in the San Angelo jail at the time, waiting to be escorted back to prison. He was released from prison in 1961 and died from a heart attack in September 1962.

Adela "Nature Girl" Heninger Gidley

At the time of her husband's arrest on January 28, 1955, Adela and Carl were already separated and she would soon become pregnant with her new boyfriend's baby. Her pregnancy prevented her from appearing at both of Stokes' 1955 trial attempts in San Angelo. She went on to testify during the December Waco trial, and the 1957 trial in Dallas. Newspapers loved to refer to her as a "Nature Girl," a moniker they played up and one that she disliked. By the time of the Dallas trial, Adela and her new husband, Morris Gidley, had moved to Denver. They lived there with her daughter from her first marriage, her second daughter born in 1955, and her son, Morris Junior, born six weeks before Washburn's second trial. She died on September 13, 2001, just 110 days after her husband passed away. The two are buried in Mount Lindo Cemetery, Morris, Colorado. Her son, Morris Junior, died in 1987 at the age of thirty.

On Findagrave.com, a photograph of the couple's tombstone states they were married on October 11, 1953. I really don't know what to make of that. Considering the numerous sources I reviewed that reported she was married but separated from Carl Heninger in 1955, I don't see how this could be accurate. However, out of consideration for the family, I think it is best to leave this discrepancy alone.

Adela's first husband, Carlton, died from a heart attack on October 25, 1975, at the age of sixty-two. At the time, he was survived by his wife, Vivian. He is buried in Houston.

Butterfield Peak Lodge

Butterfield Peak Lodge is still in the family and is much the same now as it was in 1955.

"Butterfield Peak Lodge, San Angelo, Texas, 6/30/48"

Chapter Eight: The Stiletto Slayer of Milwaukee, 1966

Milwaukee, Wisconsin
November 11, 1966

IT ALL HAPPENED SO FAST.

Walking to school just after eight-o'clock in the morning, eleven-year-old Kathleen Dreyer froze in horror as a young man, driving a black, 1957 Chevy, slammed on the brakes, jumped out and grabbed her before she could understand what was happening. With his gloved hand over her mouth, he dragged her thirty-feet down an alley to an unpaved driveway where, after a brief struggle, he stabbed her in the back with a seven-inch stiletto.

She screamed as loud as she could and then she screamed again and again.

Scared, the man ran back to his car, hit the gas, and sped past her down the paved alley in the 4800 block of North 36th Street.

Everyone in Milwaukee knew this was going to happen. They didn't know when and they didn't know who, but they knew it was going to happen. Again. This was the guy who almost killed a married mother of four while she was on her way to work. This was the guy who had knifed, molested, and killed two young females over the last two months—one of them a ten-year-old girl. But those murders happened at night, in dark corners, and unseen places.

Stabbing little Kathy Dreyer on a residential street with a school crossing guard and neighbors nearby was just—stupid. Although it was a vicious wound, she would live. She got a good look at the short man with dark hair and thick black glasses. He was in his early twenties and wore a dark jacket and a sweater with a large, orange-colored "G" on the front.

The last two-months were a time of fear in Milwaukee. Children were being kept indoors at night. Women were taking special precautions. People carried self-defense weapons and walked in groups whenever possible. The entire Milwaukee police force worked overtime on the case, and even the fire department got involved. The only thing they had to go on was a vague description from a Catholic nun, who saw a shadowy figure walking away. In spite of all their efforts, until November 11, 1966, they didn't have a single clue that would lead them to the stiletto slayer of Milwaukee.

But with what Kathy and the other witnesses gave them that morning, they now had enough to find him. It was a lot to go on. News of the incident flashed across police band radios and then spread to local radio stations throughout the city, suburbs, and county. Off-duty cops were called in and road blocks went up. The 1957 Chevy was the most iconic car in American history. Hell, everyone knew what a black '57 Chevy looked like and if necessary, they would stop every damn one of them.

The whole city was on alert that day. Somebody would see him. Somebody would find him. He wasn't going to get away. They were finally going to get him. They were finally going to get that son of a bitch.

THE STILETTO SLAYER'S REIGN OF terror was thought to have begun on Thursday, September 1, 1966. That morning, thirty-four-year-old Mary Troyer was driving from her home in Oak Creek[1] to her job in west Milwaukee, when another motorist drove next to her and frantically waved for her to pullover. Concerned, she slowed down to a stop along the median near the 7400 block of South 27th Street and watched as the young man, driving a grey, 1956 Chevrolet, parked in front of her car. When he got out, she could hear him shouting something about sparks coming from underneath her vehicle. After getting out to look for herself, the man ran up and began stabbing her with a knife. When she started screaming, he slashed her throat, chest, and scalp. And just as quickly as the attack had begun, he got back into his car and drove away.

A passing truck driver came to her aid. He saw her assailant drive off and gave police a description of him, his car, and three letters and numbers from his license plate. Mary Troyer was taken to a nearby hospital where her wounds were treated. She remained there for nearly two weeks. When she was able to speak with Oak Creek police, she told them she didn't know the man, had never seen him before, and had no idea what his motive might be or why he had targeted her.

She described her attacker as a dark-haired man in his early twenties who was slender and stood about five-foot ten-inches tall. In spite of the description of the car and partial license plate number, detectives were unable to match them to a grey, 1956 Chevrolet. Police in Milwaukee, and other nearby cities, were asked to be on the lookout for a car driven by a man who fit the description given by Mrs. Troyer. For days, police in Oak Creek, with a population 10,000 at the time, watched for '56 Chevys and scanned license plates. However, by the time they found their first suspect, another victim would be found—dead.

At approximately 11:30 p.m. on September 3, Milwaukee police were notified that ten-year-old Julia Beckwith was missing. That Saturday night was the wedding anniversary of her parents, Alice and Gordon Beckwith. At 8:30, the couple

---

[1] Oak Creek is a suburb just south of Milwaukee.

left their nine children, ranging in age from eighteen-months to sixteen-years-old, at home so they could celebrate with dinner at a nice restaurant. When they returned to their apartment at 920 North 16th Street at 10:15, everything seemed fine. But at eleven, one of the older children told her parents that at nine-o'clock, she had asked Julia to ride her bicycle to a friend's house on West Michigan Street and return with a blouse she had left there. Julia agreed and she was last seen pedaling away on her bicycle. She had not returned.

Alarmed, the father, with two of Julia's oldest sisters and one of their friends, went looking for the ten-year-old. He first went to the duplex house at 2134 West Michigan but was told Julia left at 9:20 with the blouse. Somewhere within those ten blocks between the two residences, his little girl had disappeared.

While the father was speaking with the family at the duplex and other residents in the area, Julia's sisters traveled the same route they believed she would have taken. They walked the entire ten blocks and when they were less than 300 feet from the home where Julia had gone, they found her bicycle leaning against a tree in front of an empty lot at 2104 West Michigan. Nearby, on the ground, was the blouse.

The girls pushed the bicycle home where they met their father. A bicycle without Julia only ratcheted up the family's anxiety. It didn't make sense. Julia was a sensible girl. She should have been home by now. She wasn't the type to stay out.

At 11:30, Gordon Beckwith called the police.

When several patrolmen arrived at the Beckwith home, they went back over the same route Julia's sisters had taken. The girls showed them the empty lot where they found the bicycle. While questioning area residents, officers learned that at approximately 9:30 that night, they heard the squealing tires of a car slamming on the brakes. In the glare of its headlights, they could see a child's bicycle in the middle of the street. The driver got out, picked the bicycle up, carried it over to the empty lot, set it up by a tree, then got back in his car and drove away. They were positive, they told officers, that he was alone and had not taken a little girl back to his car, described as a green, 1965 Ford.

Their accounts of this incident directed everyone's attention to the lot. It was a strange piece of land; wild, untamed, and out of place in an urban environment. Narrow but long, it featured a mound that rose up about five feet from the paved driveway of a three-story apartment building to the west, and sloped down to the east, where it bordered an alley adjacent to an old, two-story rooming-house. The abandoned plot stretched back for three-fourths of the block.[2] Two sets of cement steps, divided by a long driveway, broken and overgrown for decades, indicated there may have been a house or two back there at one time. But the trees, the hostile trees with a thousand arms reaching down, and the weeds, an incredible eight to ten feet high, all made it seem as if those structures had sunk into the ground one night and disappeared forever.

Gordon Beckwith ventured forward. Alone. Ten feet into his journey, the ivory glow of a nearby streetlamp abruptly stopped, and he disappeared into the darkness. He pushed forward. Towards the back of the lot, near the edge of an embankment, in a giant swath of weeds and bushes, he found her. He found his freckle-faced little girl.

"Her face had been pushed into the muddy soil," a crime magazine writer later reported. "Her blouse was pushed up around her shoulders and her slacks were wrapped around her neck. Crimson stains covered her face, blood matted her hair, and mud caked her body."

---

[2] This lot still exists today. It has been re-landscaped and part of its boundaries were appropriated to expand a parking lot on the east side. See the "Famous Crimes Volume II Photo Gallery" on my blog after you have completed this chapter.

His screams brought the police officers. A quick examination revealed a knife wound in her back, and a contusion on her head. The black slacks she wore were wrapped around her neck tight enough to suffocate her.

It was overkill.

Julia Beckwith, 10.

The Milwaukee Police Department did not mess around. The area was roped off. Crime scene technicians, photographers, and homicide investigators were woken up and told where to go. In the middle of the night, more than a dozen support vehicles and marked and unmarked cop cars swarmed the once-quiet street in front of 2104 West Michigan.

The clamor of car doors and trunk lids opening and slamming shut, and serious men talking and shouting orders attracted the attention of area residents who came outside to witness the invasion.

They stood from a distance and peered deep into that unwelcoming patch of land and watched the flashlight beams of a dozen, shadowy men sway back and forth and up and down as if they were part of some disorganized, creepy light show. They were looking for the murder weapon. They were looking for something, anything. Bystanders in the crowd studied their faces when they appeared under the streetlamp. From their stern looks and suppressed emotion, they knew it was bad. Really bad. They had seen those kinds of faces before—on TV, when Kennedy was shot.

Under the morning sun, the platoon of investigators and experts conducted another careful, inch-by-inch search of the lot. In the middle, they found a pool of blood, and then drag marks leading to where Julia's body was found. A knife in the back should have caused Julia to scream loud enough to alert neighbors. But with the exception of the green Ford slamming on its brakes, nobody heard a thing. Whatever happened inside that lot, it went unnoticed.

By the time church let out later that Sunday, fifty detectives and fifty officers were assigned to the case.

While investigators and officers were talking to witnesses and canvassing the entire area, a squad of firemen and a ladder truck was called in to search the rooftops of eight different multi-story buildings in the area. When nothing was found, they swung their ladders out over the trees, peered into the branches, and shook them in the million-to-one shot the killer had thrown something into the limbs.

The firemen found nothing. The police found an old paring knife near the body, but it was covered in rust and soil. It had been there a long time. It was not the murder weapon.

At the city morgue, Dr. Helen Young, Medical Examiner for Milwaukee County, conducted her autopsy that Sunday morning. She had been called to the death lot soon after the body was discovered. The horrible sight she had seen under the beams of flashlights was magnified under the surgical lights. Julia had a seven-inch deep knife wound in her back. It was made by a double-edged blade, narrow, like a stiletto. The contusion on her head turned out to be a skull fracture. And although the little girl had been molested, she had not been raped.

News of what happened on that vacant lot played across radio and television stations throughout Wisconsin that Sunday. By Monday, September 5, the molestation and brutal murder of ten-year-old Julia Beckwith was reported in newspapers throughout the country. The daily *Milwaukee Sentinel* did not run a Sunday edition in those days, but the front page of their Monday morning paper featured a world war sized headline—**HUNT KILLER OF GIRL**—along with the third-grade school photo of an adorable, smiling Julia with short brown hair and freckles.

To the right of her picture was a larger photo that told the story of what was on everyone's mind: a mother waving goodbye to her three elementary-school-aged daughters in the foreground, and their public school in the background. That Monday was the first day of the new school year, and young children all over Milwaukee would be walking to and from school every day. That meant they would be vulnerable at a time when a monster was hunting little girls.

The stark contrast of the happy photograph of kids returning to school with the fear-inducing headline that one was recently murdered was unnerving to readers. A newspaper interview with a woman who lived near the crime scene reflected the fear that was flowing through the city built on the western banks of Lake Michigan.

"It sure shook up the whole neighborhood," the woman said, too terrified to give her real name. "We're shocked. I never leave our building after 7:30. It's just not safe."

Most of the residents, she added, don't go out after dark. And as the reporter spoke with her that Sunday night, he pointed out that the streets were eerily quiet.

"They're scared," she replied.

As the shock of what had happened settled over the city that Sunday, police broadcast an appeal for the only two people known to be in the area that night: the driver of the green Ford, and a man the Beckwith sisters had encountered just minutes after finding the bicycle. He was walking down the alley that lay between the vacant lot and the two-story rooming house to the east. The young, slender man was in his early twenties, and wore sunglasses—a fact the Beckwith sisters found to be odd since it was eleven o'clock at night.

"Have you seen a little girl on a bike? A girl with short brown hair and freckles?" one of the sisters asked.

"No, I didn't," the man replied.

Both of those men came forward. The young man said he was walking home from a relative's house and had not seen anything suspicious. Since it was believed Julia was abducted and killed sometime around 9:30, he was questioned and released. The driver of the Ford, who had most likely stopped for the bicycle at the same time Julia was being molested and murdered, was a forty-six-year-old man with no police record. He had not seen or heard anything suspicious that night, and no one else was in the area. He merely set the bicycle against the tree and continued on his way.

During those first forty-eight hours into the investigation, Milwaukee police followed routine procedure by going through their sex offender files, and rounding up all the known rapists, kiddie perverts, and wiener flashers.

"The parade of possible suspects was brought to headquarters for questioning," veteran journalist William T. Brannon wrote in his article for *True Detective* magazine. "Every man was given the option of having a lawyer present, but none took advantage of this. Each gave an account of his movements—nearly all seemed eager to do this—and each alibi was carefully verified."

Even among the molesters of Milwaukee, there seemed to be the consensus that Julia's killer was a monster—some fresh demon that signaled the beginning of a tragic new era in American crime.

By Wednesday, September 7, just four days into the investigation, the police department had no leads, no prime suspects, no witnesses, and no clues. The 100 men working the case were ordered back to the lot to search again, back to question all family members and neighbors, and back to an eight-block area surrounding the crime scene to search through bushes, trash cans, yards, and question everyone. All days off for detectives were canceled and the men, a top police official said, were devoted to solving the case. Most of them had children of their own and over-time hours were worked without complaint.

"The men are interested in this case," Chief Inspector Leo Woelfel told *Milwaukee Sentinel* reporters. "They're eager beavers."

That Wednesday was also the same day the ten-member Beckwith family buried Julia. Seventy people attended the graveside services at Wisconsin Memorial Park Cemetery. As the four pallbearers carried the little, white casket, Alice, her mother, kept her eyes shut tight. She held back the tears until after the service, after the mourners and well-wishers had left—and then she sobbed uncontrollably.

Julia should have been in a fourth-grade classroom that day.

Over the next forty days, the case went in circles. The city sewers were dredged, the lot was cleared, and a suspect in the Mary Troyer stabbing case was questioned and released after Mrs. Troyer failed to identify him in a line-up.

Detectives investigating the Beckwith murder weren't back to square-one because they had never left square-one. For them, unfortunately, the break in the case would not come until Milwaukee's stiletto slayer made a mistake—but only after he had struck again and again.

On Sunday, October 16, Joris Thompson gave his daughter, Sherryl, a ride to her job at the Pancake House Restaurant where she worked as a waitress. Her shift began at 5 p.m. and when she got off work around 9:30, her father would normally be there to take her home. However, on that particular evening, Joris and his wife, Clarion, were going to watch *The Jimmy Dean Show*, which was filming in Milwaukee that night. They weren't due to get home until 11:30. To get to her house eleven blocks away, Sherryl would have to make the fifteen-minute walk alone that night.

The attractive eighteen-year-old graduated from St. John's Cathedral High School that June, and in July, she began her waitressing job at the popular Pancake House located at 3001 West Wisconsin Avenue. She was a good employee, and described by her employer as "a very respectable girl, a very sweet and darling girl." Sherryl lived at home with her parents and four siblings. Since her boyfriend had started college at the University of Wisconsin that September, she never went out at night, and had never been one to give her parents or teachers any trouble.

After her shift ended at 9:30, Sherryl called home and spoke with her twin sister, Sharron. She told her that before going home, she was going to stop at a store and buy a tube of toothpaste. She asked Sharron if there was anything she wanted.

Soda and snacks, her sister told her.

Instead of walking west, toward the direction of home, Sherryl walked three blocks east where she was seen by family friends in two stores nearly adjacent to each other on North 27th Street. In one shop, she bought the toothpaste. In another, she bought soda, potato chips, and two taffy apples. Before she left the second store, she tried to use the telephone, most likely to call and tell her sister she was on her way home. For some reason, the call did not go through. It was the last time anyone saw her alive.

Except for her killer.

WHEN HER PARENTS RETURNED AND learned that Sherryl had not come home, they got back in their car and drove around on that cold night to look for her. Sharron stayed behind and left the porch light on. If her sister returned while her parents were gone, she was to turn the light off. This was the signal to let them know Sherryl was home safe.

"We went from every street in the area, up, down and sideways, looking," her mother told a reporter the next morning. "Finally, we came home (at 1:30 a.m.) and we waited."

The Thompsons lay in bed and waited for the sound of the front door opening and closing. It never came. At five in the morning, they called police and reported their daughter missing. Their activity in the home went unnoticed by their three youngest children, Shirley, 13, Terry 12, and Susan, 10. When they came down for breakfast shortly before seven, only their son, Terry, asked why his sister Sherryl wasn't home.

After they ate, Mr. Thompson drove all four[3] to their schools, dropping the youngest three off at St. Rose of Lima Catholic School located one block south of the Pancake House restaurant. The St. Rose of Lima Parish, with church, school, rectory, convent, and other buildings, occupy an entire city block between West Michigan and Clybourn Streets, and North 30th and 31st Streets. Young boys attending the school were required to serve as altar boys. On that particular morning, Terry was tasked with helping Father Francis

---

[3] It's unclear what school Sharron was attending. All of the Milwaukee daily newspapers were removed from Google News Archives, without notice, while the author was working on this chapter.

Siemanowski conduct the eight o'clock mass. Ten minutes before it started, the priest sent him on an errand to the rectory, west of the church, to bring him more wine cruets.

Still wearing his surplice and cassock, Terry exited the front of the church, ran around to the west side, and near a breezeway between the church and the rectory, he spotted his sister lying in the grass. He recognized her distinctive coat, plaid with fur sleeves. She was nude from the waist down and covered in blood. Next to the body were her bloodstained sneakers. Her girdle had been removed but was still attached to her stockings, which were pulled down to her ankles.

"It's my sister! It's my sister!" he cried out. He screamed so loud Father Siemanowski could hear him inside the brick church.

Sherryl Thompson, 18.

About a minute or two before Terry saw his blood covered sister, her body had been discovered by a resident of the church's old rectory, which was being rented out. The tenant saw her body when he was walking by and had run to notify several assistant priests to call the police. The tenant and priests were just arriving to the location when Terry saw his sister lying face down against the west wall. As the boy sobbed and cried out, one of the priests administered last rites while the tenant ran back to his house to retrieve a blanket to cover her body.

The same medical examiner who performed the autopsy on Julia Beckwith later reported that Sherryl Thompson had been stabbed twenty-two times including wounds to the head, left eye, abdomen, both legs, and three to the heart, which killed her. The knife wounds were similar to the one found in young Julia: narrow, double-edged, and seven-inches deep. The killer had used a killer's knife: a stiletto.

Despite Sherryl being naked from the waist down, Dr. Young found no evidence she had been raped, although a sexual motive seemed certain.

Besides the possible sex motive, Milwaukee investigators would soon learn the killer had taken some souvenirs. After he killed Sherryl, he scavenged the contents of her woven handbag, which had spilled on the ground. A little red pocketbook, containing about twenty-dollars in cash, her social security card, a St. Rose of Lima Catholic Youth Organization card, and a photograph of Sherryl, were missing. Also missing was the paper sack containing the toothpaste, soda, apple, and potato chips she had purchased less than fifteen minutes before she was killed.

Two people heard Sherryl scream around the same time she was thought to have been killed. A nun, Sister Mary Celestina, said she heard five piercing shrieks around 10:15 the night before. She took no great interest in the noise since the yelling and shouting of half-feral teenagers running around at night was common in that neighborhood. Even so, curiosity got the best of her when the screaming abruptly stopped. She looked out her window and saw a man walking away from where the body was later found. He was walking south, near 30th Street, from the church to the school's playground. She described him as about twenty-years-old, with dark hair and possibly wearing thick, dark glasses. He wore a jacket and appeared to be putting gloves on his hands as he walked away.

Another witness, who had been on a date with the tenant's daughter, said he heard the same screams but dismissed them as feral cats, another common problem in that neighborhood.

The Milwaukee police launched their investigation into Sherryl Thompson's death with the same level of intensity in which they began their investigation into Julia Beckwith's death. More than one hundred detectives and uniformed officers searched a twenty-five square block area that morning. And just as it was with Julia, the gruesome details of Sherryl's murder were told in newspapers across the United States, but with significantly more coverage. A brother, serving as an altar boy, finding his murdered, half-nude sister lying next to the church ten minutes before the eight o'clock mass, was a story editors from Texas to New York, and West Virginia to California found too terrifying to pass up.

Almost immediately, connections between Thompson's murder and that of Julia Beckwith were being made by the local media as well as in the Associated Press and United Press International wire reports. While police were contemplating the same thing, Julia's mother was certain it was the same man.

"There is no doubt, in my mind, whatsoever, that the killer is the same man as our Julia," Mrs. Beckwith told the *Milwaukee Sentinel.* The paper pointed out to its readers that the two murders occurred at approximately the same time, and nine blocks apart along West Michigan Street.[4]

"I feel badly for those poor people (Sherryl's parents)," Julia's mother continued. "I have all of the confidence in the world that the Milwaukee police will catch Julie's murderer, but it is too bad they couldn't have caught him before this happened."

---

[4] The church is on the corner of 30th and West Michigan streets.

Like the investigation into her own daughter's death, the Thompson case provided no solid clues that would lead them to the killer. They would have to wait; wait until the killer screwed-up so bad they could get him. A mistake so big, it was almost as if he wanted to be caught.

The stiletto slayer's blunder came when he made an impulsive decision to try and murder little Kathy Dreyer in broad daylight. The golden-haired fifth-grader was just one block from home when she was grabbed while walking to school that November 11.

"The car stopped and that man suddenly jumped out and put his hand on my mouth," Kathy later told authorities from the hospital. She had bit his fingers, and they tasted like leather. He was wearing gloves, they surmised.

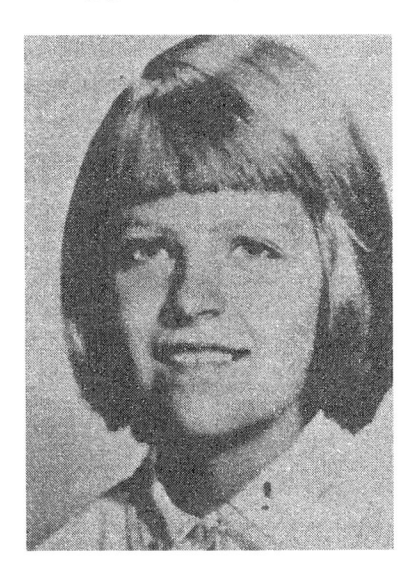

Kathy Dreyer, 11.

After he had dragged her down an alley about thirty-feet to a spot behind a small garage, he shoved her face into the dirt. Then, he flipped her over until she was on her back. "I kicked him and he shoved again," she continued. The kick angered him and he rolled her back over to her stomach, pushed her face down into the mud, and plunged the stiletto into her back, just below the right shoulder blade.

"I screamed and screamed and screamed loud," she said with excitement, the memory still fresh in her mind. Those screams saved her life. She heard him run back up the alley, get in his car, and drive past her as she lay on the ground. She got up, staggered forward a few steps and knocked on the back door of the nearest house.

A school crossing guard later told investigators that she was just arriving at her post when she heard the little girl cry out.

"I saw a car come out of the alley at a high-rate of speed," Mrs. Elden Balanger said. "A little boy was pointing at the alley. I went up there and found Kathy."

The girl had gone to the home of Mrs. Irving Colrud and was ringing the bell when the crossing guard arrived. Mrs. Colrud was in her kitchen sewing and as they waited for her to open the back door, Mrs. Balanger could see a large bloodstain forming on the back of Kathy's jacket.

While the two women were helping the injured girl inside, Balanger noticed a man in the alley she recognized as a local fireman. She motioned for him to come help.

His name was Jerome Engle and he had served in the Navy as a medical corpsman. When he came through the backdoor, Kathy was sitting in the kitchen "looking pale, like she would faint," he later said. He placed her on the floor, opened the back of her dress, and found a bleeding wound about one-inch wide.

"He hurt me, he hurt me," Kathy cried as he applied pressure with a wet towel.

Mrs. Colrud telephoned police at approximately 8:30 a.m.

Kathy's description of a young, clean-cut man of medium height, short dark hair and thick, black-framed glasses, along with that of his car, was the break the Milwaukee Police Department had eagerly been awaiting. Shortly after nine o'clock that morning, the police chief issued an order to all his officers to drop whatever they were doing and find that Chevy.

"All squads are to concentrate their efforts to locate suspect," the order read in-part.

Local radio stations, tuned into the police scanner, heard the call go out and soon all of Milwaukee knew about the attack on a little girl, the suspect's description, and what kind of car he was seen driving.

At 10 a.m., he was spotted at a gas station only one-half mile east of the Dreyer crime scene. A young boy, who knew about the stabbing, saw the black '57 Chevy and ran to the alley and told officers what he saw. Two detectives got in their car and sped toward the station, but by the time they got there, he was gone. The fuel attendant confirmed the boy's account that the driver matched the suspect's description.

"He looked like a college student to me," he told detectives. The young man purchased two-dollars in gas, and was wearing a dark jacket over a sweatshirt which had some writing on it.

Thirty minutes later, the same driver was pulled over by a motorcycle cop. When asked what he was doing that morning, Michael Lee Herrington told him that he had been at work, but left early because he felt sick.

"I've got ulcers," the twenty-three-year-old said.

But if he was sick, why wasn't he home? the officer wanted to know.

Herrington then explained that he, his pregnant wife, and mother-in-law were going away that weekend and he was out running errands before they left.

Although suspicious, the officer decided to let him go. Herrington's story seemed plausible, and he wasn't nervous. He was calm and matter-of-fact with his replies. Before he handed back Herrington's driver's license, he noted the address: it was an apartment at 2211 West Wells Street.

His decision to let the suspect go was one he immediately regretted. Ten minutes later, the officer knocked on his apartment door. He wanted to know in what city Herrington was going to be that weekend, and where he was staying. The slender young man, with dark brown hair neatly combed to the side and thick black glasses, showed him the reservations he had for a Bahá'í Faith religious conference. He and his attractive wife, Patricia, were married in a Bahá'í Temple earlier that April. They were leaving that evening to go "up north, to Green Lake."

He thanked Herrington, left, and then went to a nearby police call box to inform his commanding officer. At noon, with hundreds of police officers searching for a car like his, Michael Lee Herrington got in his black '57 Chevy, and drove to a service station to purchase a new tire when he was pulled over by a patrol car. Two officers got out, inquired about his destination, and then politely suggested he should follow them to the 5th District Police Station.

The captain wants to talk to you, he was told. He wasn't under arrest, they just wanted to talk.

"I know," he replied with a mock sigh. "It's about a stabbing. I was stopped by a motorcycle cop downtown."

Even though he agreed to follow the patrol car, one of the officers rode with him. They were taking no chances. Before leaving, one of them made sure he advised Herrington of his Miranda rights.

You have the right to remain...

Across the country, law enforcement offers were adjusting to this new requirement mandated by the United States Supreme Court with their June 13, 1966, decision in *Miranda v. Arizona*. This action by the officer was just one of many that the Milwaukee Police Department would take to protect the legal rights of their top suspect in a high profile, multi-victim murder investigation. They weren't just protecting his rights, however, they were protecting the integrity of their case. God forbid they lose it on a technicality to a savvy defense attorney.

But what those two patrolmen didn't know in that moment was—they had the right guy. It was *him*. This was the SOB they were looking for.

At the station, Herrington was formally arrested for aggravated assault in the stabbing of Kathleen Dreyer nearly four hours earlier that Friday. Before his interrogation began, Detective Dorsey Tisdale once again advised him of his rights, which he chose to waive.

When asked about it, Herrington denied having anything to do with stabbing the Dreyer girl.

"You know why you are here?" Tisdale asked.

"Yes," the prisoner replied. "Listen, my wife's pregnant. If she should have a daughter, I certainly wouldn't want her out on the street with a guy like that running around."

For the next one and one-half hours, Tisdale continued asking questions and Herrington continued his denials. By 2 p.m., the higher-ups ordered Tisdale and several other detectives to quietly move the suspect to one of the department's central offices downtown. Reporters were on to them. They had seen the black, 1957 Chevrolet parked outside and were beginning to ask questions no one was ready to answer.

The plain-clothed detectives managed to sneak him out in an unmarked car. At the downtown building, they escorted Herrington to a meeting room used by detectives. Tisdale bought him a steak sandwich, a soda, and posted guards outside the door so they wouldn't be interrupted.

"Would you like to tell me exactly what happened?" Tisdale began.

With a sigh of resignation, Michael Lee Herrington finally said the words: "I'm the guy you want."

He was "the guy" all right. He not only stabbed Kathleen Dreyer, but he also murdered Julia Beckwith and Sherryl Thompson. Over the next several hours, Herrington's replies to Tisdale's questions were recorded by a stenographer and documented in a forty-seven-page confession.

Beneath his camouflaged layers of mild-manners, and clean-cut appearance, lurked the heart of a monster who struggled to understand why he was the way he was: a monster

Michael Lee Herrington

who was able to fool everyone into believing that he was just a normal guy; a monster that had molested a little girl when he was seventeen; and a monster who had already served time in federal prison.

"Why did you stab the Dreyer girl?" a detective asked.

"I don't know," Herrington replied.

"Did something come over you?"

"I really don't know."

As for the two murdered girls, the *Milwaukee Sentinel* was correct in their observation that both occurred at approximately the same time for a reason: his wife got off work from her job as a nurse's aide at Children's Memorial Hospital at 11 p.m. In those dark hours before eleven, Herrington was a predator on the streets of Milwaukee searching for a victim "with an urge to destroy someone," a psychiatrist would later report.

On September 3, he spotted little Julia Beckwith as she was bicycling down the driveway of the duplex, where she had picked up her sister's blouse, and was on her way home. When she came near the empty lot, Herrington said he stepped out and kicked the rear wheel of her bike, knocking both her and the bicycle over. He then dragged her deep into the lot, where the weeds hid them from the adjacent world, and molested her.

And then he strangled her to death with her slacks.[5]

After driving away, Herrington said he realized he had left his knife behind. He sped home, got a flashlight, and drove back to the area, parking a short distance away.

"After finding it, I stabbed her in the back," Herrington stated in his confession.[6]

Instead of walking out toward the front, where he risked exposure from the street lamp, he exited the lot onto the alley that runs between the vacant land and the two-story rooming house. As he walked south toward West Michigan Avenue, he met the victim's sisters.

"Have you seen a little girl on a bike? A girl with short brown hair and freckles?" one of them asked him.

Although they couldn't have known who he was, and what he had done, those young girls were smart enough to know something was off about that guy. Who wears sunglasses at night? They told their father and police about him. When it was reported in the papers, Michael Lee Herrington contacted

---

[5] A different account claimed Julia Beckwith was strangled with a rope. This is unclear, but slacks is mentioned in the research more frequently than a rope is.

[6] His version did not match the evidence found in the lot. Detectives reported finding a pool of blood, and then drag marks. If he stabbed her post-mortem, there would not have been "a pool of blood" as large as the one they found.

investigators to say he was in the alley about eleven o'clock that night, after visiting a nearby relative. He was just one of a thousand people police interviewed and with his normal guy persona, he was able to fool them into dismissing him as a suspect.

His confession continued with an account of how he murdered Sherryl Thompson forty-four days later and nine blocks to the west. After she had gotten off work at 9:30 the night of October 16, she walked three blocks east along Wisconsin Avenue to the two shops where she was last seen alive. As she walked, her head down to block the cold wind, a black, 1957 Chevrolet slowly rolled past her.

She didn't notice it.

Herrington continued driving east, then circled back around and spotted Sherryl after she had left the two stores. She was walking south along North 28th Street and then she made a right turn onto West Michigan Street. From the forty-seven-page report, Herrington said he parked on Michigan, and then began following her on foot. When she reached the Catholic Church on the corner of Michigan and North 30th, he attacked.

"I came up behind her and forced her behind the church. She screamed, and I stabbed her."

He didn't just stab her, he speared her twenty-two times in a brutal assault with wounds to her head and left eye, among others. And then he carefully took her shoes off and pulled her pants down just to see how she looked, or to demonstrate his power by leaving her in a humiliated condition next to a Catholic Church; the same denomination in which he had been raised before he was introduced to the Baháʼí Faith.

Herrington then revealed to police that after killing the eighteen-year-old, he realized he had dropped his tobacco pouch. As he reached down to pick it up, he spotted Sherryl's red French purse, which had fallen out of her handbag. He decided to take it, along with her shopping bag with the items she had just purchased. He took them home and the next day, he drank the two sodas and ate the .39-cent bag of potato chips. His wife ate the taffy apples—the fruit of her husband's poisoned mind—unaware of their origin.

After his confession, detectives, high-ranking police officials, and an assistant district attorney took Herrington on a little sightseeing trip. They brought along a stenographer whose recordings were added to the confession.

First, they went to Allied Tool Products where their suspect worked as a shipping clerk. There, underneath a heavy metal cabinet near his workstation, detectives retrieved the murder weapon: a British war surplus commando knife manufactured by the Fairbairn-Sykes Company. It was a well-known dagger among knife enthusiasts and World War II history buffs.

It was a mean looking piece of steel; eleven and one-half inches long with a seven-inch double-edged blade. Anyone looking at that weapon could immediately understand its purpose—to kill.

Herrington never brought the knife home with him, he told them. After every attack, he would hide it underneath the metal cabinet at work.

Fairbairn–Sykes British Commando knife, similar to the one used by Herrington.

From the tool factory, the small parade of cars drove to West Michigan Street where Milwaukee's Dr. Jekyll demonstrated to authorities how Mr. Hyde brutally murdered two young ladies. He finished his macabre tour at North 36th Street where he attacked the Dreyer girl earlier that day.

The one place they didn't go was South 27th Street where Mary Troyer was attacked at 6:30 in the morning while on her way to work. Herrington steadfastly denied having anything to do with that incident. Mrs. Troyer later confirmed that he was not the man who almost killed her.

He also denied murdering Diane Olkwitz[7] on November 3 in Menomonee Falls twenty miles northwest of Milwaukee; or murdering Valerie Percy, the twenty-one-year-old daughter of United States Senator-elect Charles Percy. She was stabbed to death inside the family home on September 18 in Kenilworth, Illinois, seventy-six miles south of Milwaukee. Both cases remained unsolved and Percy's murder was described, for a time, as America's number-one unsolved murder. It was the Jon Benét Ramsey mystery of its day.[8]

His answers may have cleared up *how* he committed the crimes, but they didn't explain *who* Michael Lee Herrington really was, or *why* he did it. It would take eight months to peel back the layers of that onion.

But for now, the stiletto slayer of Milwaukee's was off the streets and at six o'clock that evening, Milwaukee police held a press conference. Chief Harold A. Breier thanked local citizens for their cooperation in leading them to Herrington.

"Everyone can sleep a little easier tonight," Breier stated with confidence.

And he was probably right. Herrington's reign of terror was over. Detectives and regular patrol officers had not had a day off since September 4. Nearly all of them had also worked overtime. Since the knife attacks began, many parents walked with their children to and from school, or gave them rides.

---

[7] It was later confirmed that Herrington was at his job during the time Olkwitz was murdered inside the Kenworth plant where she worked. Diane is fondly remembered by her sisters and friends on a Topix.com message board.

[8] FBI files released in 2014 name William Thoresen III, the mentally disturbed son of a wealthy industrialist, as their top suspect for the Percy murder. Thoresen was shot and killed by his wife in 1970. Before he died, he told her that he had killed several people. More information can be found on the on the Famous Crimes Volume II photo gallery on my blog.

Those same parents watched out for other children, giving them rides or corralling them together to walk in one large group.

One woman, interviewed the day Kathy Dreyer was stabbed, said she was carrying an umbrella to defend herself. "They won't let us carry defense weapons, so this will have to do," she said with a determined twist of the parasol handle.

Shortly after Sherryl Thompson's murder, which came after Troyer, Valerie Percy in Illinois, and Julia Beckwith, residents of Milwaukee's west side took special precautions.

"…an entire metropolitan area was apprehensive, especially that near the west side section, where the two girls had lost their lives," Brannon wrote in his magazine article. "Many persons, particularly women, refused to open their doors even to policeman until they were convinced of the officers' identities."

"I've lived here over fifteen years and I've never seen things as bad as they are now," an unidentified man told a *Sentinel* reporter. "I don't like to go alone myself at night anymore, and now my wife says she's afraid to walk through the alley in back, even in daylight."

Other neighbors interviewed by the *Sentinel* after the Beckwith and Thompson murders also said they no longer went out at night, and if they did, they carried police whistles and a wide variety of self-defense weapons.

While the city breathed a sigh of relief, those close to Michael Lee Herrington were either in shock or complete denial.

"He was the kind of man I would recommend any woman to marry," said a neighbor who lived in the apartment above Herrington and his wife Patricia. The young couple used to babysit her three children on occasion. He was always kind to them and that Halloween, gave her kids an entire bag of candy. She added that he never drank and she never saw him lose his temper.

With his conservative, clean-cut appearance, complete with glasses and a pipe he often smoked, Herrington cultivated the look of a quiet, erudite young man. "[He seemed] so scholarly he looked as though he was one of the college kids [around] here," the woman said.

Other neighbors described him as introverted, but friendly, and good with children. "Herrington seemed to make young children happy," said a woman who lived near him on State Street, before he got married.

In spite of his confession, the witnesses, and the evidence against him, the one person who still believed in Herrington was his wife, seven-months pregnant.

"He's not guilty. He's not guilty. I wish the police would get this silly business over with. He didn't do it. He didn't do it," Patricia said during a *Milwaukee Journal* interview in her apartment later that Friday night. "They'll have to prove it to me. I know he'll prove he's innocent."

She met her husband at the children's hospital, where she worked as a nurse's aide and he worked in the supply department maintaining equipment. For a young woman pregnant with his child, she didn't seem to know very much about her husband. He had moved to Milwaukee the year before and lived with his mother and younger brother on State Street. He was born in Kansas City where his father, Claude, was a twenty-five- year veteran of the police force. She knew he was on parole for some minor crime, but she didn't know what it was for. All he told her was that when he was young, he made a stupid mistake, and it wouldn't happen again.

"Mike is an easygoing guy who everybody could like," she continued. "He (gets) along with even the hardest person."

She was there the next day when her husband was arraigned in court and ordered held on $65,000 bail: $15,000 for the attack on Kathy Dreyer, and $25,000 each for killing Beckwith and Thompson. Before he was taken back to jail, the judge ruled Herrington an indigent, and assigned him an attorney.

The murder warrants against him cited his forty-seven-page confession, witness statements, and the discovery of the murder weapon. Reporters also learned that police searched his car and found the black leather gloves he wore when he grabbed the Dreyer girl, as well as some surgical instruments and unspecified narcotics. The surgical instruments, they assumed, were stolen from the hospital where he once worked. While searching his home, they found a dark sweatshirt that looked similar to the one his last victim reported seeing.

The Associated Press and United Press International spread the news of Herrington's arrest across the country from El Paso to Boston, and Burlington, North Carolina, to Pocatello, Idaho. In Wisconsin, his attack on the Dreyer girl and consequential apprehension was covered by every radio and television station with a news department. On New Year's Eve, his reign of terror over the city was named the top news story in the entire state that year.

Although the term didn't exist in 1966, Herrington's horrible crimes distinguished him as Milwaukee's first serial killer, a *Chicago Tribune* reporter claimed in an article published twenty-five years later.

The national publicity generated by his arrest also shined a light into his dark past; he had done this sort of thing before. His criminal record dated back to his young teens when he was placed under the jurisdiction of the juvenile court for unspecified offenses. A month after his seventeenth birthday, he admitted to molesting a ten-year-old girl after striking her on the head with a blackjack. He was again turned over to juvenile authorities and released when he was eighteen.

Before his next birthday, Herrington pled guilty to three counts of mail theft when he was caught stealing letters that contained money from an insurance company. He served time in federal prison, was released in 1964 or 1965, and traveled to Milwaukee where he moved in with his mother, Eva

Schlaitzer, and his thirteen-year-old brother. After she had divorced Michael's father, she married a soldier and the couple moved to Milwaukee. That marriage also failed and by 1965, the three of them were living in a small apartment above a grocery store at 1529 West State Street. It took newspapers and investigators a few weeks to realize that this apartment, where the killer once lived, was just 300 feet north of the Beckwith's home on North 16th Street.

Following a brief courtship, he moved out when he married his wife in April. Patricia was the first and only woman in his life—besides his overbearing mother.

IN THE MONTHS AFTER HIS arrest, Herrington regretted his confession and his lawyer requested a sanity hearing stating his client was "probably insane or feeble minded." In December, Herrington was committed to a state mental hospital for thirty-days of observation. During a January 20 hearing, which cleared the way for his trial to proceed, hospital psychiatrists shot down his lawyer's claims and declared his client was fit to stand trial.

"Our evaluation of Michael Lee Herrington shows no evidence of organic brain disease or severe mental illness," their report read. It further stated that although sane, Herrington did have a personality disorder.

On January 16, 1967, his wife Patricia gave birth to a baby girl. During a jail house meeting nine days later, in which a reporter was present, Herrington met his daughter for the first time—a daughter he once told police he wouldn't want on the streets "with a guy like [him] running around."

Three weeks later, the circuit court judge overseeing the Herrington case granted the defendant funds to employ his own psychiatrist and psychologist. For the first time ever, he also granted a defendant his own investigator. It was an unusual step but one taken to guarantee that Herrington received "a totally fair trial." With their own mental health experts, Herrington and his lawyer were finally able to get the diagnosis they wanted and on March 17, he pleaded innocent, and innocent by reason of insanity.

On April 6, Herrington's mother was found dead inside her car in a sealed garage near her apartment. The ignition was on and the gas tank was empty. She left behind a suicide note, which blamed her four children for her death.

"May I congratulate my children [here she names them.] They have given me so much hell they have pushed me over the brink," she wrote.

Her naming of all four children seemed unfair to the other three. One daughter was married, another was a Catholic nun, and her youngest child, a son, was only thirteen-years-old at the time. Her suicide was a selfish and thoughtless act that blamed others for her own misery. It also gave amateur psychiatrists some idea from where her eldest son had inherited his personality disorder. Although his mother's suicide didn't seem to effect Herrington, he apparently used the incident to his advantage.

One month after her death, and just one month before his trial began, model prisoner Michael Lee Herrington began throwing temper tantrums. On May 5, he was found screaming in his cell and pounding on the walls. When officers responded, they found he had torn his mattress cover into strips and tied them together to make a rope, which he fastened to a bar high in his cell. When asked why he did it, Herrington replied: "I did it to show what could happen—that I might hang myself."

Four days later, on May 9, deputies were back in his cell after he failed to get out of bed for morning roll call. There, they discovered he had swallowed a large quantity of sedatives prescribed to him for a "nervous condition" believed responsible for his ulcer. He was taken to the hospital, treated, and returned to the county jail the next day.

During a May 12 hearing to consolidate the three charges against him into one trial, Herrington surprised everyone when he unexpectedly told the judge that deputies had attacked him in an unprovoked incident several days earlier. The sheriff disputed those claims and reported Herrington had to be restrained after launching into a tirade in which he spit and cursed at officers. Always mindful of the defendant's rights, the judge ordered Herrington moved to the state mental hospital until his trial began on Monday, June 26, with jury selection.

During those first few days, Herrington's defense attorney began strong with a three-pronged attack to have the confession thrown out because: his client claimed he did not receive his Miranda warning; to have the evidence gathered from his car and apartment ruled inadmissible because they were illegally obtained; and a renewed request for a change of venue. The jury was dismissed while the motions were argued, and Herrington himself sat in the witness chair to deny that he was Mirandized.

He was lying, and the judge believed the officers who said they twice read him his rights. The judge's rejection of his three motions effectively put an end to Herrington's entire defense before his case even began. However, since this was a bifurcated trial–one in which the jury would have to first decide guilt or innocence and then decide if he was insane–he shifted his hope to his own mental health experts.

Over the next five business days, the prosecution presented their slam dunk case. It began with a tour of the crime scene and then opened with testimony from detectives and eyewitness. The only remarkable event during the entire trial came from a fearless, unintimidated Kathleen Dreyer.

The young victim, with her long blonde hair, wore a peach-colored sleeveless dress tied in the back with a bow, and knee-length white socks with brown loafers. She looked like exactly what she was, a sweet, innocent girl—but an incredibly strong one.

From the stand, she gave a coherent, irrefutable account of what the defendant had done to her in that alley. After the prosecution asked her to point to the man who stabbed her, he went one step further and asked her to do something that would be unthinkable in a 21st Century courtroom.

"Then [the prosecutor] asked her to touch the man she was pointing to, so there could be no mistake in the minds of the jurors," the *Milwaukee Journal* reported. "The child walked about twenty feet, stopped at the table where Herrington sat, and touched him on the left shoulder. She said nothing. Herrington sat expressionless."

On the fourth and last day of the prosecution's case, July 5, 1967, all forty-seven transcribed pages of Herrington's confession was read to the jury.

When it came time for the defense, his attorney examined one inconsequential witness and his entire presentation was over in twelve minutes. He further surprised the courtroom when he waived his closing argument.

The jury took just thirty-five minutes to find Michael Lee Herrington guilty on two counts of first-degree murder, and one count of attempted murder.

The real battle to mitigate Herrington's punishment was during his sanity trial that began immediately after his guilty verdict was pronounced. With two psychiatrists for the defense, and four more for the prosecution and court, the combined findings of six experts provided conflicting but revealing insight into why this small, reserved, and nervous little man by day, was a cold-blooded killer of young innocents by night.

For the latter group, Herrington's evil was simply rooted in the fact that he was a sociopath with anti-social personality disorder characteristics. He wasn't insane, they told the court, because he knew what he did was wrong, although "he had no use for people," he was quoted as saying during one of his interviews.

But for his defense experts, Herrington's fragile mental disorder was more complicated, more severe, and in his own mind, *he* was the victim.

"He has the tendency to blame everyone else for his hurts—a paranoid tendency," Dr. Donald J. Carek testified. Paranoid was the keyword in his statement. He diagnosed Herrington as a paranoid schizoid[9], but not a schizophrenic. Not yet, anyway. Even so, he wasn't just a man who perceived himself as a victim of others, he was also a victim of his own mind—incapable of overcoming the demons that drove him.

"The viciousness of his disease is that people are objects to him. They can be disposed of if they satisfy his urges. He is like an iceberg, a little bit on the surface, but so much going on beneath."

The iceberg metaphor sounded great in the courtroom, but it was a comparison that could be said of any human. However, Dr. Carek knew how to twist it for the benefit of the defendant. With all that was beneath the surface of Michael Herrington, other people–ordinary people–could not "appreciate the full danger."

That "danger," the doctor specified, was present when Herrington "walked the streets of Milwaukee with the urge to destroy someone, but the right person did not come along."

Well, yes they did, three times in fact, but the doctor was trying to make a point that Herrington chose his victims "like a person going to the pantry. He says to himself, 'I feel like eating something. Who cares where it comes from?' If he finds something to his taste, he eats it."

Interesting hypothesis: one that puts a man who murders in cold blood on the same level as a shark in the ocean. A fish

---

[9] Schizoid Personality Disorder is not the same as schizophrenia. According to psychcentral.com, Schizoid Personality Disorder is characterized by a long-standing pattern of detachment from social relationships. A person with schizoid personality disorder often has difficulty expressing emotions and does so typically in very restricted range, especially when communicating with others.

swims by, the shark eats it. It's not the shark's fault for doing what sharks do. Extrapolate that to Michael Herrington, and he's not responsible either.

At the time of the stabbings, Dr. Carek concluded, Herrington was "dictated and dominated by an unconscious conflict within him. He was at the mercy of his impulses."

Doctor Basil Jackson, also a university professor, agreed with his colleague, but was less eloquent and metaphorical. When asked why Herrington preferred to attack young people, his succinct reply was: "He has a reason."

The two defense psychiatrists gave the jury of seven men and five women something to think about as they deliberated on July 7 for two hours and fifteen minutes. But in the end, on the fifth ballot, they sided with the prosecution: Michael Lee Herrington was sane.

But in 1966 Wisconsin, guilty of two counts of first degree murder and one count of attempted murder wasn't all it was cracked up to be. Wisconsin didn't have the death penalty and hadn't executed anyone since 1851. Immediately after the jury ruled on Herrington's sanity, presiding Judge John L. Coffey was ready to pass sentence. It was an emotional case for him and as he gave his statement condemning the defendant, his voice steadily rose in volume until it thundered out across the crowded courtroom.

"…ONLY ALMIGHTY GOD HAS THE RIGHT TO TAKE A LIFE…"

"I'm not deaf, your honor," Herrington interrupted.

"But the people you killed are deaf," Coffey fired back. "I hope someday God forgives you. I can't."

He sentenced the twenty-four-year-old to nearly the maximum the law allowed: two consecutive life sentences for the Beckwith and Thompson murders, and thirty-years to run concurrent for the attempted murder of Kathleen Dreyer.

However, a life sentence in 1966 did not mean life without parole. Milwaukee reporters did the math: Michael Lee

Herrington would be eligible for release in just twenty-one years and three months. As he was led off to prison the next day, he was smug in the knowledge that he would one day be free. Realistically he knew it wouldn't be in twenty-one years, but one day, before he was sick and old and feeble, he would walk out of prison, alive.

Epilogue

OR SO HE THOUGHT

During a 1984 interview with the *Milwaukee Journal*, a forty-one-year-old Herrington speculated on his eventual release from prison.

"I'll be fifty before I get out," he told the reporter, his first visitor in fifteen years. His wife, who did not attend his trial, divorced him in 1968. By 1984, after serving seventeen years in prison, he had not seen or heard from any family member in years.

"All he knows," the *Journal* reported, "is that his former wife and daughter are somewhere in New York."

The estrangement from family was extended to his brother and sisters with whom he had not been in contact with for years. "My sisters just quit writing. When they quit, I quit. I figure when I at least don't get a Christmas card back, why bother to waste postage?"

Seventeen years had given him plenty of time to think about the lives he had taken, and the people he hurt. He was sorry for what he had done, and without the benefit of counseling, he thought he understood why he did it.

"Well, probably the biggest factor was, that it was a kind of an explosion of anger," he said. "As a kid, my mother wore out one of my dad's uniform belts on me, among other things. And it didn't seem to impress me too much. But I think that probably it was an explosion of all this anger that I built up over the years."

Herrington added that when he was twelve, he took the belt away from his mother, unwilling to tolerate her spankings anymore. But then she found other ways to make his life miserable, by forbidding him to associate with girls.

And although three of his victims were ten and eleven-years-old, and another just eighteen, he claimed his victims were chosen entirely at random.

"Was there a reason for selecting the victims?" the reporter asked.

"There was no selection," he replied.

"Were they chosen at random?"

"They were available," he said.

"You were there and they were there?"

"Right," he responded. "There was no selection."

Herrington said he had not known any of his Milwaukee victims and blamed his selection process on his anger, saying he was "pretty hostile throughout the period of the killings, just hostile. There wasn't any particular aim or reason."

Apparently, the young age and sex of his victims ws just a coincidence.

While expressing his remorse, real or not, he understood that being in prison was the only measure of satisfaction the victims' families could point to.

"The fact I did it, I am sorry," he said. "I am sorry I did it. It is something that should not have happened to those people, to them, to their families. No matter how long I am in prison, these people still are dead. There is nothing that can bring them back; there is nothing that can make their families feel better other than the fact that I am in prison."

He was right about that. In that same feature special, another *Journal* staff reporter interviewed three members of the Joris Thompson family to discover how the crime had affected them for nearly twenty years. As they spoke of their love for Sherryl, the pain of losing her was written on their faces, and could be heard in the cracks in their voices.

The interview took place in the living room of Joris Thompson's home—a room with a picture of Sherryl prominently displayed on a wall.

Susan said she also had a picture of Sherryl in her own home.

"I wonder how I'm going to explain it to my kids when they get old enough," Susan began. She was ten-years-old when her big sister was murdered. "The man literally tore our lives apart for a while. He changed our lives. We can never turn back. I grew up very fast because of it. I went from ten to fifteen overnight. I was about fifteen [when] I [started] having real bad nightmares, that he got out and he killed my mom and dad—" her voice trailed off.

"I always have this fear that something's going to happen to my kids," the twenty-seven-year-old continued. "My oldest started school this year. I watch that door to make sure he comes home from school. I wonder if my kids will be OK—if they're going to grow up and I'm going to lose them like my mother did my sister."

Sharron, her twin sister, shared her trauma-driven anxiety. "I'm even afraid sometimes to go out at night. You still get that fear—somebody's going to be there. I think you carry it with you. I don't like to go out after dark alone."

According to sentencing and parole guidelines in 1966, a murderer serving a life sentence was automatically eligible for parole in eleven years and three months. For Michael Lee Herrington, his two consecutive life sentences followed some other kind of math, one which added just ten years from his second to his first life sentence. As he sat for that interview with the *Milwaukee Journal*, he was just four years away from his first parole hearing scheduled in 1988.

But Michael Lee Herrington was too impatient for 1988. Prior to his interview, he had tried to consolidate his life sentences to run concurrent, which would have made him eligible for parole years earlier. According to Harlan Richards, a Wisconsin inmate currently serving a life sentence, up until the 1980s, killers were usually paroled after serving thirteen to fifteen years. During the 1970s, it was standard procedure for Wisconsin governors to commute life sentences to fifty years in prison, allowing murderers to be parole-eligible after serving only five years.

Although his interview took place in 1984, Herrington had been living with the state's lenient parole standards for seventeen years. In his mind, he felt certain that he would be paroled sometime after 1992. Other killers had gone free after serving a comparable number of years, and he would too. Parole would come, eventually, and he was fully justified in thinking that.

"In the 1980s, release on parole was virtually assured based on past practice," Richards writes in his *Wisconsin Lifers* blog. "Back in the 1980s a person with a life sentence (lifer) would serve on average thirteen to fifteen years before release on parole. It was so rare for a lifer to spend more than 20 consecutive years in prison that in 1980 there were only two prisoners with that distinction."

But what Herrington didn't understand at the time of his interview was that the public's attitude toward violent and repeat offenders, as well as lax parole boards, was in the process of a radical reversal. Criminal rehabilitation was out, warehousing was in.

"Times have changed," Richards continued in his 2009 blog post. "The constant drum beat of vengeance, retribution, and punishment has changed the political landscape. From only two lifers with twenty or more consecutive years served in 1980, there are now 255. The number is increasing every year. There are six lifers (in 2009) who have served over forty years."

When Joris Thompson heard in 1984 that his daughter's killer had tried to have his sentences consolidated so he come up for parole, his face expressed disgust.

"As far as I'm concerned, he can rot there," Mr. Thompson said.

Sharron said, "I'm just afraid if he gets out somebody else is going to get hurt. I think he'll just keep doing it."

In spite of their hatred for the man who took their daughter and sister away, all three were against the death penalty. Suitable punishment for Sherryl's killer would be a lifetime in purgatory hell.

"Why kill him off? Leave him to suffer in jail," Sharron continued. "I lost a sister, a friend. They say twins are close.... I don't have a sister. There is no way we can bring my sister back. I don't want him dead because that's not going to serve anything."

The Thompsons got their wish—Michael Lee Herrington was never paroled. Now seventy-three, he has been behind bars for more than fifty-years since his arrest on November 11, 1966. As of March 2017, he is incarcerated at the medium security prison, Stanley Correctional Institute, in Stanley, Wisconsin, as prisoner number 27378. His next parole hearing is August 6, 2018.

Michael Lee Herrington, 2014. (Courtesy Wisconsin Department of Corrections.)

Images Available Online

The forty-one images and photographs presented in this eBook or paperback book you are holding are ALSO available for viewing on my blog, **HistoricalCrimeDetective.com**, under the **"Famous Crimes Volume II Photo Gallery."** A link to this gallery can be found in the right sidebar of the blog.

That online photo gallery includes an additional 120 story-related photographs, maps, and other images, which do not appear in this book. The online Famous Crimes II photo gallery is divided into eight different sub-galleries, one for each chapter.

Before viewing the Famous Crimes II Photo Gallery on my blog, I want to caution you that the sub-galleries also contain photographs of the killers. If you view the blog gallery before you finish reading this book, it will spoil your enjoyment of the stories. Please wait until after you have read the book to view the gallery. Thank you.

Acknowledgments

A book like this cannot be written alone and I would like to identify some very special people who helped me along the way.

I end this work with a warm and special appreciation for my editors, Cherri Randall, Tiffany McNab, and true crime writer Tobin Buhk, who each did an outstanding job while offering kind words of encouragement. They also dug into the work with great tenacity and came up with many helpful suggestions to smooth out the rough spots and improve the content.

My research brought me into contact with many helpful people who volunteered their time and energy—people like Patterson Smith, who owns the largest collection of crime magazines, as well as author Skip Hollandsworth, who shared with me his contacts within the Texas Department of Criminal Justice.

I also want to thank the men and women from the following agencies that assisted me with my requests for more information and photographs. They include: the California State Archives, the Washington State Archives, the Texas Department of Criminal Justice – Classification and Records, the Nevada State Libraries and Archives, the Tulsa Public Library – Reference Department, the Houston Public Library, the Oklahoma Historical Society, and Kevin Blinn, reference librarian with the Tom Green County Public Library in San Angelo.

Two individuals who should be singled out praised for the time, patience and generosity include: Richard T. Callery M.D. F.C.A.P. Forensic Pathologist, who consulted with me about the symptoms of arsenic poisoning once it is ingested, the devastation it causes, and finally, the horrible way in which leads to death. The material he provided guided my narration of the symptoms and suffering Susie and Louis Belew endured before they died, and Tess Keehn, granddaughter of Helen Harris Weaver and author of *Alchemical Inheritance*. Her assistance with the complicated and in-depth story presented in Chapter Seven was priceless. I encourage everyone to purchase her book, *Alchemical Inheritance*, to learn more about her family who are among the central characters presented in that chapter.

I would also like to thank all of the dedicated fans who follow my blog, HistoricalCrimeDetective.com. It was their enthusiasm in the early stages of my journey into the historical true crime genre that encouraged me to continue with what was then just a hobby

Sources

Chapter One: The Last Supper, 1897

1897

"Poison is Poured in the Well," *San Francisco Call*, November 10, 1897, page 3.

"Poison in Well Causes two Deaths," *San Francisco Chronicle*, November 10, 1897, page 1.

"Victims of Cunning Murderer," *San Francisco Call*, November 11, 1897, page 3.

"No Clew to the Dixon Poisoners," *San Francisco Chronicle*, November 11, 1897, page 1.

"Unable to Solve the Mystery," *SF Call*, November 12, page 1.

"Little Progress," *Woodland Daily Democrat*, Woodland, California, November 12, page 1.

"Poison in the Beef Broth," *SF Call*, November 13, page 3.

"Poison in the Beef Stew," *SF Chronicle*, November 13, page 4.

"Poisoned Food," *Woodland Daily Democrat*, November 13, page 1.

"Seeking Clews to Dixon Poisoner," *SF Chronicle*, November 14, page 16.

"Each Says the other is Guilty," *SF Call*, November 15, page 3.

"Belew and Allen Cry Innocent," *SF Chronicle*, November 15, pages 1 and 2.

"Dixon Tragedy," *Woodland Daily Democrat*, November 15, page 1.

"Belew and Allen Cry Innocent," *SF Chronicle*, November 15, page 1.

"Say Frank Belew is Innocent," *SF Call*, November 16, page 3.

"Officers Hint at a Surprise," *SF Chronicle*, November 16, page 1.

"Still a Mystery," *Woodland Daily Democrat*, November 16, page 1.

"Curtin in Charge of the Case," *SF Call*, November 17, page 3.

"All at Fault in Dixon Case," *SF Chronicle*, November 17, page 4.

"All in the Dark," *Woodland Daily Democrat*, November 17, page 1.

"Poisoned Water for the Dying," *SF Call*, November 18, page 3.

"Past Records," *Woodland Daily Democrat*, November 18, page 1.

"What Drug Store Sold the Arsenic?," *SF Call*, November 19, page 3.

"Belew Mystery," *Woodland Daily Democrat*, November 19, page 1.

"Poisoned Even the Potatoes," *SF Call*, November 20, page 3.

"Tubers Poisoned," *Woodland Daily Democrat*, November 20, page 1.

"No Sales of Arsenic in Dixon," *SF Call*, November 21, page 3.

"Admit the Innocence of Allen," *SF Call*, November 22, page 3.

"Belew Inquest," *Woodland Daily Democrat*," November 22, page 3.

"Poisoned by Persons Unknown," *SF Call*, November 23, page 3.

"Belew Inquest," *Woodland Daily Democrat*, November 23, page 1.

"Accuses No One of the Poisoning," *SF Call*, November 24, page 4.

"Still a Mystery," *Woodland Daily Democrat*," November 24, page 1.

"Probing Frank Belew's Past," *SF Call*, November 25, page 3.

"Not Reconciled to her Husband," *SF Call*, November 29, page 3.

"Brevities," downloaded from the DixonLibrary.com on July 27, 2015. "Brevities" is a 930-page document containing local news and notes compiled from the *Dixon Tribune* by local historian, Ardeth Sievers Reidel during the 1970s. It covers items published from the late 1800s to 1950. Background material on Belew family, and the Byrd Photography Studio were found by the author on pages: 230, 274, 316, and 434.

1898

"Murderer Belew Caged, Dixon's Poisoner behind the Bars for Killing his Brother and Sister," *SF Call*, February 4, 1898, pages 1 and 2.

"Heard Him Confess," *SF Call*, February 4, page 2.

"Frank Belew's Threat to Murder his Brother and Sister," *SF Call*, February 4, page 2.

"Frank Belew Confronted by Bird, Hangs his Head when Accused of Crimes," *SF Call*, February 5, page 1.

"Guilt of Blood upon His Soul," *SF Call*, February 5, page 1.

"The Awful Secret Carried by Bird," *SF Call*, February 5, page 1.

"The Call's Enterprise Everywhere Commended," *SF Call*, February 5, page 2.

"Belew in Danger of the Noose," *SF Chronicle*, February 5, pages 1 and 2.

"Frank Belew has Confessed, in His Lonely Cell with a Call Reporter, the Fiend Breaks Down," *SF Call*, February 6, page 1.

"His Relatives Appalled," *SF Call*, February 6, page 1.

"All Solano County Smiles," *SF Call*, February 6, page 1.

"The Sheriff Notified," *SF Call*, February 6, page 1.

"Belew, the Prisoner, was also Thief," *SF Call*, February 6, page 2.

"Frank Belew Makes Confession of the Dixon Double Murder," *SF Chronicle*, February 6, page 13.

"Story of the Crime," *SF Chronicle*, February 6, page 13.

"Belew Deserted by His Brothers," *SF Chronicle*, February 6, page 13.

"Belew Anxious to Plead Guilty, Does not Want a Trial and Wishes it was all Over with," *SF Call*, February 7, page 1.

"Public Confession of Frank Belew," *SF Call*, February 7, page 1.

"Talks to the Laws Executor," *SF Chronicle*, February 7, pages 1 and 3.

"Belew to Fight for his Life," *SF Call*, February 8, page 3.

"Murderer Belew to Plead Not Guilty," *SF Chronicle*, February 8, page 4.

"Belew Hopes to be Freed," *SF Call*, February 9, page 4.

"Bird's Testimony," *SF Call*, February 9, page 4.

"Murderer Belew Gains a Few Days Delay," *SF Chronicle*, February 9, page 4.

"His Crime Long Planned," *SF Chronicle*, February 9, page 4.

"Another Crime Charged to Belew," *SF Chronicle*, February 9, page 4.

"Watching the Dixon Poisoner," *SF Call*, February 10, page 2.

"Murderer Belew Fears Solitude," *SF Chronicle*, February 10, page 9.

"Thinks he May Evade the Noose," *SF Call*, February 11, page 4.

"Belew Held for Slaying His Sister," *SF Call*, February 12, page 3.

"Murderer Bunkoed for a Confession," *SF Call*, February 13, page 8.

"Frank Belew in Better Spirits," *SF Call*, February 17, page 10.

"Arraignment of Frank Belew," *SF Call*, February 24, page 8.

"Belew's Wife Calls upon Him," *SF Call*, March 9, page 4.

"Frank Belew's Wife Visits Him in Prison," *SF Call*, March 20, page 8.

"Thrusts His Head into the Noose," *SF Call*, March 30, page 4.

"Belew on Trial for his Life," *SF Call*, April 6, page 5.

"Frank Belew to Yield his Life on the Gallows," *SF Call*, April 10, page 3.

"Belew Will Die in June," *SF Call*, April 14, page 4.

"Claims the Belew Reward, Brother-in-Law Bird after that $800," *Sacramento Record-Union*, May 4, 1898, page 4.

"Belew Will Not Appeal," *Sacramento Record-Union*, May 13, page 3.

"Frank Belew Accuses Bird," *SF Call*, May 14, page 3.

"Bird is Accused," *Woodland Daily Democrat*, May 14, page 1.

"Belew Hanged, He Was the Coolest Man in the Whole Crowd," *Woodland Daily Democrat*, June 16, page 3.

"Frank Belew is Executed," *San Francisco Chronicle*, June 17, page 4.

"Execution of Frank Belew," *SF Call*, June 17, page 3.

"Claims Against the State," *Sacramento Record-Union*, September 7, page 6.

No Title, The American Lawyer, Volume VI, December, 1899, page 441.

Other

"Tennessee Dixie "Tennie" *Martin* Corrigan," (Frank's wife), Findagrave.com, Retrieved August 10, 2015. URL: http://www.findagrave.com/cgi-bin/fg.cgi?page=gr&GRid=112207655

"Merritt Linn Belew," (Frank's son), Findagrave.com, Retrieved August 10, 2015. URL: http://www.findagrave.com/cgi-bin/fg.cgi?page=gr&GRid=58656958

"Thomas Raymond *Belew* Kavanaugh," (Frank's son), Findagrave.com, Retrieved August 10, 2015. URL: http://www.findagrave.com/cgi-bin/fg.cgi?page=gr&GRid=130444529

"Franklyn "Frank" Belew," Findagrave.com, Retrieved August 10, 2015. http://www.findagrave.com/cgi-bin/fg.cgi?page=gr&GRid=111832782

"Acute and Chronic Arsenic Toxicity," by Ranjit N Ratnaike, *Postgraduate Medical Journal*, 2003;79:391-396. PDF Link

"The Inheritor's Powder: A Tale of Arsenic, Murder, and the New Forensic Science," 1st Edition, by Sandra Hempel, W. W. Norton & Company, 2014.

---###---

Chapter Two: The Crystal Cool Killer, 1922

1922

"Shot Dead in Bed by Burglar who Feared his Awakening," *New York Evening World*, August 14, 1922, page 1.

"Lakehurst Man Found Slain, Wife Gagged," *Philadelphia Evening Public Ledger*, August 14, 1922, page 1.

"Seek Writer of Love Letters to Wife of Murdered Man," *Buffalo Evening News*, August 15, page 3.

"Hold Jersey Woman for Killing Husband," *New York Times*, August 15, 1922, pages 1 and 5.

"Bronx Man Named in New Jersey Murder, Insist That Burglars Killed Giberson, Whose Wife is now Under Arrest," *New York Evening World*, August 15, pages 1 and 2.

"Harold A Ganun Goes to Lakehurst in Giberson Case," *New York Evening World*, August 15, pages 1 and 2.

"Wife is Accused of Killing Man While he Slept," *New York Tribune*, August 15, page 1.

"Love Letters Clue in Jersey Murder," *Philadelphia Evening Public-Ledger*, August 15, pages 1 and 2.

"Third-Degree Grilling of Accused Wife in N.J. Brings Protest," *New York Evening World*, August 16, page 1.

"Chloroform a Clue in Giberson Killing," *New York Times*, August 16, page 1 and 10.

"Bound and Gagged Story told Twice Before by Woman," *New York Tribune*, August 16, pages 1 and 4.

"Wife's Letters Newest Clue in Man's Slaying," *Syracuse News-Journal*, Syracuse, New York, August 16, page 9.

"Giberson's Letters but Greeting Cards, Assert Ga Nun," *Brooklyn Daily Eagle*, August 17, page 2.

"Detective Sure Wife Fired Shot in N.J. Murder," *New York Evening World*, August 17, pages 1 and 8.

"Say Mrs. Giberson was Thrice Robbed," *New York Times*, August 17, page 12.

"Widow Kept from Giberson Funeral," *Philadelphia Evening Public-Ledger*, August 17, page 2.

"Giberson Murder to be Re-enacted at Scene of Crime," *New York Evening World*, August 18, page 1.

"Sleuths Come to Aid of Mrs. Giberson," *New York Times*, August 18, page 11.

"Hunt Bootlegger in Giberson Case," *Philadelphia Evening Public-Ledger*, August 18, page 2.

"Seek Drug Addict Seen with Son," *New York Evening World*, August 19, page 3.

"Counsel Defends Mrs. Giberson," *New York Times*, August 19, page 5.

"Mrs. Giberson Calm as Cameras Click," *New York Times*, August 20, page 2.

"'Innocent' Says Mrs. Giberson in First Interview," *New York Tribune*, August 20, page 7.

"Mrs. Giberson Pleads Not Guilty," *New York Times*, August 25, page 12.

"Mrs. Giberson Placed on Trial for N.J. Murder," *New York Evening World*, October 11, page 3.

"Sister of Murdered 'Sleuth' Says Gibersons Fought over Presence of Man Named Ga Nun in Home," *Buffalo Courier*, Buffalo, New York, October 12, page 1.

"Shells in Pistol at Giberson Trial are Identified," *New York Evening World*, October 12, page 1.

"Mrs. Giberson Put on Trial as Slayer," *New York Times*, October 12, page 15.

"Money Troubles of Mrs. Giberson seen as Motive," *New York Tribune*, October 12, page 7.

"Giberson Shot to Hide Crime, Police Claim," *Syracuse Herald*, October 12, page 10.

"Letters of Ga Nun to Mrs. Giberson are Read in Court," *New York Evening World*, October 13, page 3.

"Says Mrs. Giberson Altered Bank Book," *New York Times*, October 13, page 36.

"Altered Bank Book Laid to Mrs. Giberson," *New York Tribune*, October 13, page 24.

"Sister of Murdered Man Heard Fuss," *Bluefield Daily Telegram*, Bluefield, West Virginia, October 13, page 1.

"State Rests Case in Giberson Trial," *New York Times*, October 14, page 12.

"Ga Nun Letters Heavy Blow to Mrs. Giberson," *New York Tribune*, October 14, page 2.

"Wife Fought Mrs. Giberson for Love of Ganun, Notes Show: Accused Calm as Damaging Tale is Heard," *The Washington Times*, October 15, page 3.

"Army Gun a Clue in Giberson Murder," *New York Times*, October 16, page 12.

"Ivy Giberson Sure Jury Will Accept Her Death Story," *Philadelphia Evening Public-Ledger*, October 16, pages 1 and 22.

"Wife Testifies in Her Own Defense," *The Boston Globe*, October 17, page 8.

"Mrs. Giberson, Fighting Chair, Goes through Contortions on Stand to Prove her Innocence," *Buffalo Courier*, October 17, pages 1 and 2.

"Wife tells Story in Giberson Trial," *New York Times*, October 17, page 16.

"'I Never Cry,' Mrs. Giberson Says on Stand," *New York Tribune*, October 17, page 22.

"Ivy Giberson Sorry She Kept Letters," *Philadelphia Evening Public-Ledger*, October 17, page 1.

"Court Permits Jury to Visit Giberson Home," *Syracuse Herald*, October 17, pages 1 and 2.

"Giberson Case Will Go to Jury before Night," *New York Evening World*, October 18, page 3.

"Love a Stranger to Mrs. Giberson," United News Special Dispatch, *New York Morning-Telegraph*, October 18, page 1.

"Testimony Finished in Giberson Trial," *New York Times*, October 18, page 40.

"Mrs. Giberson Visibly Shaken by State's Quiz," *New York Tribune*, October 18, page 3.

"Life Term for Mrs. Giberson," *Boston Globe*, October 19, page 10.

"Find Mrs. Giberson Guilty of Murder, Sentenced to Life Imprisonment for Death of Husband; Innocent, She Says," *Buffalo Courier*, October 19, page 1.

"Mrs. Ivy Guilty of Murdering Her Husband," *Norwich Bulletin*, Norwich, Connecticut, October 19, page 1.

"Mrs. Giberson Sentenced to Life, Still Confident," *New York Evening-World*, October 19, page 5.

"Mrs. Ivy Giberson, Guilty of Murder, Gets Life Sentence," *New York Times*, October 19, page 1.

"Mrs. Giberson Guilty, Sent to Prison for Life," *New York Tribune*, October 19, pages 1 and 12.

"Mrs. Ivy Giberson, Husband Slayer, Given Life Term," *Washington Herald*, October 19, page 1.

"Mrs. Giberson Gets Stay on Writ Error," *New York Times*, October 20, page 36.

"Mrs. Giberson Gets Stay," *New York Tribune*, October 20, page 3.

"Deny Mrs. Giberson is Innocent of Slaying," *The Sun and the Globe*, New York City, December 12, page 21.

"Favors Her Pardon, Prosecutor Will Not Oppose Ivy Giberson," *Standard-Union*, Brooklyn, New York, August 23, 1928, page 20.

Crime Periodicals

"Chasing a Lisping Whisper," by T.H Trent, *Actual Detective Stories of Women in Crime*, April 6, 1938, page 30.

"Case of the Man with a Hole in His Head," by Alan Hynd, *True Police Cases*, November 1958, page 32.

"The Gay Deceiver Takes the Rap," by West Peterson, *Master Detective*, March 1958, page 56.

Other

"The Girls of Murder City," by Robert Loerzel, *Chicago Magazine* (online), August 25, 2010.

US Census, Iva M. Richmond, Year: 1900; Census Place: Manchester, Ocean, New Jersey; Roll: 989; Page: 5A; Enumeration District: 0161; FHL microfilm: 1240989. Accessed via Ancestry.com

US Census, Iva M. Giberson, Year: 1920; Census Place: Manchester, Ocean, New Jersey; Roll: T625_1061; Page: 2A; Enumeration District: 167; Image: 985. Accessed via Ancestry.com

US Census, Iva M. Giberson, Year: 1930; Census Place: Union, Hunterdon, New Jersey; Roll: 1361; Page: 1B; Enumeration District: 0035; Image: 719.0; FHL microfilm: 2341096. Accessed via Ancestry.com

---###---

Chapter Three: The Love Song of Archie Moock, 1928

1928

"Woman is Found Killed in the Valley," *Spokane Daily Chronicle*, September 24, page 1.

"Matrimony Lured Woman to Death," *Spokane Daily Chronicle*, Street Edition, September 24, page 17.

"Murder Charge will be Filed in Moock Case," *Spokane Daily Chronicle*, September 25, page 1.

"File Murder Complaint against Archie Moock," *Spokane Daily Chronicle*, September 25, pages 1 and 3 of Sport's Edition.

"Wife Stands by Her Man," *Spokane Daily Chronicle*, September 25, pages 1 and 3 of Street Edition.

"Spokane Man Faces Murder Charge for Woman's Death, AP, *Oakland Tribune*, Oakland, California, September 25, page 24.

"Woman Seeker of Husband is Murder Victim," AP, *The News-Review*, Roseburg, Oregon, September 25, page 1.

"Lawyer Declares Moock Will Not Get Fair Trial in Hatchet Murder Case," *Spokane Daily Chronicle*, September 26, page 1.

"Moock Demanding Trial in Seattle," *Spokane Daily Chronicle*, September 26, page 1 of Street Edition.

"Wife of Accused Man to Aid Him," AP, *Great Falls Tribune*, Great Falls, Montana, September 26, page 3.

"Moock Tells Chronicle Story of Murder Case," *Spokane Daily Chronicle*, September 27, pages 1 and 3 of Street Edition.

"Alleged Murderer was Former Yorktown Resident," *The Winnipeg Evening-Tribune*, Winnipeg, Canada, September 27, page 12.

"James Murphy Clews Now Piling Up," *Spokane Daily Chronicle*, September 28, page 1.

"New Hatchet Slaying Theory," *Spokane Daily Chronicle*, September 28, page 1 of Street Edition.

"Murder Ring Hired Moock," *Spokane Daily Chronicle*, September 29, page 1 of Sports Edition.

"Moock is Willing to Admit Letters," *Spokane Daily Chronicle*, September 29, page of Street Edition.

"Moock Enjoys Card Games," *Spokesman Review*, October 1, page 6.

"Moock Faces Jury Trial Today in Hatchet Murder Case," *Spokane Daily Chronicle*, December 3, page 1.

"Moock Jury Selection is Progressing Slowly," *Spokane Daily Chronicle*, December 3, page 1 of Sports Edition.

"Wrangling about Jurors in Hatchet Murder Case," *Spokane Daily Chronicle*, December 3, page 1 of Street Edition.

"Can't Secure Hatchet Murder Jury," *Spokane Daily Chronicle*, December 4, pages 1 and 2.

"Issue Call for More Jurors in Hatchet Murder Case," *Spokane Daily Chronicle*, December 4, page 1 of Tri-State Edition.

"Draw Near Moock Panel," *Spokane Daily Chronicle*, December 4, page 1 of Sports Edition.

"Noted Criminal Expert Called in Moock Trial," *Spokane Daily Chronicle*, December 5, pages 1 and 2.

"Greenough Outlines Web of Evidence which State Hopes will Hang Moock," *Spokane Daily Chronicle*, December 5, page 1 of Sports Edition.

"Get Moock Murder Jury," *Spokane Daily Chronicle*, December 5, page 1 of Tri-State Edition.

"Moock Wins First Round in Murder Charge Trial," *Spokane Daily Chronicle*, December 6, page 1.

"Ghastly Exhibits Fail to Move Moock," *Spokane Daily Chronicle*, December 6, page 1 of Sports Edition.

"Horrible Exhibits in Moock Trial," *Spokane Daily Chronicle*, December 6, pages 1 and 3 of Street Edition.

"Hatchet Murder Juror Taken Ill; Is Released," *Spokane Daily Chronicle*, December 7, pages 1 and 2.

"Moock Loses Fight over Letters, Money," *Spokane Daily Chronicle*, December 7, pages 1 and 2 of Sports Edition.

"Officer Declares Moock had Wild-Haired Stories," *Spokane Daily Chronicle*, December 7, pages 1 and 2 of Street Edition.

"Moock Already Plans to Appeal," *Spokane Daily Chronicle*, December 8, page 1.

"Lindell Tells of Seeing Coupe," *Spokane Daily Chronicle*, December 8, pages 1 and 3 of Sports Edition.

"Prosecutor Scores in Moock Trial," *Spokane Daily Chronicle*, December 8, pages 1 and 3 of Street Edition.

"Pile More Evidence on Moock," *Spokane Daily Chronicle*, December 8, pages 1 and 2 of Tri-State Edition.

"Moock's Attorneys Open Fight Today," *Spokane Daily Chronicle*, December 10, page 1.

"Moock is Unmoved by Hatchet," *Spokane Daily Chronicle*, December 10, pages 1 of Sports Edition.

"Archie Moock Battles to Escape Death Rope," *Spokane Daily Chronicle*, December 10, pages 1 of Street Edition.

"Moock on Witness Stand," *Spokane Daily Chronicle*, December 10, pages 1 and 2 of Tri-State Edition.

"Prosecutor Will Grill Moock in Murder Case," *Spokane Daily Chronicle*, December 11, page 1.

"Moock's Wife Takes Stand for Defense," *Spokane Daily Chronicle*, December 11, page 1 of Sports Edition.

"Moock's Attorneys Attacked," *Spokane Daily Chronicle*, December 11, pages 1 and 2 of Tri-State Edition.

"Moock's Jury will Visit Scene of Murder Today, *Spokane Daily Chronicle*, December 12, page 1.

"Moock Jury Visits Scene of Doping," *Spokane Daily Chronicle*, December 12, pages 1 and 2 of Sports Edition.

"Use Auto Speedometer to Help Moock," *Spokane Daily Chronicle*, December 12, pages 1 and 2 of Street Edition.

"Moock Attorneys Score," *Spokane Daily Chronicle*, December 12, pages 1 and 2 of Tri-State Edition.

"Jury will be Given Moock Case Today," *Spokane Daily Chronicle*, December 13, page 1.

"Jury Won't Get Moock Case before Early this Evening," *Spokane Daily Chronicle*, December 13, page 1 of Sports Edition.

"Moock Jury All Ready to Decide on his Fate," *Spokane Daily Chronicle*, December 13, page 1 of Street Edition.

"Fate of Moock will soon be Known," *Spokane Daily Chronicle*, December 13, page 1 of Tri-State Edition.

"Moock to Hang, Jury Declares," *Spokane Daily Chronicle*, December 14, page 1.

"Death Penalty Handed Moock," *Spokane Daily Chronicle*, December 14, page 1 of Tri-State Edition.

1929

"Sentence Moock to Death Soon," *Spokane Daily Chronicle*, January 5, page 2 of Sports Edition.

"Judge Huneke Sentence Moock, Slayer, to Hang," *Spokane Daily Chronicle*, January 17, page of Extra Edition.

"Judge Huneke Gives Moock Death Knell," *Spokane Daily Chronicle*, January 17, page 1 of Sports Edition.

"Little Chance Seen of Moock Appealing," *Spokane Daily Chronicle*, February 12, page 1 of Sports Edition.

1930

State v. Much, 156 Wash. 403, 287 Pac. 57 (1930). Note: Argued April 17, 1930.

"Supreme Court is Moock's Hope," *Spokane Daily Chronicle*, April 18, pages 1 and 2 of Sports Edition.

"Moock Hanging Date Requested," *Spokane Daily Chronicle*, June 24, page 3 of Sports Edition.

"Hatchet Murderer Dated with Death," *Spokane Daily Chronicle*, June 25, page 1 of Sports Edition.

"Wilkins Confesses to Hatchet Murder; Says Moock Clear," *Spokane Daily Chronicle*, August 15, page 1 and 6 of Fireside Edition.

"Letter Outlines Crime for which other is to Hang," *Spokane Daily Chronicle*, August 16, pages 1 and 2 of Sports Edition.

"Moock Spurned Chance for Life," *Spokane Daily Chronicle*, August 19, page 1 of Fireside Edition.

"Archie Moock Executed at Walla, Walla," *La Grande Evening-Observer*, La Grande, Idaho, September 12, page 1.

"Archie Moock, Spokane Hatchett Slayer, Hanged at Walla, Walla Today," *The Daily Inter-Lake*, Kalispell, Montana, page 1.

"Dear Diary: He Says He Loves Me," by Jack Heise, *Actual Detective Stories*, April 1940, pages 24-27, and 37-38.

"Moock, Archie F." *Legal Executions after Statehood in North Dakota, South Dakota, Wyoming, Montana, Idaho, Washington and Oregon, A Comprehensive Registry*," by R. Michael Wilson, McFarland and Company, Inc., 2011, pages 319-20.

"Mail Order Marriage," by John Shuttleworth, *Radio and Television Mirror*, June 1950, page 52, 92-94.

---###---

Chapter Four: The Highway Hunter, 1930

Guide to Abbreviations: AP = Associated Press; UP = United Press.

1929

"Young Couple Slain at Trysting Place," AP, *Joplin Globe*, Joplin, Missouri, August 31, 1929, page 2. [Author's Note: This short article reports on the unsolved murder of Ruth Laughlin and Paul Leslie Odell near Cliff Drive, Kansas City, Missouri, on August 30, 1929].

1930

"Two Teachers Slain during Theft of Car," *Daily Oklahoman*, Oklahoma City, December 29, page 1.

"Police Trail New Clues in Girls' Death," *Daily Oklahoman*, December 30, pages 1 and 2.

"Hunt Insane Man in Girl's Murder," AP, *Tulsa World*, December 30, page 1.

"Attack on Younger Girl Held Motive," AP, *Tulsa World*, December 30, pages 1 and 8.

"Suspect is Named; Search for Slayer of Girls Extended," *Daily Oklahoman*, December 31, pages 1 and 2.

"Former Convict is Hunted as Killer," AP, *Tulsa World*, December 31, pages 1 and 8.

1931

"Griffith Case Develops into Hunt for Man," *Daily Oklahoman*, January 1, pages 1 and 2.

"Quinn Search Still Futile, Two Released," *Daily Oklahoman*, January 2, page 1.

"Claims Quinn was Attacker," UP, *Lincoln Evening-Journal*, Lincoln, Nebraska, January 2, page 1.

"Evidence Web Widens, Quinn Hunt Goes on," *Daily Oklahoman*, January 3, page 1.

"New Crime is Laid at Ex-Convict's Door," *Tulsa World*, January 3, page 3.

"Woman Found Strangled," AP, *Joplin Globe*, Joplin Missouri, January 11, page 2. (Note: Unsolved murder of Mamie Houlehan).

"Boys Found Body of Slain Woman," *Sedalia Capital*, Sedalia, Missouri, January 11, page 15.

"Newton Crime Still a Mystery," AP, *Atchison Daily-Globe*, Atchison, Kansas, February 11, page 1. (Unsolved murder of Lucille Price).

"Quinn, Slayer Suspect, Caught," *Daily Oklahoman*, May 16, page 1.

"Potter will Seek Extradition Papers," *Daily Oklahoman*, May 16, page 1.

"Quinn Sought for Months by Police," AP, *Daily Oklahoman*, May 16, pages 1 and 2.

"Quinn to be Quizzed about Other Murders," UP, *Lincoln Evening-Journal*, Lincoln, Nebraska, May 16, page 1.

"Denies He Slew two Teachers," AP, *Moberly Monitor-Index*, Moberly, Missouri, May 16, page 1.

"Quinn, Nerves on Edge, is 'Surprised' at Being Held for Griffith Crime," *Daily Oklahoman*, May 17, pages 1 and 6.

"Wife Defends Quinn, Says He is Innocent, Will Aid him in Court, 'I'm Tougher than Earl is,' Mate's Boast," *Daily Oklahoman*, May 17, page 6.

"Relentless Four Month Hunt Brings Earl Quinn to Earth," *Daily Oklahoman*, May 17, page 6.

"Griffith Sees Quinn in Jail," *Daily Oklahoman*, May 22, page 1.

"Seven Name Quinn as Bridge Bandit," *Daily Oklahoman*, June 11, page 5.

"Quinn Illness a Headache," *Daily Oklahoman*, June 21, page 16.

"Lucille Price Slaying Apt to Remain Unsolved," AP, *The Hutchinson*, Hutchinson, Kansas, July 27, page 7.

"How Did the Murderers Capture Lucille Price," Supplemental feature story addition to the *San Antonio Light* by American Weekly, Inc., April 5, 1931, page 61.

"Quinn Trial First on Court Docket," *Daily Oklahoman*, September 3, page 1.

"Mrs. Quinn Hopes to Clear Husband," *Daily Oklahoman*, September 4, page 4.

First Trial

"Second Venire Due for Call in Quinn Trial," by Merle Blakely, *Daily Oklahoman*, September 24, pages 1 and 17.

"State Shows 'Case Ace' in Quinn's Trial," by Merle Blakely, *Daily Oklahoman*, September 25, pages 1 and 14.

"Result of Quinn Trial May Hinge on Ruling Today," by Walter Biscup, *Tulsa World*, September 25, pages 1 and 3.

"Mother of Slain Girl Testifies in Quinn Trial," UP, *Wichita Daily Times*, September 25, page 6.

"Evidence Net Spun by State against Quinn," by Merle Blakely, *Daily Oklahoman*, September 26, pages 1 and 2.

"Death Gun Will Confront Quinn at Trial Today," by Walter Biscup, *Tulsa World*, September 26, pages 1 and 3.

"State Pieces out Version of Dual Slaying," UP, *Wichita Daily Times*, September 26, pages 1 and 2.

"Death Weapon is Identified in Quinn Case," by Merle Blakely, *Daily Oklahoman*, September 27, pages 1 and 8.

"Defense Attacks State's Witness in Trial of Quinn," by Walter Biscup, *Tulsa World*, September 27, pages 1 and 6.

"Bits of Coat Hold Interest in Quinn Trial," by Merle Blakely, *Daily Oklahoman*, September 28, pages 1 and 4.

"State to Finish Case in Quinn Trial this Week," by Walter Biscup, *Daily Oklahoman*, September 28, pages 1 and 2.

"Sensational Developments Expected in Murder Trial of Earl Quinn as State Nears Completion of its Case," UP, *Wichita Daily Times*, September 28, pages 1 and 2.

"Quinn Defense Upsets State's Claim," by Merle Blakely, *Daily Oklahoman*, September 29, pages 1 and 3.

"Defense Scores Round for Quinn in Murder Trial," by Walter Biscup, *Tulsa World*, September 29, pages 1 and 5.

"Quinn Defense Attempting to Shift Blame," UP, *Wichita Daily Times*, September 29, pages 1 and 9.

"State Rests; Quinn Defense Opens Today," by Merle Blakely, *Daily Oklahoman*, September 30, page 1.

"Woman Witness Tells of Attack in Trial of Quinn," by Walter Biscup, *Tulsa World*, September 30, pages 1 and 8.

"Judge Refuses Instruct Jury in Quinn Case," UP, *Wichita Daily Times*, September 30, pages 1 and 11.

"Quinn Lawyer Shifts Blame for Murders," by Merle Blakely, *Daily Oklahoman*, October 1, pages 1 and 2.

"Mistrial Denied Earl Quinn; Jury is Taken to Task," by Walter Biscup, *Tulsa World*, October 1, pages 1 and 2.

"Propose an Alibi in Earl Quinn Case," UP, *Wichita Daily Times*, October 1, pages 1 and 2.

"Lawyers will Argue Today in Quinn Case," by Merle Blakely, *Daily Oklahoman*, October 2, pages 1 and 2.

"Court Instructs Quinn Jurors as Trial Nears End," by Walter Biscup, *Tulsa World*, October 2, pages 1 and 12.

"Rumors of Gun Battle Climaxing Quinn Trial Lead to Precautions," UP, *Wichita Daily Times*, October 2, pages 1 and 2.

"May Know Fate Tonight," UP, *Wichita Daily Times*, October 2, page 2.

"Quinn's Fate in Hands of Jury," by Merle Blakely, *Daily Oklahoman*, October 3, pages 1 and 2.

"Jury Holds Fate of Quinn; Verdict Probably Today," by Walter Biscup, *Tulsa World*, October 3, pages 1 and 5.

"Jury Inquires about Penalty in Quinn Case," UP, *Wichita Daily Times*, October 3, pages 1 and 2.

"Jurors Brand Quinn Slayer, Decree Death," by Merle Blakely, *Daily Oklahoman*, October 4, pages 1 and 2.

"Circumstantial Evidence Convicts Quinn; Murders Rank with Most Fiendish in State," *Daily Oklahoman*, October 4, page 2.

"Quinn Convicted, Given Death for Slaying Sisters," by Walter Biscup, *Tulsa World*, October 4, pages 1 and 6.

"Death Sentence for Quinn in Oklahoma Slaying: Found Guilty Murder Young Blackwell School Teacher; Sister Also Shot to Death," UP, *Wichita Daily Times*, October 4, page 1.

"Early Second Trial Sought in Quinn Case," *Daily Oklahoman*, November 30, page 1.

1932

"County Bitter, Mathers Tells Appeals Court," *Daily Oklahoman*, April 28, page 2.

Quinn v State 1932 OK CR 206 16 P.2d 591 54 Okl.Cr. 179. [Oklahoma Court of Criminal Appeals, Argued April 28, 1932. Decided: 11/29/1932]

1933

"The Strange Enigma of Salt Fork River," by Tonkawa Chief of Police Charles Wagner as told to Herbert Hall Taylor, *True Detective Mysteries*, January 1933, 54-58, 70-73.

"Quinn, Out of Prison, Says Next Trial, 'In My Pocket,'" AP, *Daily Oklahoman*, January 7, page 2.

"State Winner in Clash over Quinn's Wife," *Daily Oklahoman*, March 1, 1933, pages 1 and 9.

"Witness Says Many in Peril as Quinn Rode," *Daily Oklahoman*, March 2, page 16.

"Detective Magazine 'Thriller' Brings Heated Clash at Murder Trial of Quinn, Crowd Laughs at Attorney's Fiery Attack," AP, *Daily Oklahoman*, March 3, page 1.

"Quinn to take Stand Today to Defend Self against Death Charge," AP, *Daily Oklahoman*, March 4, page 7.

"Testimony is Completed at Trial in Enid," AP, *Daily Oklahoman*, March 5, page 10.

"Jury Studies Fate of Quinn," AP, *Daily Oklahoman*, March 7, page 9.

"Quinn is Given Death Verdict," AP, *Daily Oklahoman*, March 8, page 2.

"Quinn Appeals on Ten Errors," *Daily Oklahoman*, June 7, page 1.

"Earl Quinn's Last Mile," by Dick Pearce, *Daily Oklahoman*, November 19, page 46.

"Accused Man Prepared for Chair Tonight," by Irvin Host, *Daily Oklahoman*, November 23, pages 1 and 2.

"Quinn Electrocuted for Double Murder," AP, *Daily Oklahoman*, November 24, pages 1 and 2.

"Quinn Dies Claiming Injustice," AP, *Daily Oklahoman*, November 24, pages 1 and 2.

"Quinn Docile in Last Hours with Mother," AP, *Daily Oklahoman*, November 24, page 2.

"Quinn's Execution is Near Third Anniversary of Griffith Crimes, *Daily Oklahoman*, November 24, page 2.

1937 & 1941

"Solving the Baffling Murder of the Oklahoma Police Chief's Daughters," by Manley W. Wellman, *Real Detective*, October 1937, pages 32-33, 72-74.

"Who Murdered the Police Chief's Daughters?" by Aaron Green, *Master Detective*, September 1941, pages 10-13, pages 56-58.

---###---

Chapter Five: The Destiny of Luther Jones, 1936

1935

"Merry Month of May Unlucky for Ohioan," *Helena Daily-Independent*, Helena, Montana, May 19, 1935, page 17.

1936

"Ogden Youth is Kidnapped to Drive Car," *Ogden Standard-Examiner*, Ogden, Utah, October 17, page 1.

"4 Nevadans Shot to Death," *Reno Evening Gazette*, October 17, page 1.

"4 Men Murdered in Elko," *Nevada State Journal*, October 18, pages 1 and 2.

"Lynching of Elko Killer Feared, Slayer of 4 will be Tried with No Delay," *Nevada State Journal*, October 19, pages 1 and 1.

"Slayer Details Murder of Four," *Nevada State Journal*, October 19, page 1.

"Ex-Convict Admits Nevada Killings," by Jack Welter, *Ogden Standard Examiner*, October 19, pages 1 and 2.

"Railroad Men Relate Jones Capture Story," by Charles A. Esser, *Ogden Standard Examiner*, October 19, page 2.

"Former Convict Tells of Killing Four for $40," *Salt Lake Tribune*, October 19, page 5.

"Jones Repudiates Story Told of Slaying of Four Nevadans in Elko Shack," *Reno Evening Gazette*, October 19, pages 1 and 3.

"Jones Makes Two Confessions Concerning Slaying in Elko," *Reno Evening Gazette*, October 19, page 1.

"Former Local Felon Admits Slayings, Confesses He Slew Four in Nevada Cabin," AP, *Billings Gazette*, Billings, Montana, October 19, pages 1 and 2.

"Former Belfry Ranch Hand," *Billings Gazette*, Billings, Montana, October 19, page 2.

"Luther Jones to Fight Murder Charge, Man Who Confesses Four Slayings in Elko Now Says He Merely was Accomplice in Killings," UP, *Nevada State Journal*, October 20, pages 1 and 2.

"Change of Venue Likely; Elko Attorney Declines Case," UP, *Nevada State Journal*, October 20, page 1.

"Jones Pleads Not Guilty to Slaying of Four Men in River Cabin in Elko," *Reno Evening Gazette*, October 20, pages 1 and 3.

"Prisoner Hints Not Guilty Plea in Mass Killing," *Salt Lake Tribune*, October 20, pages 1 and 2.

"New Witness Found in Elko Mass Murder," *Nevada State Journal*, October 21, pages 1 and 2.

"Jones is Placed at Slaying Scene by two Men at Elko," AP, *Reno Evening Gazette*, October 21, page 14.

"Funeral Services of Gun Victim Held Today," *Reno Evening Gazette*, October 21, page 14.

"Jones under Heavy Guard; Fear Suicide," *Ogden Standard Examiner*, October 21, pages 1 and 2.

"Jones Presents Not Guilty Plea in Elko Killing," *Salt Lake Tribune*, October 21, pages 1 and 2.

"New Evidence Found in Elko Mass Murder," UP, *Nevada State Journal*, October 22, page 7.

"Nevada Killer Suspect Trial in November," UP, *Ogden Standard Examiner*, October 23, page 1.

"Trial of Jones in Elko Set for Nov. 16," AP, *Reno Evening Gazette*, October 30, page 20.

"Money Hidden by Arrascada Found in Truck," *Reno Evening Gazette*, November 10, page 8.

"Federal Expert to Testify in Jones Case," *Reno Evening Gazette*, November 14, page 2.

"Trial Jones Opened Today for Slaying 4 Men," AP, *Reno Evening Gazette*, November 16, page 12.

"Confession of Admitted Today in Evidence at Trial," AP, *Reno Evening Gazette*, November 17, page 16.

"Jury May Get Elko Slaying Case Tonight," UP, *Nevada State Journal*, November 18, pages 1 and 2.

"Jones Says 'Mind was Blank,' in Elko Slaying Testimony," AP, *Reno Evening Gazette*, November 18, pages 1 and 2.

"Jones Convicted of Slaying at Elko and Faces Execution, Pistol Fashioned from Soap Found in Prisoner's Cell," AP, *Reno Evening Gazette*, November 19, pages 1 and 3.

"Luther Jones Guilty! Unanimous Verdict Reached on First Ballot by Jurors," UP, *Nevada State Journal*, November 19, pages 1 and 2.

"Jones Execution in Gas House is set for Week of Jan. 24," AP, *Reno Evening Gazette*, November 23, page 14.

"Slayer on Way to Prison at Carson," AP, *Reno Evening Gazette*, November 24, page 20.

"Slayer of Four Sent to Prison," UP, *Nevada State Journal*, November 25, page 1.

"Jones Execution Set for Jan. 26," *Reno Evening Gazette*, December 12, page 14.

"Indiana Friends of Jones Ask Sentence Commutation in Petition Sent to [Governor] Kirman," *Reno Evening Gazette*, December 17, page 17.

"Mercy is Petitioned for Indiana Killer," AP, *Indianapolis Star*, December 18, page 5.

"An Appeal is Made for Jones' Life," Editorial, *Nevada State Journal*, December 26.

1937

"Condemned Man's Sister Appeals for Board Action," *Nevada State Journal*, January 12, 1937, page 3.

"Fate of Slayer of Four Will Be Determined Today," NSJ, January 22, page 3.

"Court Denies Stay to Luther Jones," UP, *Ogden Standard Examiner*, January 22, page 5.

"Religion Aids Luther Jones in Death House," UP, *Nevada State Journal*, January 23, page 1.

"Plans Complete for Execution of Jones," *Reno Evening Gazette*, January 25, page 12.

"Luther Jones Dies at Dawn in Gas House, Slayer of 4 Executed in State Prison," by Ernest A. Foster, UP Correspondent, *Nevada State Journal*, January 26, pages 7 and 9.

"Luther Jones is Executed in Prison Gas House Today," *Reno Evening Gazette*, January 26, page 14.

"Luther Jones, 8th Man to Die in Gas House, Will be Buried Today in Carson City," UP, *Nevada State Journal*, January 27, page 6.

"Pallid Kidnapper and the Missing Cattle Kings," by Detective Sergeant C.K. Keeter [Ogden, Utah], as told to Jack DeWitt, *American Detective*, February 1937.

US Census Records

Year: *1920*; Census Place: *Marion Ward 4, Grant, Indiana*; Roll: *T625_434*; Page: *18A*; Enumeration District: *98*; Image: *1080*. Accessed through Ancestry.com, *1920 United States Federal Census* [database on-line].

Year: *1930*; Census Place: *Sims, Grant, Indiana*; Roll: *589*; Page: *4A*; Enumeration District: *0037*; Image: *996.0*; FHL microfilm: *2340324*, Accessed through Ancestry.com. *1930 United States Federal Census* [database on-line].

Year: *1940*; Census Place: *Sims, Grant, Indiana*; Roll: *T627_1048*; Page: *5A*; Enumeration District: *27-42B*, Accessed through Ancestry.com. *1940 United States Federal Census* [database on-line].

---###---

Chapter Six: The Tomato Killer, 1943-44

1933

"Louis E. Brooks to Testify Friday, Six Men Are Involved in Case Now," *Marshall Evening-Chronicle*, Marshall, Michigan, November 28, pages 1 and 4.

"Wanted to Kill Brooks, Lyle Daly Tells Attorney Prevented Joe Medley from Murdering Louis Brooks," *Marshall Evening-Chronicle*, December 4, pages 1 and 5.

"Daly Breaks Down as He Tells Story," *Marshall Evening-Chronicle*, December 12, pages 1, 2, and 5.

"Jane Edwards Will Probably be Freed of Robbery and Armed Charge but Held as Witness," *Marshall Evening-Chronicle*, December 13, pages 1 and 6.

1934

"Louis Gonyou Hiding in Tijuana, Mex., Nabbed as Crosses Border into U.S.," *Marshall Evening-Chronicle*, February 15, page 1.

"Medley Caught at Flint, Last of Brooks Suspects Surprised in Apt House by 16 Police Officers," *Marshall Evening-Chronicle*, March 24, pages 1 and 2.

"Four Brooks Robbers Sentenced, Brown Gets 40-60 Years at Marquette," *Marshall Evening-Chronicle*, March 31, pages 1 and 2.

1944

"Woman is Found Dead in Bathtub," *New Orleans Times-Picayune*, New Orleans, Louisiana, December 25, page 1.

"Identity of Dead Woman Unknown," *New Orleans Times-Picayune*, December 26, page 3.

"Police Hunt Man in Bathtub Case," *New Orleans Times-Picayune*, December 27, page 14.

"Records of FBI Identify Woman," *New Orleans Times-Picayune*, December 28, pages 1 and 2.

"Bathtub Victim's Past is Studied," *New Orleans Times-Picayune*, December 29, page 15 of Part Two.

1945

"Bathtub Death Not from Poison," *New Orleans Times-Picayune*, January 23, page 7.

"Mystery Covers Woman's Death in Loop Hotel," *Chicago Daily Tribune*, February 18, page 17.

"Spur 2 Hunts in Mysterious Hotel Death," *Chicago Daily-Tribune*, February 19, page 1.

"Second Bathtub Death is Probed," *New Orleans Times-Picayune*, February 19, page 1.

"Quiz Woman in Hotel Tub Mystery Death," *Chicago Daily-Tribune*, February 20, page 8.

"Signatures Link Bathtub Deaths," *New Orleans Times-Picayune*, February 22, page 3.

"Convict Sought in Hotel Death," *Chicago Daily-Tribune*, February 23, page 1.

"New Clew Links Fugitive to Two Deaths in Tubs," *Chicago Daily-Tribune*, February 24, page 1.

"Fugitive Sought in Bathtub Death," *New Orleans Times-Picayune*, February 24, page 1.

"Handwriting Test Awaited in 2 Tub Deaths," *Chicago Daily-Tribune*, February 25, page 12.

"2 Gun Gambler Hunted in Hotel Bathtub Death," *Chicago Daily-Tribune*, February 25, page 15.

"Search Westwego for Murder Clues," *New Orleans Times-Picayune*, February 26, page 4.

"Blame Alcohol and Benzedrine in Tub Death," *Chicago Daily-Tribune*, February 28, page 15.

"Poison Test Set in Bathtub Case," *New Orleans Times-Picayune*, February 28, page 1.

"Testifies Woman used Benzedrine," *New Orleans Times-Picayune*, March 1, page 9.

"Medley Indicted in Bathtub Death," *New Orleans Times-Picayune*, March 2, page 16.

"Rich Woman Found Slain in Capital Home," AP, *Cumberland Evening-Times*, Cumberland, Maryland, March 9, page 1.

"Medley Hunted in Another Killing," *New Orleans Times-Picayune*, March 10, page 1.

"Woman is Killed in Capital Apartment, Warrant Will be Sworn Out for Ex-Convict," AP, *New York Times*, March 10, page 19.

"Roads Blocked in Hunt for Medley, Reportedly Seen near Lansing, Mich.," *New Orleans Times-Picayune*, March 13, page 1.

"Officers Expect Medley to Fight," *New Orleans Times-Picayune*, March 18, page 1.

"FBI Seeks Convict in Deaths of 3," *New York Times*, March 18, pages 18 and 35.

"Medley Captured in St. Louis Hotel," *New Orleans Times-Picayune*, March 19, page 1.

"Man Seized Here is Sent East for Woman's Murder," *St. Louis Post-Dispatch*, March 19, page 3A.

"Man Suspected in Slaying of Three Seized," AP, *Joplin News Herald*, March 19, page 8.

"Medley Objects to Examination," *New Orleans Times-Picayune*, March 20, page 1.

"2 Women Tell How they Met Medley," by Anne Hagner, *Washington Post*, June 1, page 5.

"Charges Medley Went Broke at Poker at Mrs. Boyer's," AP, *St. Louis Post-Dispatch*, May 29, page 9.

"Mrs. Boyer's Ring Evidence against Joseph Medley," AP, *Somerset Daily-American*, Somerset, Pennsylvania, May 30, page 1.

"Killer Tries to Sell Mrs. Boyer's Furs," AP, *Somerset Daily-American*, June 1, page 2.

"Woman Says Medley Wanted Coat Sold," AP, *St. Louis Post-Dispatch*, June 1, page 5C.

"Only Other Man at Boyer Party Admits Using Alias," by Winifred Nelson, *Washington Post*, June 1, pages 1 and 5.

"Maid Testifies to 'Fear' Held by Mrs. Boyer," by Winifred Nelson, *Washington Post*, June 6, pages 1 and 2.

"Medley Murder Case Heads toward Jury," AP, *The Daily-Mail*, Hagerstown, Maryland, June 7, page 2.

"Medley Fate to be Put in Jury's Hands Thursday," by Winifred Nelson, *Washington Post*, June 7, pages 1 and 2.

"Medley Convicted on Murder Count, Death Mandatory," AP, *New Orleans Times-Picayune*, June 7, page 1.

"Jury Returns Mandatory Death Verdict in 3 Hours," by Winifred Nelson, *Washington Post*, June 8, pages 1 and 4.

"Medley, Found Guilty in Murder, Gets Death," AP, *St. Louis Post-Dispatch*, June 8, page 5A.

"Monster of Murder: Crimson Trail of Joseph Medley," by Clayton D. Carter, *Inside Detective*, July 1945.

"Clew of the Friendly Little Game," by Harland Mendenhall, *Actual Detective Stories*, July 1945.

"State Prison Scandals Bared, 17 Charges are Studied by Dethmers," *Detroit Free-Press*, July 15, pages 1.

"Jackson Prison Scandal Bared, Cupid Club for the Lovelorn is Discovered," UP, *Traverse City Record-Eagle*, Traverse City, Michigan, July 24, pages 1 and 3.

"Washington Scene," column by George Dixon, *Tucson Daily Citizen*, Tucson, Arizona, December 21, 1945, page 12.

"Laxity of D of C Jails Irks 'Voteless' Citizens," column by Sam Tucker, *Decatur Sunday Herald and Review*, Decatur, Texas, December 23, 1945, page 6.

1946

"Two Slayers Flee Jail in Guards' Garbs," UP, *Mount Carmel Item*, Mount Carmel, Pennsylvania, April 3, 1946, page 1.

"Hunt for Escaped Slayer Spreads over Wide Area," AP, *Rochester Democrat and Chronicle*, Rochester, New York, April 5, page 6.

"Felons Freed to See Girls, Quiz Told, Revels Bared at Michigan Prison Inquiry," *Chicago Daily-Tribune*, April 11, page 1.

"Jail Guards and Killers Played Cards for a Month," by Al Hailey, *Washington Post*, April 11, pages 1 and 2.

"Convicts Went out on 'Dates,' Probers Told," *Chicago Daily-Tribune*, April 12, page 17.

"Witnesses Tell More of Vice and Graft at Michigan State Prison," by Roberta Applegate, *Escanaba Daily-Press*, Escanaba, Michigan, April 12, page 2.

"Probers Told How Medley Ruled Roost," by Al Hailey, *Washington Post*, April 12, pages 1 and 2.

"Secret Witness Tells Story in Prison Inquiry," *Chicago Daily-Tribune*, April 13, page 4.

"Inside Story of State Pen Escape Bared," by Roberta Applegate, *Escanaba Daily-Press*, April 13, pages 1 and 10.

"Jackson Aides' Laxity State's Big Weapon," by Owen C. Deatrick, *Detroit Free-Press*, April 14, page 34.

"Appeals Court Affirms Joseph Medley Conviction," AP, *St. Louis Post-Dispatch*, April 17, page 9.

"District Jail Changes Due after Report," *Washington Post*, April 20, pages 1 and 2.

"Convicting Mr. Gill," Editorial, *Washington Post*, April 25, page 10.

"Ex-Warden Turns upon Assistants," by Owen C. Deatrick, *Detroit Free-Press*, April 30, page 11.

"Jailhouse Jamboree," by James W. Booth, *Front Page Detective*, July 1946. PDF File Download.

"Defense Holds Little Hope for Medley," *Washington Post*, December 10, page 2.

"Final Appeal Denied, Medley to Die Today," *Washington Post*, December 20, page 1.

"Killer Medley Dies with Prayer on his Lips, Death Hour Delayed by Futile Court Maneuver," by Charles Yarbrough, *Washington Post*, December 21, pages 1 and 5.

Other

"Hot Bullets for Washington's Poker Party Hostess," by Wilson Handrow, *True Crime Detective*, August 1963.

"States of Violence: Zones of Autonomy and Regimes of Control, the Case at Jackson Prison," Fernando Coronil and Julie Skurski, Editors, University of Michigan Press, 2006.

"No Speed Limit: The Highs and Lows of Meth," by Frank Owen, St. Martin's Press, 2007.

US Census, Joseph D. Medley, Year: 1930; Census Place: Blackman, Jackson, Michigan; Roll: 995; Page: 31A; Enumeration District: 0056; Image: 518.0; FHL microfilm: 2340730. Accessed via Ancestry.com

---###---

Chapter Seven: A Soft Touch, 1955

1955

"Mrs. Weaver is Explosion Victim," *San Angelo Standard-Times*, January 19, pages 1 and 2.

"Car Bomb Blast Kills San Angelo Woman," AP, *Abilene Reporter-News*, January 19, page 1.

"Grand Jurors Set to Open Probe in Blast," *San Angelo Standard-Times*, January 19, page 1.

"New Quiz of Houston Bomb Suspect Hinted," by Ed Freitag, *San Angelo Standard-Times*, January 20, pages 1 and 2.

"Houstonian Quizzed in Angelo Bombing, Car Blast Kills Wife of Architect," AP, *Abilene Reporter-News-Morning*, January 20, pages 1 and 2B.

"Bombing Probe Shifts to Angelo," by Reporter-News Service, *Abilene Reporter-News-Evening*, January 20, page 1.

"Suspect Freed in Car Bomb Slaying," *Houston Chronicle*, January 20, pages 1 and 10.

"Probe Continues in Bomb Death," *San Angelo Standard-Times*, January 21, page 1.

"Church Sets up Memorial Fund," *San Angelo Standard-Times*, January 21, page 2.

"Long Probe Due in Angelo Killing," AP, *Abilene Reporter-News-Evening*, January 21, page 1.

"Call Seeks Cash for Bomb Killer," by Ed Freitag and Joe North, *San Angelo Standard-Times*, January 23, pages 1 and 10.

"Estate Left to Husband, Daughters," *San Angelo Standard-Times*, January 23, pages 1 and 10.

"Phantom Caller Trap Fails to Solve Angelo Bombing," AP, *Abilene Reporter-News*, January 23, pages 1 and 5.

"Stokes Says Arrest in Bomb Case 'Just a Matter of Time,'" *San Angelo Standard-Times*, January 24, page 1.

"Police Comb Mrs. Weaver's Residence for Hidden Bomb," AP, *Abilene Reporter-News-Morning*, January 24, page 60.

"New Bombing Fears Scare Man in Angelo," *Abilene Reporter-News*, January 24, page 17.

"San Angelo Prosecutor Hints Bombing Clue Found," UP, *Valley Morning-Star*, Harlingen, Texas, January 24, page 2.

"Guard Increased; Plane Trip Made," *San Angelo Standard-Times*, January 25, pages 1 and 2.

"Guard is Doubled at Bombing Scene," AP, *Abilene Reporter-News*, January 25, page 1.

"Arrest Slated in Bomb Death," AP, *Abilene Reporter-News*, January 25, page 17.

"Officers Know Bomb Killer," UP, *Lubbock Evening-Journal*, Lubbock, Texas, January 25, pages 1 and 8.

"Weaver Family offers $10,000 to Get Killer," *San Angelo Standard-Times*, January 26, page 1.

"Hubby Offers $10,000 for Bomb Slayer," AP, *Abilene Reporter-News-Evening*, January 26, page 1.

"Exclusive! 'I Didn't Murder my Wife' --- Weaver," by Jack Donahue, *El Paso Herald-Post*, pages 1 and 2.

"Pretty Divorcee Knew Weaver as Shrewd Bargainer," UP, *El Paso Herald-Post*, January 26, page 8.

"Reward to Stand, Lawyer Indicates," by Ed Freitag, *San Angelo Standard-Times*, January 27, page 1.

"Bomb Victim's Husband Told Not to Take Lie Test," AP, *Abilene Reporter-News-Evening*, January 27, page 1.

"Bomb Victim's Husband Puts up Big Reward," AP, *Abilene Reporter-News-Evening*, January 27, page 7A.

"Mate of Woman Killed by Bomb Fears Death," UP, *El Paso Herald-Post*, January 27, pages 1 and 2.

"Mystery Woman in Weaver Case Called before Special Grand Jury," by Jack Donahue for the *El Paso Herald-Post*, January 27, pages 1 and 2.

"Weaver—," *Longview Daily-News*, Longview, Texas, January 27, page 8.

"Brownwood Man Denies Weaver Extortion Attempt," *San Angelo Standard-Times*, January 28, page 1.

"Extortion Suspect Jailed in Angelo Bomb Death," *Abilene Reporter-News-Evening*, January 28, page 1.

"Angelo Bomb Study Goes to Houston," AP, *Abilene Reporter-News-Evening*, January 28, page 30.

"2 Houston Men Jailed in Angelo Bomb Death," AP, *Abilene Reporter-News-Evening*, January 29, page 1.

"Ex Son-in-Law Charged in Weaver Slaying," AP, *Corpus Christi Times*, January 29, pages 1 and 3.

"Mrs. Weaver's Ex-Son-in-Law Charged in her Bomb Murder," by Jack Weeks and Stan Redding, *Houston Chronicle,* January 29, pages 1 and 5.

"Weaver is Sorry for Washburn," *Houston Chronicle*, January 29, page 5.

"Weaver Family Shaken by Washburn Arrest," by Zarko Franks, *Houston Chronicle*, January 29, page 5.

"Bomb Suspects Jailed Here; Grand Jury Move is Awaited; Pair Held in Murder," by Ed Freitag, *San Angelo Standard-Times*, January 30, pages 1 and 2.

"Kin of Slain Woman Slow to Comment," *San Angelo Standard-Times*, January 30, pages 1 and 2.

"From Blast to Murder Charges, Bombing Slaps San Angelo into National Spotlight," *San Angelo Standard-Times*, January 30, page 4.

"Text of Official Report on Probe Given by Detective," AP, *San Angelo Standard-Times*, January 30, page 5.

"Stokes Drops Husband as Case Suspect," *San Angelo Standard-Times*, January 30, page 5.

"Man who Wired Car Bomb Sought," *Houston Chronicle*, January 30, pages 1 and 12.

"Washburn's Arrest Shocks Neighbors," by Norman Baxter, *Houston Chronicle*, January 30, page 12.

"Weaver Cleared, but Pain Remains," *Houston Chronicle*, January 30, page 12.

"Weaver's Attorneys Ask D.A. for Public Apology," *Houston Chronicle*, January 30, page 12.

"2 Bomb Suspects Jailed in Angelo," AP, *Abilene Reporter-News-Sunday*, January 30, pages 1 and 2A.

"Former Son-in-Law, Carpenter Held in San Angelo Bomb Death," *Lubbock Avalanche-Journal*, January 30, page 10.

"Texas Rangers, Police Route Two Suspects," UP, *Valley Morning Star-Sun*, Harlingen, Texas, January 30, page A3.

"Weaver Case Gun Said Sold for $5," AP, *San Angelo Standard-Times*, January 31, page 1.

"Lawyer Says Blast Suspect Defense to be Hard Job," AP, *Abilene Reporter-News-Evening*, January 31, page 1.

"Plenty of Questions Still Unanswered in Bomb Slaying," AP, *Abilene Reporter-News-Evening*, January 31, page 4A.

"D.A. Predicts Indictment in Weaver Killing," by Zarko Franks, *Houston Chronicle*, January 31, pages 1 and 2.

"Washburn's Kids' Fate Undecided," *Houston Chronicle*, February 1, page 3 of Section 5.

"Murder, Extortion, Kidnap? 3 Major Crimes Revolve around Bombing in Angelo," AP, *Abilene Reporter-News-Evening*, February 1, page 1.

"Kidnaping of Washburn's 2 Children Feared by Ex-Wife," AP, *Abilene Reporter-News-Evening*, February 1, page 7A.

"Suspect in Weaver Bomb Slaying Freed," *Houston Chronicle*, February 2, page 1.

"Law Officers Disagree, Angelo Bombing Suspect Freed, Charge Dropped," AP, *Abilene Reporter-News-Evening*, February 2, page 1.

"Bomb Slayer Known; Extra TNT Sought," AP, *Abilene Reporter-News-Evening*, February 3, page 1.

"Ex Lady Wrestler Enters Bomb Plot," AP, *Abilene Reporter-News-Evening*, February 4, pages 1 and 3.

"'Nature Girl' Says She was Offered $10,000 to Murder Texan," UP, *El Paso Herald-Post*, February 4, pages 1 and 2.

"Washburn's Lawyer Quits; Grand Jury to Meet Soon," AP, *Abilene Reporter-News- Evening*, February 5, page 1.

"Grand Jury May Get Angelo Bombing Case," AP, *Abilene Reporter-News-Evening*, February 7, page 1.

"2 Saw Washburn, Angelo Grand Jury to Get Bomb Evidence Thursday," AP, *Abilene Reporter-News-Evening*, February 7, page 7B.

"Ex-Con Says He Bought Dynamite," AP, *Abilene Reporter-News-Morning*, February 10, Page 1.

"No Nature Girl: Grand Jury Begins Study of Angelo Bomb Slaying," by Garth Jones, AP, *Abilene Reporter-News-Evening*, February 10, page 1.

"Angelo Grand Jurors to Deliberate Today," AP, *Abilene Reporter-News-Evening*, February 12, page 8A.

"2 Men Indicted for Bomb Death," by Garth Jones, AP, *Abilene Reporter-News-Evening*, February 13, pages 1 and 5.

"Money Motivated Bombing, Victim's Husband Asserts," AP, *Abilene Reporter-News-Evening*, February 14, page 1.

"'Money, Money, Money,' Brought on Bomb Slaying," AP, *Abilene Reporter-News-Evening*, February 14, page 7A.

"Two Plead Innocent in Car Bomb Murder," UP, *EL Paso Herald-Post*, February 18, page 4.

"The Murder that Shook Texas," by Paul McClung, *Front Page Detective*, May 1955.

"Bomb Murder Suspect's Bond Granted," AP, *Abilene Reporter-News-Evening*, May 13, page 3.

"Nelson Taken to State Pen," AP, *Abilene Reporter-News-Evening*, May 17, page 1.

"Trial of Henry Washburn Begins Monday in Angelo," *Abilene Reporter-News-Morning*, September 25, page 7A.

"Moving of Washburn Case Asked by State," AP, *Abilene Reporter-News-Evening*, October 1, page 1.

"Angelo's Washburn Trial sent to Waco, Judge Changes Site of Hearing," AP, *Abilene Reporter-News-Evening*, October 2, page 1.

"Dec. 5 Slated as Trial Date for Washburn," AP, *Abilene Reporter-News-Evening*, October 6, page 2.

First Trial, December 1955

"All Jurors Selected Here in Bomb Death Trial of Washburn," by Bob Sadler, *Waco News-Tribune*, December 6, pages 1 and 4.

"Court Photography Cleared Way for TV," *Waco News-Tribune*, December 6, pages 1 and 2.

"Weaver, Husband of Auto-Bomb Victim, Testifies in Trial of Harry Washburn," UP, *Brownwood Bulletin*, Brownwood, Texas, December 6, pages 1 and 9.

"Weaver Testifies Life Threatened," AP, *Corpus Christi Times*, December 6, pages 1 and 16.

"Defense Fires Questions at Testimony by Weaver," by Bob Sadler, *Waco News-Tribune*, December 7, pages 1 and 18.

"Little Helen Not Present during Trial," by Chris Whitcraft, *Waco News-Tribune*, December 7, page 18.

"Weaver Wary of Questions by Defense," *Waco News-Tribune*, December 7, page 18.

"Criminal Juries Barred from Public Contacts," *Waco News-Tribune*, December 7, page 18.

"Witness Says He and Another Man were Hired to Kill Weaver; Houston Man Names Washburn in Murder Plot at San Angelo," UP, *Brownwood Bulletin*, December 7, pages 1 and 10.

"Judge Leaves Bed to Answer London Reporter's Call about TV in Court," UP, *Brownwood Bulletin*, December 7, page 1.

"Witness Bares Payoff Effort," AP, by Jim Bowman, *Denton Record-Chronicle*, Denton, Texas, December 7, pages 1 and 2.

"Witness Claims Washburn Tried to Hire for Killer," AP, *Paris News*, Paris, Texas, December 7, page 1.

"State Witnesses Build Case against Washburn, 34 Testify at Trial Wednesday," by Bob Sadler, *Waco News-Tribune*, December 8, pages 1 and 4.

"London Reporter's Call gets Judge out of Bed," *Waco News-Tribune*, December 8, pages 1 and 4.

"State Rests Prosecution against Harry Washburn," UP, *Brownwood Bulletin*, December 8, pages 1 and 11.

"Murder Trial Disrupts Normal Waco Activities," UP, *Brownwood Bulletin*, December 8, pages 1 and 11.

"Woman Tells Murder Plot, Lady Wrestler Puts Finger on Washburn," UP, *Galveston Daily-News*, December 8, pages 1 and 3.

"Testimony is Concluded; Jury May Get Case Today," by Bob Sadler, *Waco News-Tribune*, December 9, pages 1 and 5.

"Old Man Weaver Called Murderer of his Wife, Washburn Defense Attorney Hurls Charge in Arguments at Trial of Harry Washburn," UP, *Brownwood Bulletin*, December 9, page 1.

"Washburn Guilty of Murder with Malice; Jury Fixes Sentence at Life in Prison," *Waco News-Tribune*, December 10, pages 1 and 9.

"Witnesses Came from Every Area," by Betty Dollens, *Waco News-Tribune*, December 10, page 9.

1956

Harry L. Washburn v. State of Texas, 299 S.W.2d 706 (Tex. Crim. App. 1956), October 3, 1956.

"Washburn Sentence Reversed on Appeal, Car Bomb Trial Conduct Rapped," AP, *Abilene Reporter-News-Evening*, October 3, 1956, page 1.

1957

"Harry Washburn to go on Trial Again," AP, *Denton Record-Chronicle*, June 16, page 3.

Second Trial

"Three Witnesses Testify at 2nd Washburn Trial Today," AP, *Abilene Reporter-News-Evening*, June 22, page 1.

"Weaver Says Washburn Demanded $20,000," AP, *Abilene Reporter-News*, June 23, pages 1 and 3.

"'Nature Girl' Says $10,000 Offered to Plan Murder," AP, *Abilene Reporter-News-Evening*, June 24, page 1.

"Brunette Tells of Washburn's Offer," AP, *Longview Daily-News*, June 24, pages 1 and 10.

"Convict Nelson Offered Immunity, He Testifies," AP, *Abilene Reporter-News-Evening*, June 25, page 1.

"Con Says Showed Bomb-Rigging to Washburn," AP, *Paris News*, June 25, page 1.

"Convict is Offered Immunity in Trial," AP, *Longview News-Journal*, June 25, page 1.

"Washburn Jury is Expected to Hear County Judge Today," AP, *Denton Record-Chronicle*, June 27, page 2.

"County Judge Testimony Due at Washburn Trial," AP, *Paris News*, June 27, page 1.

"Washburn Given 99-Year Term," AP, *Abilene Reporter-News-Evening*, June 29, page 1.

"99-Year Term for Washburn," AP, *Denton Record-Chronicle*, June 30, page 2.

"Washburn Plans to Appeal Again," AP, *Abilene Reporter-News-Evening*, June 30, page 5.

"Wife of State's Star Witness in Trial Dies Sunday," UP, *Lubbock Evening-Journal*, July 1, page 2.

"Star Witness' Wife Died Natural Death," UP, *Waco News-Tribune*, July 2, page 1.

1958-2016

Harry L. Washburn v. State of Texas, 318 S.W.2d 627 (Tex. Crim. App. 1958), June 25, 1958.

"Washburn Due to Start 99 Years in Pen," AP, *The Eagle*, Bryan, Texas, January 5, 1959, page 10.

"Washburn's Last Appeal is Denied," AP, *Abilene Reporter-News-Evening*, April 21, 1959, page 1.

"Woman Wrestler Seeks Reward in Bombing Case," AP, *Waco News Tribune*, June 13, 1959, page 7.

"I Killed the Wrong Person!" by Pat Clausen, *Master Detective*, July 1959.

"25 Claim Reward in Washburn Case," AP, *Abilene Reporter-News*, October 21, 1959, page 5.

"Hearing Set on Awarding Reward," AP, *Amarillo Globe-Times*, October 26, 1959, page 5.

"13 Persons Get Reward Money in Murder Case," AP, *Lubbock Avalanche-Journal*, December 23, 1960, page 6A.

"New Hope is Sought for Harry L. Washburn," Letters to the Editor, *Waco News-Citizen*, February 21, 1961, page 6.

"A Stick of Dynamite for his Fancy In-Laws," by Ted Wiley, *Confidential Detective Cases*, November 1963.

"Hearing Set in Washburn Case Today," AP, *Abilene Reporter-News-Morning*, June 2, 1964, page 4A.

"Harry Washburn Appeal Denied," AP, *Corsicana Daily-Sun*, November 11, 1964, page 8.

"Texas Heiress Slain in Bomb Plot," by Bill Cox, *Master Detective*, April 1965.

"Harry Washburn Claims Rangers Violated his Constitutional Rights," AP, *Waco News-Tribune*, July 13, 1967, page 11.

"Lawyers: There is No Better than Me," *Time*, March 21, 1969.

"$3 Million Suit Filed in San Angelo Case," AP, *Odessa American*, Odessa, Texas, December 30, 1969, page 10A.

"Man Files 2 Suits in Angelo Slaying," AP, *Abilene Reporter-News*, December 31, 1969, page 5.

Ex-Parte Harry L. Washburn, Court of Criminal Appeals Texas, November 10, 1970

"Release Bid is Refused," UPI, *Longview News-Journal*, November 11, 1970, page 2.

Harry L. Washburn, v. W. J. Estelle, Director, Texas Department of Corrections, 476 F.2d 278 (5th Cir. 1973)

"Famed Trial Lawyer Percy Foreman Dies," *Washington Post*, August 26, 1988.

Alchemical Inheritance: Embracing what is, Manifesting what Becomes, by Tess Keehn, MS, with H. Harris Willcockson, Edited by Mary Ellen Ryder, M. Div., Balboa Press, 2015.

"Washburn, Harry L., ID 149130," Texas Department of Corrections, Basic Information Relating to Offender (Inmate), obtained by author August 5, 2016. This file included:

> Certified Copy of Judgement and Sentence: Plea of Not Guilty, State of Texas vs Harry L. Washburn, No. C-2485-H. Judgement on June 28, 1957, signed, J.K. Smith, Jury Foreman. Sentenced on September 6, 1957. Mandate on January 3, 1959, signed Bill Shaw, Clerk Criminal District Courts, Dallas County, Texas.
>
> Mandate from the Court of Criminal Appeals, Austin, Texas, Harry L. Washburn Appellant vs. The State of Texas, signed Bill Shaw, January 5, 1959, Clerk of the Criminal District Courts, Dallas, Texas.
>
> Three Proclamations by the Governor of the State of Texas authorizing Harry L. Washburn to be at the deathbed of his critically ill mother on January 23, 1968; February 6-8, 1968; and to attend her funeral, April 22, 1968.

Email exchanges between Robbie Moore, wife of Tom Moore, and author, October 30-November 10, 2016.

Email exchanges and telephone conversations with Tess Keehn, February 2017.

Other

Certificate of Birth, Harry L. Washburn, Texas State Board of Health, May 13, 1916.

Harry L. Washburn, 1930 Census. Census Place: Houston, Harris, Texas; Roll: 2346; Page: 7A; Enumeration District: 0060; Image: 59.0; FHL microfilm: 2342080. Ancestry.com. 1930 United States Federal Census [database on-line]. Provo, UT, USA: Ancestry.com Operations Inc, 2002.

Harry L. Washburn, 1940; Census Place: Houston, Harris, Texas; Roll: T627_4194; Page: 8A; Enumeration District: 258-135.

Ancestry.com. 1940 United States Federal Census [database on-line]. Provo, UT, USA: Ancestry.com Operations, Inc., 2012.

1938 Births, Texas Births Index, Washburn, Harriet Louise, Texas Department of Health, Bureau of Vital Statistics, page 2111.

Harry, Helen, Sadie Gwin and Helen Weaver, 1940 Census. Census Place: Houston, Harris, Texas; Roll: T627_4196; Page: 11B; Enumeration District: 258-184. Ancestry.com. 1940 United States Federal Census [database on-line]. Provo, UT, USA: Ancestry.com Operations, Inc., 2012.

Certificate of Death, 4732, Texas Department of Health, Bureau of Vital Statistics, Helen Harris Weaver, January 19, 1955.

Certificate of Death, 4338, State File 38, Texas Department of Health, Bureau of Vital Statistics, Harry E. Weaver, April 18, 1970.

Certificate of Death, 4109, State File 30, Texas Department of Health, Bureau of Vital Statistics, Carlton Joseph Heninger, October 25, 1975.

Certificate of Death, 4275, Texas Department of Health, Bureau of Vital Statistics, Harry L. Washburn, December 31, 1979.

---###---

Chapter Eight: The Stiletto Slayer of Milwaukee, 1966

Sources Currently Not Available. Both Milwaukee daily newspapers, the *Journal*, and *Sentinel*, were removed from Google News Archives, without warning, when the author was almost finished with this chapter. Until the relevant articles are republished (paid only access) on the newspaper's website, this section will remain unfinished.

---###---

About the Author

Jason Lucky Morrow is a Gulf War veteran and former award winning newspaper reporter who now researches and writes vintage true crime stories for his blog, HistoricalCrimeDetective.com. His focus is on obscure but significant criminal cases that are nearly forgotten and have not been adequately explored in decades. Mr. Morrow has lived and worked in Nebraska, Texas, Alabama, Romania, and Oklahoma where he currently resides in the Tulsa area with his wife, Alina, and his sweet, beautiful, wonderful daughter, Alison.

Please visit HistoricalCrimeDetective.com for more vintage true crime stories and follow along for new story updates on our Facebook page.

Also by Jason Lucky Morrow

The DC Dead Girls Club:
A Vintage True Crime Story of Four Unsolved Murders in Washington D.C.

Famous Crimes the World Forgot: Volume I
Ten Vintage True Crime Stories Rescued from Obscurity

Deadly Hero:
The High Society Murder that Created Hysteria in the Heartland

One Last Thing…

Thank you for reading *Famous Crimes the World Forgot*, Volume II. It means a lot to me that you selected this book. If you enjoyed these eight stories and found them interesting, **I would be truly grateful if you would take a minute or two and write a review on Amazon.com.** Your support really does make a difference. As an independent researcher and writer, notification through my blog, Facebook page, and word of mouth are my only sources of advertising. I don't have a publicist, literary agent, manager, or marketing team.

In general, I believe the author's work should speak for itself, not the author. This can only be done by readers like you who share their opinions for others. With your review, and sharing this book with your friends, I hope to continue my work of introducing new readers to these old, forgotten crime stories.

Thank you for reading my book. If you are interested in reading more historical true crime stories, I invite you to visit my blog, where there are plenty of stories and photographs.

Sincerely,

Jason Lucky Morrow
March 15, 2017

Printed in Great Britain
by Amazon